Battle Ground Academy - Voices From Back in the Day

Battle Ground Academy
Voices From Back in the Day

Edited by Paul Clements

Copyright © 2025 by Clearview Press ~

All rights reserved. No part of this publication may be reproduced, distributed, or transmitted in any form or by any means, including photocopying, recording, or other electronic or mechanical methods, without the prior written permission of the publisher, except in the case of brief quotations embodied in critical reviews and certain other noncommercial uses permitted by copyright law.

Library of Congress Control Number (LCCN): 2025919598

ISBN: 979-8-9893496-2-3

Contents

Preface	1
George Isaac Briggs, Class of 1903	5
Daly Thompson, 1910	8
Martha Hatcher Whitaker, Class of 1925	11
Gaston Buford, Class of 1925	17
J. B. Akin, Class of 1926	19
Dr. Harry Guffee, Class of 1931	21
Bill Baker, Class of 1937	25
BGA in 1939	35
Proctor System, 1940	37
World War Two	39
George Briggs, Marble Champion	40
Van Montague, Class of 1943	41
A Snow Day in 1943	47
Bob Short, Class of 1944	48
Mama Haynes	51
John Green, Class of 1945	53
Glenn Eddington	57
Bobby Gentry, Class of 1946	59
Ralph Brown, Class of 1949	67
Henry Brown	84
Walter Reed Capps, Class of 1950	87
Gale Pewitt, Class of 1950	92
Jonas Coverdale	100

Paul Redick	*102*
Bunny Akin, Class of 1951	*106*
Leaving the Mid-South Athletic Association	*113*
Carl Smithson	*114*
Tiger Grimes, Class of 1953	*116*
David Wood, Class of 1954	*123*
The BGA Museum	*135*
Winder Campbell, Class of 1955	*137*
Richard Ashworth, Class of 1957	*145*
Larry Stumb, Class of 1957	*152*
J. B. Akin, 1957	*157*
Mike Hudgins, Class of 1957	*159*
Britt Knox, Class of 1957	*167*
Buddy Benedict, Class of 1960	*176*
Larry Brown, Class of 1961	*183*
John Coleman, Class of 1961	*189*
Charles Trabue, Class of 1961	*197*
Cora Miller Spencer	*207*
Billy Adair, Class of 1965	*210*
Kenneth Phelps, Class of 1965	*221*
Steve Plonka, Class of 1965	*229*
Paul Clements, Class of 1965	*238*
Bill Armistead, Class of 1969	*252*
Bob Smithson, Class of 1970	*262*
Anne Smithson Wallace	*270*
John Bragg	*274*
Index	*293*
Acknowledgements	*316*

Preface

BGA Campus, circa 1952

When Battle Ground Academy was dedicated on October 5, 1889, Senator William B. Bate, a former Confederate General, was the principal speaker. He stood very close to the spot where, 25 years earlier, the horse he was riding was shot during the Battle of Franklin. As he spoke, he mentioned the soldiers—presumably men from both sides—who "fought and fell on this historic ground." He said that the new school would be a place of transformation, from "the haversack of the soldier, into the satchel of the schoolboy." What had been a killing field would become a campus where students learned, and where boys shot marbles instead of guns.

Only seventeen days later, a child named Daly Thompson was born in a rural section of northern Arkansas. Daly would eventually come to Franklin, and he graduated from BGA in 1910. When my classmates and I showed up to start seventh grade nearly fifty years later, Daly Thompson was the oldest teacher on the faculty. He occasionally disciplined students in a way that was in keeping with what had taken place back in the 1800s. While some of the social and political perspectives we encountered also reflected an earlier time, the traditional values embraced by BGA gave the school a distinct and authentic atmosphere.

After Battle Ground Academy relocated several miles to the north in 1996, the old campus, where so many lives unfolded over the years, quickly changed. Buildings were soon being torn down, or renovated beyond recognition, and parking lots and new structures erased more and more familiar places. It was clear that the essence of what had once taken place there would be lost to time as well.

Around 2011, I was talking to my long-time friend, Patrick Roberts, who had become the assistant head of school at BGA. We both understood the need to preserve the school's history, as did Jason Gregg, a senior member of the BGA staff, who soon became part of the conversation. I suggested that the best way to preserve what had taken place at BGA over the years would be to record interviews with former teachers and some of the school's older graduates. At some point, those interviews would be available to craft autobiographical narratives which, taken together, could form a mosaic that conveyed what Battle Ground Academy had once been.

Initially, Jason Gregg contacted a number of individuals, and along with filming the interviews, he also asked some questions. Beginning with Bill Baker, a member of the class of 1937, the recollections of some thirty older graduates and teachers were gathered. Although the project began to lose momentum after a couple of years, by the time the project fell into dormancy, a wealth of old stories and details about BGA had been recorded.

It had been anticipated that younger alumni would eventually be interviewed, but when the work was discontinued, only two individuals who graduated after 1965 had been recorded. Therefore, not only are a number of earlier classes not represented in this volume, there are no recollections of anyone who graduated after 1970. Consequently, the achievements of several state championship teams are not chronicled. Along with adding accounts from unrepresented classes and highlighting athletic triumphs, a subsequent volume could focus on some of the outstanding students and faculty members who went unmentioned in this book.

Bill Armistead, a 1969 graduate of BGA and one of those who had been interviewed a decade earlier, remembered the earlier intention to put together a book. In 2024, he asked what was necessary for a book to be produced. When he learned that the interviews needed to be transcribed, he offered to underwrite the cost of those transcriptions. Individual narratives have been supplemented with articles from *the Review-Appeal,* the Franklin newspaper owned for decades by the Armistead family. Those articles, as well as articles from old editions of the school newspaper, *the Cannonball*, underwent various degrees of editing.

Oral history interviews are, by their nature, subjective. Different interviewers will ask different sets of questions. The same holds true for editing interviews into narratives. Different editors will edit identical material in different ways. When asked about a past event, a number of follow-up questions are generally required before a person pieces together a complete description. In order to accurately convert a memory into a readable narrative, it is almost always necessary for an editor to rearrange disjointed fragments into chronological order, and then paraphrase and supplement the original verbiage. With regard to editing, the goal of this book has been to present a narrative that is as close as possible to what a subject was trying to relate, and at the same time provide a clear account for the reader.

Along with preserving a sense of what it once was like to attend Battle Ground Academy, some of the unique lives and friendships that were molded in those years have been included in these accounts. I suspect that if an entirely different group of former students had been interviewed, the essence of the school would have come to light as well. As time goes by, and as education continues to change, I hope that reading about BGA—with all of its rough edges and all of its virtues—will add some understanding to how things were back in the day. Back before athletics in schools became a business. Back before the era of school shootings. Before the era in which intrusive parents, and the continual threat of litigation, altered the nature of interactions between teachers and students. Before the time when electronic devices left so many students both isolated and homogenized.

Paul Clements

George Isaac Briggs, Class of 1903

In the thirty years that George I. Briggs has devoted to teaching, he has endeavored to impress his students with one idea. "Give to the world the best you have, and the best will come back to you."

An only son with five sisters, he was born in Nashville in 1886 to George Isaac and Matilda Harrison Briggs. His mother was born 12 years before the Battle of Franklin in an old two-story house just over Winstead Hill on the Columbia Highway. Her father was a Confederate soldier. After the battle, their home, known today as the Harrison House, was filled with the wounded. She was kept busy waiting on the soldiers. Every morning she gave a blossom from her mother's garden to each sufferer. For several weeks, a yellow flag waved over the home, signifying that it was a Confederate hospital.

When George Briggs was five, his father died, and his mother came back to Williamson County with her children. George entered the public school when he was six, and he was around fourteen when he started Battle Ground Academy, which was more commonly called the Mooney School. He was instructed by Professor Arthur Watkins, who had graduated from the school in 1893. Briggs stood out as a member of the baseball team, and he also won the declamation medal. The original building burned in 1902, and George graduated the following year.

Home of George Briggs, 1928

He attended college at Southwestern University, then located in Clarksville, where he studied under a pair of noted scholars. He took part in a number of athletic activities, and along with being named captain of several teams, he won the Bible Medal in his senior year. After receiving his degree, he went to Chattanooga and taught and coached all of the athletic teams at the McCallie School. He was there for six years, but the low pay led him to resign his position. (Note – on September 3, 1913, Briggs married Miss Nell Tague of Memphis, in Buncombe County, North Carolina. Their daughter, Jane, was born August 6, 1914, but the marriage soon ended.) Briggs moved to Memphis and formed a small insurance company, but the venture only lasted for one year. Briggs, convinced that teaching was his God-given profession, accepted the headmastership of Darlington School in Rome, Georgia.

George Briggs remained at Darlington until America entered World War One. He was sent to Camp Gordon, near Atlanta, and received his commission as a first lieutenant, but he was never sent to Europe. At the close of the war he came back to Franklin, and taught under Prof. R.G. Peoples. Briggs coached all the athletic teams at BGA, and in 1919, his basketball squad played and defeated the Vanderbilt varsity. At the close of the term, he accepted a position at the Baylor School in Chattanooga. He returned to Franklin and married Susie Lee Roberts at the close of 1919. George Briggs and his wife remained for six years at Baylor, and their daughter, Sarah, was born there in 1921. With the resignation of Professor Peoples in 1925, Briggs returned with his wife and two daughters, and became the headmaster of BGA.

George Isaac Briggs

His popularity has grown each year, and the academic standard achieved by his predecessors has been raised even higher. Every year he turns out students who go to universities, and they reflect credit on the school where they were educated.

This edited article, which was supplemented by corroborative research, was written by Miss Jane Owen, and appeared in the Review-Appeal on February 11, 1937. George Isaac Briggs died at his home, across the street from the BGA campus, in 1944 at the age of 57. He was survived by his wife, Susie, two daughters, and one grandchild.

Daly Thompson, 1910

Daly Thompson was born in 1889, and was reared on a farm in Randolph County, Arkansas, in the foothills of the Ozark Mountains. He and his brother worked all summer in the cotton fields, and attended school through the winter. Rarely going into town, they knew little of bright lights and other city attractions. Their greatest pleasures were fishing and hunting with neighbor boys. Daly tramped the hills with a gun and his dog, looking for squirrels and quail. He fished in the streams, and although his mother didn't want him to get in the water, that is where he learned to swim.

He was eventually sent to a local prep school, and when he was around the age of 18, while he was still a student, he took an examination to become a teacher. After he passed, he secured a position at a school in the Ozarks. It was 20 miles from a railroad, and five miles from the nearest post office. He had 45 pupils covering all eight grades. His salary was $33 per month, and boarding in a mountain farmhouse cost him $7.50 a month. His good-hearted landlady would fix him a lunch consisting of onions, cabbage, cornbread, and sorghum molasses, and on Monday there would be a generous slice of cake, saved from Sunday dinner. He kept this up for four summers, and used the money he earned to help put himself through school. He learned lessons in thrift and contentment, and his experiences with mountain folks left a lasting impression on his life.

Hearing of Battle Ground Academy and the famous Peoples brothers, he decided to come to Franklin to prepare for college. He graduated from BGA in 1910, and went on to attend Vanderbilt University. He worked as a waiter to pay for his boarding expenses, and went into debt for the part of his tuition that his summer work failed to cover. After receiving his degree from Vanderbilt in 1914, he returned to BGA to teach. (He is shown as a member of the faculty on the BGA composite for the 1913-1914 school year, so he must have had some teaching duties prior to graduating from Vanderbilt.)

Daly Thompson, back row, fourth from right

He taught at BGA for three or four years, before his career was interrupted by World War One. He served for 18 months in the 526th Engineers, which was attached to the 89th Division. He was in the Battle of Saint-Mihiel and in the Meuse-Argonne Offensive, and was overseas for one year and twenty days, during which time he rose from buck private to sergeant.

Returning at the close of the war, Professor Thompson worked as the principal of a high school for four years at Collinsville, in Shelby County, Tennessee. From there, he became school superintendent in Pocahontas, Arkansas, where he married Ouida Blankenship, an accomplished musician. Then, through the influence of old schoolmates at BGA, he was offered the superintendency of the Franklin city schools.

He arrived in the fall of 1929, soon after the erection of the handsome new high school building. Two years later, he completed work on his Master's degree at Peabody. Franklin High School had eight teachers and 38 graduates in Mr. Thompson's first year, and four years later there are 13 and 61 graduates. At the time he came, some members of the faculty only had two years of college. Now all the teachers have degrees. The library has progressed from a few books in the corner of the study hall, to a room with 3000 volumes, and a full-time librarian.

Mr. and Mrs. Thompson live in a house on Lewisburg Avenue where their children, Daly Jr. who is four-and-a-half, and Sarah Evelyn who is two, were born. Mr. Thompson attends the Methodist Church, and not only teaches a Bible class for young men, he is a member of the congregation's Men's Quartet.

Daly Thompson is one of the most outstanding educators in the South. He stands at the top of his profession, and is often consulted on important educational matters. He is guided by a principle that was expressed by British Prime Minister Gladstone. "What is really wanted is to light up the spirit that is within the boy… There is in every boy the material for good work in the world. It is in every boy, not only those who are brilliant, not only those who are quick, but in those who are solid, and even in those who are dull."

This edited article was written by Miss Jane Owen in 1936. Daly Thompson died in 1967 at the age of 77. He was survived by his wife, Ouida, two children, and four grandchildren.

Martha Hatcher Whitaker, Class of 1925

My mother, Kathleen Kennedy, was the daughter of a Confederate veteran. She was born in Memphis, but my father, Milton Hatcher, was a country boy from Arno, out in Williamson County. He started his business, the Memphis Broom and Brush Company, around 1904. I was born in Memphis in 1907. I was the youngest of three girls. When we were older, our parents decided that my middle sister, Kathryn, and I needed to go away to school. I imagine there must have been some problem between my mother and father, and that was what brought us to BGA.

My sister and I stayed with Mrs. Lee McEwen on Lewisburg Pike. I lived there for two years. We'd come home for Christmas, but not for Thanksgiving or Easter. We would've had to catch the train, and it was too much to go back and forth to Memphis. I went home in the summer, but then I'd go to a YWCA camp in Arkansas.

Kathryn was three years older than I was, but she was only one year ahead of me at Battle Ground.

My father gave Kathryn money for both of us. He told her to be careful with it, but she just kept it all for herself. She wouldn't give me my allowance. One day BGA had a ball game, but it cost 25 cents to go. Sarah Roberts, the daughter of Walter Roberts, who owned a big store in Franklin, gave me a quarter so I could go to the game. After that, I found out where Kathryn was keeping the money, and I started taking what I needed. Kathryn was mean to me when we were at Battle Ground. She was the most selfish human being I ever knew. She was a monster.

Of all the people I've met through the years, I would say that Professor R.G. Peoples was the most solid, quiet, thoughtful individual I ever met. He never made any waves, but he stood up for what was best for the school and best for the students. We called him Mr. Peoples. His wife was the sister of the famous educator, Sawney Webb, who started Webb School in Bell Buckle. She was a nice, pleasant person, and she was extremely nice to me.

I don't think Mr. Peoples wanted to have girls at BGA, but he didn't have a choice. Wealthy board members like Walter Roberts had daughters, and they wanted them to go to Battle Ground. At least we had the Girls Room. It was a room at school that was just for us. There were no physical activities for girls. No sports. Nothing. And there were no dances. My friend Maxie Howlett and some of the other girls would invite me to their luncheons. Other than that, there wasn't much of a social life, but we were allowed to walk to Franklin to get a hot dog at the hot dog wagon, or go see a movie.

R.G. Peoples

There was a reenactment of the Battle of Franklin in 1923, very close to the BGA campus. A film was being made on the site where the battle took place. BGA boys were recruited as soldiers, but they refused, dogmatically, to put on Union uniforms. Mr. Peoples had to give them a talk to get them to wear the uniforms. He said, "It's okay for you to dress like a Yankee. It doesn't mean that you *are* a Yankee."

There were times when Mr. Peoples would call a student to his office. He'd say something like, "Son, come with me." They'd go into his office, and sometimes he'd paddle the daylights out them with a wooden paddle. I never saw him do it, but I heard it. He never had to paddle any of the girls. We behaved ourselves, but the boys were different.

One time there was going to be a big fight. Walter Cotton and Bob Jennings were mortal enemies. Walter was smart. He was a scholar, but Bob was stupid. Mr. Peoples stopped school, and made us all come to a big room behind his office. It was the room where he taught all his classes. He told all of us that we were going to watch the fight. So Bob and Walter started fighting, and they fought and fought until they wanted to stop. But Mr. Peoples wouldn't let them. He said, "No, you're not going to stop. Just keep on fighting. They fought until they were both exhausted, and he finally let them quit. After that, the boys didn't fight much anymore.

We had homework assignments from Monday through Friday, but not too much on weekends. I got all my lessons done every night before I went to bed. We had to be prepared for each one of our classes, but we never knew which class we would have the next day. All we did was study, go to school the next morning, and wait to hear which classes would be called. I had to get help with solid geometry. Mr. Peoples had a lovely house on Lewisburg Avenue, right across the street from where Kathryn and I lived. He let me come over to his house three nights a week. He tried as hard as he could to explain solid geometry to me, but it was a total loss.

I think we would get to school around eight in the morning. and classes ended around three in the afternoon. We could sit outside and study when the weather was nice, but we never knew whether it was First Latin or Third Latin or First French or English that was about to start. We didn't know, so we had to be ready.

Students on front lawn, undated

I have very few memories of some of my classmates, but there are others I remember quite well. My friend, Lula Mai Boaz, lived across the street from the campus. She was a brilliant girl, but the lady I stayed with, Mrs. McEwen, said that Lula Mai and I shouldn't be friends. Lula Mai's father was a salesman for the J.R. Watkins Company, and that wasn't seen as a proper profession. Maxie Howlett was another one of my friends. She was a good student, and she ended up graduating from Randolph-Macon in Virginia. And Mary Sam Tulloss was an outgoing, happy girl who was fun to be around.

William Moss was a little bitty guy. His nickname was Chigger, and he became a preacher. And there was Theodore Lillie, who was a quiet, serious boy. Somebody paid for Theodore to go to BGA. He wore the same pair of pants, day in and day out. He was not very outgoing, but he became a Church of Christ minister. Tom Bond was a nice young man. He seemed like a country boy, but he lived in Franklin. He didn't go to college, but he took a business course and got a big job later on.

Frank Gray was a very good student, but he was not socially inclined. I always had the feeling that Frank noticed me, but he never said anything. His father owned the drug store in Franklin, and Frank eventually became a federal judge. Many years later he presided over the trial of Jimmy Hoffa, the head of the Teamsters Union. Courtney Marshall was the son of the postmaster. Courtney was a ball player and a good looking boy. I always liked Courtney and I enjoyed being around him, but I was not one of those girls that was boy-crazy.

Gaston Buford was a quiet boy. You never knew Gaston was around. His father was a minister who was killed trying to save the lives of several people in a shooting. He received a Carnegie Medal for heroism, and Gaston, along with his brother and two sisters, were all educated with money that came from what their father did. After BGA, Gaston went to the University of North Carolina. He married, served in the war, and then came back and taught at BGA for several years. Sam Fleming, who later did so well in banking, was in the class ahead of me. He was wonderful to me. He was very strong, and he went from BGA to Vanderbilt.

Main Building

George Paschall lived out in the country. During our senior year, his father was put on trial for killing his mother. One day when George wasn't in school, Mr. Peoples called all of us together. He said that George was in a sad situation, and not to say anything about what was going on. He wanted us to act like we didn't know anything about it. George was a pre-med student at Vanderbilt when he killed himself a few years later.

And Sam Compton was one of my classmates. His mother was Mazie Henderson. The Hendersons were an upper echelon family in Franklin. Sam's mother married a man from Texas named Robert Compton, and Sam was their only child. The Henderson family apparently didn't approve of Compton, and there was eventually a divorce. When Sam was little, his father had gone to San Francisco. Sam and I would walk to school together. He was my friend, but he wasn't my boyfriend. We'd just walk to school and talk. Sam was very bright, but he wasn't interested in being a scholar, and he didn't go to college.

My sister, Kathryn, fell in love with Walter Cotton. Walter was a smart boy. I told her to let him get his education and then they could get married. But the summer after they graduated, and just before I started my senior year, they got married anyway. Eight years later, after they had three children, they divorced. My family took the children in, and took care of them. Walter went on to get his doctorate at the University of Wisconsin in animal husbandry. He married six times, but he ended up owning a large dairy farm near Arrington.

My senior year was the last year Mr. Peoples was at BGA. He must have realized that the school was struggling, but he never let on. I noticed that there were times when the furnace didn't work. The rooms would be cold and we'd all huddle up in the Girls Room, but we assumed that everything was all right. We never thought that the school might be in danger of closing. There were about 25 students in my class, but there were only around 80 students in the whole school. Mr. Peoples was able to conceal that it was his last year.

The Honor Code was very important when I was a student. I don't recall any cheating going on at BGA while I was there. I wouldn't even say the word, *cheating*. I made good grades except for math, and I don't know how Mr. Peoples gave me my diploma. But when I got the diploma, it didn't say it was from Battle Ground Academy. It was from Peoples School. Mr. Peoples left Franklin at the end of the school year. He went to teach in a college in Missouri, and I never saw him again.

After I got out of BGA, I didn't do much of anything for a couple of years, and then I enrolled at Memphis State. I went there for one year, and then I met Nelson Whitaker. We got married in 1929, the Depression hit, and we had a little talk about whether we should become parents. I said, "Well, I don't know about having children." He said, "Who knows what's going to happen next? Under the circumstances, I don't think we should have a family either." I agreed. It would be a burden for everybody. He quietly said, "I'll take care of that." And so a family was out.

There I was with one year of college, no skills, and nothing to sell. So I went back to Memphis State and got my degree in education in 1934. When I went to interview for a teaching job, they went through all my records, and everything seemed fine. I was even assigned to a school, but then they saw that I was married and living with my husband, and I left with no job. After that I became a caseworker in emergency relief.

Even though my oldest sister, Dorothy, was never a student at BGA, the school became a big part of her life. She married Bob Lea and had three children, and she eventually went back and got her bachelor and masters degrees in geography at the University of Wisconsin. Her son, Milton Lea, graduated from BGA in 1943. He was Phi Beta Kappa at Vanderbilt in Physics, and worked in the steel industry. Dorothy taught in the public schools in Franklin until they integrated, but she couldn't cope with that situation, and she taught at BGA in the 1970s. She and Kathryn both died in Franklin. Dorothy was 95 and Kathryn was 91.

I did not want to go to my 50th BGA reunion. I didn't want to see all those old people, but after I got there, I was glad I went. I think the main reason that my husband, Nelson, wanted to go was because I was in better shape than the rest of my class. The party was at Frank Gray's house, and at some point he showed me a photograph of President Kennedy appointing him as a Federal judge. My advice to any young person is to put as much knowledge in your head as you can. You can lose your money and your worldly possessions, but nobody can take away your skills and your knowledge. If you put it in your head, it's yours.

Everybody who came to the reunion would have known what happened to our classmate, Sam Compton. His mother and father eventually remarried, and he went to California and lived with them for a time. After I graduated from Memphis State, I went out to California. While I was there, I called Sam and we got together. He rented a car, and we drove around San Francisco. We had a wonderful day.

His parents invited me for dinner that night. I was already married, but Sam was still single. His father, Mr. Compton, was a nice man, and he was being playful with Sam. He said, "Boy, you're a fool. Why didn't you get busy back then?" Sam just laughed and said I was already spoken for. We were still just friends. There was never any romance, but I could have fallen in love with Sam later, I'm sure. His mother and father only lived a few years after that. Sam came back to Franklin, and it wasn't long before he killed himself while he was sitting in his car out in the western part of the county.

The information contained in this narrative came from an interview conducted in 2004 by then BGA headmaster, Dr. George Elder, Class of 1965, and from subsequent research by the editor. Martha Hatcher Whitaker died in Memphis in 2005 at the age of 98.

Gaston Buford, Class of 1925

Gaston Buford was born in Franklin in 1907. His paternal grandfather, the late James L. Buford, ran away from home at the age of 15 and joined the 15th Mississippi regiment. He took part in several military engagements, and fought at the Battle of Franklin, where his colonel and a number of devoted friends lost their lives. He lost a leg after being wounded at Bentonville, North Carolina. His maternal grandfather, Dr. William Caffey, was a physician during the war. He saved both the lives and the limbs of wounded Confederate soldiers, and eventually turned his home into a hospital.

When Gaston was six months old, his family moved to Louisville, where his father studied to become a Presbyterian minister. Reverend Buford then became pastor of a church in Atlanta, but after his death in 1917, his widow and children returned to Franklin. (Note – Rev. Buford was killed after rushing to the aid of two women who were shot by a former mental patient.) Young Buford entered the local elementary school when he was around ten, and received his high school education at Battle Ground Academy. During the summer months, he worked in Rose's Grocery, and was considered to be one of the most efficient boys Mr. and Mrs. Rose ever employed.

Gaston Buford graduated from BGA in 1925. Although two of his uncles graduated from Harvard, and his older brother, Jim Buford, had gone from BGA to Princeton, Gaston decided to attend the University of North Carolina. After graduating in 1929, he accepted a position with a real estate firm in Birmingham, and two years into the Depression, he went to work as a traveling salesman. In 1936, Headmaster George Briggs was searching for a teacher who was mentally, morally, and physically fit, and also had enough personality and tact to cope with the younger boys who attended Battle Ground Academy. He decided that Gaston Buford, who had graduated from BGA a decade earlier, was just the man he wanted.

When he began his teaching career that fall, he was a dormitory counselor. He teaches English and History to the sub-freshmen, as well as first and second year Latin, and his school duties are coaching the midget football and basketball teams, and doing track work. He is a great favorite with both dormitory and day students. One day he went into class and found that Richard Courtney had carved a somewhat true to life caricature of Mr. Buford. The ears were prominent, and the mouth was wide open. With it were the words, "Our beloved professor in a characteristic pose."

Mr. Buford possesses a fine baritone voice. On another occasion, he had taken a solo part in a chorus at the Presbyterian Church. Afterward, a BGA student, Mike Nolan of Birmingham, was standing outside on the steps. He said, "Don't feel bad, professor, I can't sing either." Mountain climbing and fishing are his favorite sports. When asked if he had fashioned a motto into the pattern of his life, he said, "keep good company, and you shall be of the number."

This edited article was written by Miss Jane Owen, and appeared in the Review-Appeal on August 18, 1938. Gaston Buford died in 1971 at the age of 64, survived by his wife, Emma, one son, one daughter, and two grandchildren.

J. B. Akin, Class of 1926

J.B. Akin, circa 1913

Several generations before James Boyd Akin was born in 1907, members of his family came from North Carolina and settled in what became the 4th District of Williamson County. His grandfather, after whom he was named, fought in a unit of Confederate cavalry, and served under General Hood at the Battle of Franklin. J.B. Akin's father, Millard Fillmore Akin, was the oldest of twelve children. He was born three years before the Civil War, and went on to run a country store in the settlement of Burwood, in western Williamson County. Young J.B. Akin was the fourth of five children. He received his early education in the Burwood community, and in 1924, when he reached his third year of high school, he entered Battle Ground Academy. That was the last year that Professor R.G. Peoples was headmaster, and George Briggs was headmaster when Akin graduated in 1926.

He went on to the University of Tennessee. He worked both before and after classes, as well as on Saturdays, to help defray his expenses. He jerked soda in a drugstore near the campus, and even took a job in an undertaking establishment. On one occasion, he and another employee were sent on a call to dress a corpse. It took several hours, and he recalls that it was the hardest work he ever did. He received his degree in science and physical education in 1930.

That fall, he went to Ashland City, where he would teach science and serve as coach and athletic director for several years. In 1931, he married Katherine Beckett of Columbia. They set up housekeeping, but while they were visiting Burwood that Christmas, their home in Ashland City burned to the ground, and they lost everything they owned.

When his father, Millard, died in 1934, J.B. and Katherine Akin moved to Burwood, where J.B. took his father's place in the store. He helped his elderly uncle run the business for a time, but J.B. wanted to return to teaching. The store was closed out, and for the next five years he was the principal of Burwood School. He and Katherine lived in the house his father had built in the early 1890s, and in 1938, when electricity was extended to Burwood, the Akin home was one of the first to have it installed.

J.B. Akin has a milking house that is equipped with electricity. A radio keeps the ten Jersey cows contented, and whoever is milking is entertained. Mrs. Akin takes great pride in her flock of White Leghorn chickens, in her flower and vegetable garden, and in the care of her home and her daughters, eight-year-old Janice and four-year-old Polly. Last fall, J.B. joined the faculty at Franklin High School, where he teaches general science, biology, and physics. He also assists Professor W.C. Yates with coaching football.

Mr. and Mrs. Akin are members of Burwood Methodist Church. He teaches the adult Bible class, and she is superintendent of Bible Study. Their aim in life is to abide by the Golden Rule, and "live by the side of the road, and be a friend to man." Their home is not many yards from Carters Creek Pike, and all who pass know a welcome awaits them, and a helping hand is extended to those who need it.

This edited article was written by Miss Jane Owen, and appeared in the Review-Appeal on February 12, 1942.

Dr. Harry Guffee, Class of 1931

Harry Guffee was born in 1913 in a three-room cottage in Callie, seven miles south of Franklin on Lewisburg Road. When he was two years old, his parents, Albert and Jane McGee Guffee, bought the 130 acre Dr. Barnett farm. Harry's mother, who is of Cherokee and Irish heritage, is one of ten children. His father, who is of Irish extraction, is one of twelve. Harry remembers making the trip in the family buggy, and moving into an eight-room frame house, where electric lights, running water, and a bathroom were soon installed. Mrs. Guffee is a wonderful manager. She raises turkeys and chickens, and cans everything grown in her garden and on the fruit trees. She puts to advantage everything she has.

Albert Guffee raises tobacco, corn, and hay on his farm. And like generations of his ancestors, he is not only a farmer, but a livestock trader. He can tell the weight of an animal by looking at it, and his judgment rarely fails. Harry's brother, Paul, was just 16 months older, and their father taught them to ride a pony before either of them could walk. When they began school at Harpeth, they came in a cart pulled by a pony. But as soon as they outgrew the cart, they rode to school on their ponies. Paul and Harry loved horses, and there were always dogs at their heels as they went about their farm chores. They shared the same bed at night during the winter, but when summer came, they pitched a tent in the yard and slept on cots.

They entered Battle Ground Academy when they were older, and they each had splendid records, both as students and as athletes. Then, for the first time, their paths divided. Paul elected to get a college education with the idea of becoming a doctor. Harry decided to stay on the farm with his father. But when Paul was killed in a motorcycle accident in the summer of 1931, Harry decided to fulfill his brother's aspiration to be a doctor. He enrolled in Vanderbilt.

He was on the football team at Vanderbilt. He was captain of the team, and was also an outstanding wrestler. He is six-feet-tall and weighs 185 pounds, and he has a wonderful physique. After receiving his undergraduate degree in 1935, he entered medical school. In 1937, he married Dorothy Brady of Springfield, whom he had met in Vanderbilt. He graduated from medical school in 1939, and the day after completing his internship at General Hospital, he came back to Franklin to work with Dr. Dan German and Dr. Tandy Rice at the German-Rice Hospital. Focusing on surgery allows Dr. Guffee to relieve the suffering of people he has known all his life,

After moving to Franklin, Dr. Guffee bought a brick bungalow on a 15-acre farm just south of town on Hillsboro Road, giving him room to keep the pair of saddle horses he and his wife are fond of riding. There is a picture of his wife and their three-month-old daughter in his office. He is happy in his work, and hopes to spend the rest of his life in the county where his parents have been living for years. Seeing Dr. Harry Guffee seated in his office, everything seems to be in perfect order.

(Miss Jane Owen, 1941)

When I met Harry Guffee, he was a legend in the making. The way he practiced medicine in those days was a throwback from another era. He made house calls. He went to patients' homes at all hours of the night, attending to their ills, and even delivered babies there. He made calls in rural areas of the county, and there were times when he had to park his truck, get his horse out of his trailer, and ride horseback the rest of the way. Because many of his patients were poor, he frequently didn't charge for his services. If, because of their pride, they insisted on paying, he rarely charged more than four dollars. Harry had grown up with many of them in a section of the county called "Little Texas." It was a rough and tumble area where, if he wasn't careful, a man could get hurt or killed. He told me about a fellow from Little Texas who had killed more than one man. He said that the man wasn't that bad. He wouldn't kill a man who didn't need killing.

Harry and his brother Paul grew up in the rural area of Williamson County. They knew what hard work was. They even delivered ice in Franklin out of a horse-drawn wagon. The boys were strong and very smart, and with some scholarship help from Headmaster George Briggs, they came to Battle Ground Academy. Both played on the football field their father, Albert Guffee, had helped build years earlier, when he had worked on the excavation using mules and a scoop. Paul was the older of the two, and he planned to attend college after BGA, and go to medical school. But Paul was killed in a motorcycle accident in West Tennessee. That hit Harry very hard, and he was determined to play out Paul's dream of college and medical school.

Harry Guffee was a star player, and a member of BGA's undefeated football team of 1930. He received a football scholarship from Coach Dan McGugin at Vanderbilt University, where he became a star player. Aside from football, Harry made excellent grades in his pre-medical studies. Then he excelled at Vanderbilt Medical School. While he was in medical school, he married Dorothy Brady, who eventually became the mother of their five children.

When World War II erupted, Dr. Harry Guffee entered the Army Medical Corps as a surgeon, and was stationed in Europe. He was eventually captured and became a prisoner of war. He experienced horrible treatment as a POW, and suffered from malnutrition and from the cold of the German winter. He was a victim of frostbite in his feet, and had problems with his feet for the rest of his life.

After the war, Harry made his way back home to Franklin, and to his wife, Dot. They already had four children. Along with Betty Jane, Harry Jr., and Paul, his youngest son, Johnny, had been born after Harry went overseas. Their last child, Dottie, was born in 1947.

Dr. Guffee resumed his medical practice and soon took up an activity that would play a huge part in his life for years to come—the breeding, training, and riding of quarter horses. He became one of the most renowned breeders of quarter horses in the country. Harry was a founder of the Franklin Rodeo, which became the biggest rodeo east of the Mississippi River.

Harry was not only a good doctor and an excellent horseman, he was a shrewd businessman. Through his lifelong friend, Dr. Thomas Frist, Harry became an initial investor in Hospital Corporation of America. Harry was enjoying the good life, practicing medicine, watching his children grow, and raising his beloved quarter horses. But he never lost sight of who he was and what he was about. His name had become a household word in the community, and there has probably never been a more revered and respected small town doctor in the country.

Harry Guffee had a lifelong interest in BGA, and he served on the BGA Board of Trustees for many years. While his boys played on the BGA football team in the 1950s and 1960s, he acted as team doctor, rarely missing a game. He was a permanent fixture on the sidelines, wearing his cowboy hat and boots and cheering the team on. Harry was my doctor and took good care of my family. He made many calls to our home, regardless of the time of day or night. Our daughter, Becky, worshiped Dr. Guffee.

I taught all the Guffee boys English at BGA. When Paul was a student at Vanderbilt, he was taking an Advanced Literature course. He was studying the symbolism in Lewis Carroll's Alice in Wonderland.

He was having difficulty grasping the material, and he called me in desperation at 11:00 p.m. He asked if he could come talk to me about it. After all the times his Dad had come to our home late at night to minister to our daughter, I couldn't refuse. Paul arrived about 11:30 p.m. and we started discussing Alice in Wonderland. By about 2:30 a.m., Paul said he finally understood the underlying meanings of the book, and he thanked me profusely when he left. Paul Guffee was one of the best students I had in my years of teaching English. He majored in English at Vanderbilt, and after he graduated, I tried to bring him back to BGA as a teacher and coach. But he had decided to pursue an acting career. He died in 1968. His parents never recovered from his loss. Harry told me later, "I've had trouble holding on to Paul's in my life. First my brother, and now my son."

Harry Guffee was one of the first people to urge me to apply for the job as headmaster at BGA. And throughout my 21-year tenure as headmaster, Harry was there when I needed him, giving me advice and encouragement. I couldn't have asked for a better friend.

Dr. Guffee retired in 1975. In their later years, both Harry and Dot suffered through various medical problems. Time had taken its toll. Harry's beloved Dot died first, and Harry followed her in 1996. Harry Guffee was very proud of BGA, just as BGA was proud of him. In 1997 the school honored Harry and his friend Ralph Brown by naming the new north campus football field and stadium, The Guffee-Brown Stadium.

(John Bragg)

This narrative includes both an edited article written by Jane Owen in 1941, and an undated article by John Bragg. When Dr. Harry Guffee died in 1996 at the age of 83, he had been preceded in death by his son, Paul, and was survived by four children and a number of grandchildren.

Bill Baker, Class of 1937

My birthday is in August, and if I last that long I'll be 92. I don't know if anybody else in my class is still living. Here is how I got to BGA. My mother got the idea that she wanted to spend the winter on the Gulf Coast. There was an old military school in Gulfport, Mississippi, and she thought she could put me there while she spent the winter in Gulfport. It was a disastrous experience.

I got the living hell beaten out of me by the upperclassmen. It was a very unhappy experience. The next fall, I went back home to Paducah. My mother wasn't very enthusiastic about me going to a public school. The next thing I knew, she had found another military school to put me in. It was up at Alton, Illinois—a place called Western Military Academy. I had a series of misfortunes while I was there.

For one thing, they had what they called an annual "Gunman Inspection." The army used to send retired officers around the country to inspect military schools. Under the program, if a student graduated from military school and was approved, he received a commission as a second lieutenant in the Army Reserve Corps. As part of the inspection, one of the things you had to do was demonstrate that you'd been trained in firearms.

They had an old World War I Browning water-cooled machine gun that had been donated to the school by the government for training cadets. For part of the inspection, you went to a firing range they had set up. You had to lay down behind the machine gun, and a target was set up a hundred yards away. It was a plywood cutout that resembled a World War I German soldier with a spiked helmet. You were supposed to fire 30 rounds at that thing.

I laid down behind the machine gun in the firing pit, and put my finger on the trigger. When I got it lined up with the target, a great big wasp came in and lit on my right hand – the one I had on the trigger. I let out a yell and jumped back. The first round had been fed into the breech, and when I jumped, the damn machine gun started firing. Nobody was wounded, but several windshields in the faculty parking lot were hit. That's part of how I got to BGA.

Back then Franklin was a town of about 5,000 souls. There isn't much resemblance between the way Franklin was then and what's there now. Well, I liked BGA. All the athletic guys were Greers, but unfortunately I was a Plato. So I would have the pleasure of getting my butt dragged through the Harpeth River in two tug-of-wars, in 1936 and 1937. As for the food at BGA – if you liked things like pork and beans, it was alright. I'll tell you this, they didn't spend a whole lot of money on food.

Football Practice

The headmaster, George Briggs, was really good at playing marbles. Boy, if you ever played marbles with him, you had better be prepared to lose all your marbles. He was an ace. Mr. Briggs was also big on football. He figured that because I was big, I'd be a football player. I didn't mind playing football and getting tackled and stuff like that, but the idea of going out there every afternoon after being in class all day – that didn't appeal to me. I liked to spend my afternoons hiking or doing things I wanted to do. That didn't sit too well with Mr. Briggs, and it didn't put me in very good standing with the faculty. I had constant problems.

Unfortunately, I had a very strong penchant for mischief. I was looking for a way to sneak off to Nashville. You know, enjoy some of the pleasures of the big city. The main thing I wanted was a set of wheels, but one of Mr. Briggs' commandments was, "Thou shalt not have an automobile if you're a student at BGA".

Well, I went into Franklin, and they had a character named Guy Wallace, who was in the car business. Mr. Wallace said, "Well, young man, what can I do for you?" I said, "Mr. Wallace, I need a set of wheels real bad." I think I was 15 years old. I wasn't even old enough to have a driver's license, but that didn't bother Mr. Wallace. The first thing he wanted to know was how much money I had to spend. When I told him I had a twenty dollar bill, he said, "Young man, I've got just the thing for you!"

It was an old Model T Ford Coupe. It had three pedals that you'd push on to shift gears. I think some farmer had traded it in on a new car. I didn't even know how to drive, but that didn't worry Mr. Wallace either. All he was thinking about was getting that $20. I said, "Will it run, Mr. Wallace?" And he said, "Oh, *yeah*." He called over one of his mechanics. "Joe, crank up the coupe for this young man." So the guy cranked it up and got it running, and I said, "If you'll show me how to operate it, it's a deal."

He showed me how to use the pedals, and then he told his mechanic to open the garage door. I got in the thing and I pushed on the pedals, and after I got it out on the street, I drove it up and down West Main Street four or five times. After doing that, I could drive as good as anybody. I didn't have any insurance or a driver's license, but Mr. Wallace said, "You have to get a license tag." Well, I went down to the courthouse, and I think the tag cost me $2.

I knew a girl named Martha Williams. She was beautiful and natural, and I used to call on her, but we never were romantic or anything. She was just a real good friend. Her daddy operated a bulk distributing plant for some gas company down at the end of West Main. I would stash my car down there at Martha's daddy's fuel depot, and then I'd walk from her house to BGA.

I ended up driving that damn car to Nashville and back, but somebody squealed on me. One of the professors said, "Baker, I understand you've got an automobile. That's against the rules," and blah blah blah. He said, "Get rid of it." So I took it back to Mr. Wallace, and said, "I'm going to have to get rid of this car." He said, "Well, that's fine, because I've got another car here that you might like." It was a 1928 Whippet. Mr. Wallace said, "Frank North traded in his Whippet. I could let you have it for five more dollars." So I handed over the $5 and drove around in this Whippet for about a month.

But one day my roommate and I were headed into Franklin. We were approaching Five Points, and Mr. Briggs had been to the post office to check his mailbox. Mr. Briggs was standing on the curb in front of the post office, and he was carrying a big stack of mail. He wasn't watching what he was doing. When I was just a few feet from the intersection, he decided to cross the street to where he'd parked his car. I stomped on the brakes and laid on the horn. Unfortunately the fool riding with me yelled out. "Jesus, Baker, it's Old Man Briggs!" Well, that caught his attention, and I was in trouble.

George Briggs in classroom

I was hauled into his office the next day. He announced the different punishments for what I'd done. One punishment was that every day after school, I had to go around to each one of my professors and get extra homework assignments. But the worst part was that I was indefinitely restricted to the campus. While the other guys were enjoying themselves out on the town, I'd be sitting in my room. And each weekend, there was a teacher keeping up with whoever wasn't supposed to go on liberty. I'd have to report to him every hour so he would know that I hadn't slipped off and left the campus.

Well fortunately, one of Franklin's bootleggers was a guy called Todd. He had a little store about an quarter of a mile south of BGA on Columbia Pike. That was close enough for me to sneak off to Todd's and buy half a pint of whiskey to take back to my room. Every time I would report to the teacher in charge, I'd have to gargle some Listerine so he couldn't smell my breath. It was all to defy authority.

But one thing I was allowed to do was take hikes. Well, it was a whole lot of fun to go hiking in the hills. I used to go hiking almost every afternoon. Mr. Briggs was always looking for somebody to work for him for free. He had an old colored man named Uncle Henry who worked for the school as kind of the janitor. Since I was on the punishment list, Mr. Briggs would call on me to do some of the work he paid Uncle Henry to do.

One day, here came Old Man Briggs. He said, "My boy, Bake." When he was in a good mood he'd say, "My boy." He said, "I wonder if you'd run down to the Franklin Library and check out a copy of *War and Peace*." The Briggs' had a daughter, Sarah Ewing Briggs, who was about my age. She went to Franklin High School, and she was supposed to make a book report on *War and Peace*. He handed me the keys to his Chevrolet and said, "Just take my car." I was very happy to do anything to get off campus for a while.

Somebody's big old home had been converted into the town library, and there was a real handsome blonde girl working there. Her name was Mary DeGraffenreid Voorhees, and she was around 24 years old at the time. She had been a real popular girl when she was in high school, and I guess she yearned to go back to that kind of life. Well, Mary took to me.

The next thing I knew, she wanted me to have dinner with her at the Voorhees home. Well, Mrs. Voorhees and Mrs. Briggs were in a bridge club together, and she told Mrs. Briggs that she wanted to invite me to have dinner with her and her daughter. So Mr. Briggs excused me from my restriction. Well, Mrs. Voorhees liked me, and Mary and I started having regular dates.

Mary had a brand new 1936 Chevrolet two-door sedan and she liked to dance, so she would pick me up on campus, and we would head out Hillsboro Road to Nashville. We'd go somewhere to dance like Hettie Ray's on Nine Mile Hill, or the Wagon Wheel on Harding Road.

I'd just turned 16, so you could say that was kind of a May-December relationship. That didn't sit very well with my mother. She didn't like the idea of her Little Billy being infatuated with a 24-year-old girl. I think nowadays people would say she was a "cougar," but it was never anything like that. Back in those days, most girls wouldn't take that kind of a risk. In a little town like Franklin, she wouldn't have been a librarian very long if it got around that she was engaged in any hanky-panky.

Mr. Briggs was a big Methodist, and when Sunday came around, we were herded out and walked down to his church. Some kids are inclined to have a disrespect for authority, and I guess I had my share of that back then. But I didn't dislike Mr. Briggs. When I got caught and he punished me for having the car, he was just doing his job.

Mr. Briggs had bought two or three houses across from the school on Everbright Avenue, which was a little gravel street back then. The residences were bought in the name of the school, and they were used as dormitories. But I stayed in the main dormitory. The gymnasium was right behind it.

One of the teachers I had was Glenn Eddington, who was the mathematics professor. He didn't have much to say. He was married to this massive woman. Mr. and Mrs. Eddington had an apartment on the first floor in one of the houses across Everbright. He had a personality that you'd think would be difficult for somebody who taught math.

We had an English teacher named Alton Bryant. He dyed his hair blonde, and we called him as "Altie." One time I happened to be out in the hall, and Mr. Bryant was standing outside the door of his room. He had a room in the dormitory with the students. He pulled out his pipe and said, "Well boys, I'm going to read a while and then go to bed." But when he opened his door, the entire room was filled with feathers. One of the guys had gone into his room and torn open his pillows and scattered feathers all over the place.

Altie's face looked like a storm cloud. He said, "Everybody is staying on campus until I find out who did this!" That was the way that the BGA faculty handled things. If somebody did something, everybody lost the privilege of going to town on the weekend. That made everybody mad, and the miscreant would finally confess and receive his punishment, whatever it was.

James Tolbert in classroom

We had another professor named James Tolbert. He taught English and French. He had graduated from some noted college, and he had been a brilliant student. Mr. Tolbert was a tall, lanky sort of fellow. He was Professor Briggs' tennis coach. He wore a vest and was always dressed properly. He was a Phi Beta Kappa, and wore an Omicron Delta Kappa key on a chain across his vest. He'd take that chain in his hand and twirl his key when he was talking to you. He had a real good opinion of himself. He'd stand up and lecture us little country boys, but looking back, I feel sorry for him. He had been a Phi Beta Kappa and all that, and the best he could do was to get a job teaching English in a little country school like BGA.

It's been 75 years since I graduated, but I still think about some of the guys I knew at BGA. There was a kid in my class named Jack Daniel Motlow. He was a relative of the man who founded Jack Daniel's whiskey. He was a good ole boy and got along with everybody. Mr. Tolbert called on him one time to read in French class. Motlow came to the French vowel "o," instead of pronouncing it "eu", he pronounced it "oo". Well, Tolbert had a fit. He said, "That's all wrong, Motlow. It's 'eu!' Now say 'eu'." Jack gave kind of a silly grin, and said "oo" again. "No, no, no that's not right! Say 'eu'. Round your lips, Jack, round your lips when you say 'eu'."

Some guy at the back of the class hollered out, "Round your lips, Park Cotton." Well, Park Cotton was an old guy from Franklin – I think he was a postman – and he was a notorious homosexual. Well, that broke up the class.

And there was Capers Andrews. That boy had some kind of a genetic problem. He had the worst case of body odor of anybody I've ever known. You wouldn't believe it. His nickname was B.O. I think he was sweet on a girl named Joanna Bransford. I came back one night from liberty, and when I walked by B.O. Andrews' room, he was boohooing. I asked somebody, "What's the matter with B.O.?" They said, "Well, Joanna Bransford dumped him." Evidently, he got too close to her.

Bill Culbreath was a nice guy, but he was one-legged. He had been out hunting with a shotgun. It went off somehow, and he had to have his leg—I believe it was his right leg—taken off at the hip. Well,

Bill had a pair of wooden crutches. You wouldn't believe the speed he could get up to on his crutches. He'd take those crutches, and he'd move faster than a lot of people with two good legs.

I had another classmate named Doc Ingram. His nickname was Doc because his initials were M.D. As fate would have it, he grew up to be a real doctor. He was a surgeon connected to Vanderbilt Hospital. He had a missing leg too. He was a saxophone player, and he could play a wicked saxophone.

BGA Orchestra, 1937 (Bill Baker with guitar, front row)

Music is one thing I got into at BGA. Professor Briggs decided the school ought to have an orchestra, so he hired this old lady named Mae Dickens to come and start one. Well, we had a boy from Gallatin named Kenneth Thompson. He was a real talented piano player, and we had Doc Ingram with his saxophone, and Bill Culbreath played the trumpet. I decided I wanted to get into that, so my mother had this old guitar she brought me from up in our attic.

That got me a special dispensation. Once a week I'd walk to Franklin and hop on the Interurban bus, and go to Nashville for a guitar lesson. This old lady would give me guitar lessons upstairs somewhere on Fifth Avenue. That was a way to get a little freedom to go somewhere. Take the Interurban and visit the big city. I used to love to ride that Interurban.

In Professor Briggs' mind, one of the worst things anybody could do was sneak off and go to Nashville. Nashville used to have this enormous red-light district, and Mr. Briggs' didn't want his boys being contaminated by women of easy virtue.

There was a BGA student who made a trip to Nashville and got infested. The question came up about what he could do about it. I was in the room and I said, "Did you ever try Sloan's Liniment?" It was supposed to be good for aches and pains, but it was an irritant. Well, one of the guys produced a bottle. The guy started applying the liniment, and at first he was okay. But in a minute or two he started hollering. He was dancing around, and then he made a dash for the showers and turned on the cold water. We didn't have anything but cold water in the dorm. Briggs wouldn't have any hot water in the barracks. Anybody who wanted to take a bath had to go to the gymnasium.

The Corner Drugstore was on the Northeast corner of Five Points. It was owned by an old guy named Virgil Jenkins. There was a soda fountain, and we used to go down there all of the time. That's where I used to buy my cigarettes, my pipes, and my pipe tobacco. And old Doc Jenkins had let somebody slip a couple of slot machines in the back of his drugstore. I used to go back there and play those slots. He was a real nice guy, and he took care of the BGA boys. I mean if a student slipped off to Nashville and got a case of – well, let's just say lice – he'd sell them a bottle of medicine without reporting it to Professor Briggs.

Joe Pursell was my roommate. He was a good old boy, and a right good saxophone player. We got to be pretty good friends, but Joe didn't like waking up in the morning. When the bell would ring for everybody to get up and dress and go eat breakfast, Joe would just lay in bed. One thing I did to get him out of bed was squeeze a wet wash rag onto his face. He'd come out of that bed cussing. "Goddammit, Baker!"

Willis Postlethwaite was a Franklin boy. His family owned a hotel on the public square called Post Hotel. My mother and daddy used to stay there when they came to check on me. It wasn't a bad hotel. They had a dining room, and even though the food wasn't all that good, we used to go down there on Sunday and eat lunch.

Harrison Rue and his older brother, Waitt, were the kind of guys it would be nice to have with you if you had to go into a dark alley. Both of them were great big broad-boned country boys. They were two guys you didn't want to mess with, but neither one of them ever gave anybody trouble.

John Still was from Boston, Massachusetts. He was a real Boston Bean. He'd say, *"Jeez!"* And if something was real egregious, he'd say, *"Jesus H. Christ!"* But if something was ordinary, he'd just say, *"Aw, balls."* Jimmy Akin was a right nice young fellow. Nobody ever had any problems with him. He used to date Joanna Bransford. Jimmy was a pilot in World War II. He got shot down.

We weren't allowed to get more than 100 demerits. One day Professor Briggs called me into his office. He said, "Baker, you've got 100 demerits. Now you've got a choice, you can either pack up and go home, or you can take a hand whipping. That will take off 25 demerits, so you'd only have 75. You can take your choice right now." I said, "Professor Briggs, I guess I'll have to take the hand whipping. I'd rather take a hand whipping than have to explain to my mother why I was coming home from school."

The old man got a yard stick or something, and I held out my right hand. He said, "You're the first senior in the history of BGA that ever had to get a hand whipping." I said, "Well, I guess that's some distinction." By the time they got to be seniors, most guys had enough sense not to do the sort of stuff I did.

I had a long list of escapades. One time I was arrested and handcuffed by some deputy sheriffs. I'd been on the roof of a canning company. It was close to the school, and I was exploring. I was just looking around. Professor Briggs was friends with the sheriff, and he got me out of that one. I was pretty good with a slingshot, and I occasionally broke windows at Franklin High School. I also did things like sneak into the kitchen pantry at night, and another time I let the air out of Professor Briggs' tires on Halloween. But my biggest caper happened during spring vacation when I was a senior.

There'd been a lot of rain and the Harpeth River was way up. I wanted to take a canoe trip, but I didn't have a canoe. So I borrowed a couple of paddles from the BGA Museum, and then I enlisted my roommate, John Hoskins. We went down to a pig farm I'd seen beside the river, and we saw a new wooden trough. We carried it down to the river. By the time the farmer came running down to the water, we were floating away on the current. We made it a few miles, but the farmer was waiting for us at a bridge downstream. We had to load the trough in the back of his truck. Mr. Briggs threatened to kick me out of school, but he didn't do it.

I finally managed to work off all my demerits. For every week I'd go without getting a demerit, some would get taken off. And others would get removed for doing yardwork. I was going to graduate with a clean slate. But one night, a bunch of us were in Nance Jordan's room. He was a big old guy who coached the football team. I was big, and he hated me because I wouldn't get out and serve as a tackling dummy for his football squad.

Anyway, I was in his room with some other boys, and I lit up a cigarette. There was a room at the end of the hall that was designated as a smoking room. Everybody would stand around down there, or sit on benches, and smoke. There was a sandbox in the middle of the floor where anybody who liked to chew tobacco could spit tobacco juice. But Mr. Jordan said, "Baker, you're not supposed to smoke. That'll be 10 demerits." That was Mr. Jordan's way of getting even with me.

The next year I went off to college. My mother decided the best cure for Mary Voorhees would be to put a lot of distance between us. So I went to Westminster College in Fulton, Missouri. The next year, I talked my mother into letting me go to Vanderbilt. That's where I spent the next three years. When I went in the Navy, I enlisted in a program where I trained to be an electronic technician.

The information for this narrative came from an interview conducted on January 18, 2012, and was supplemented with information from a pair of brief accounts written by Mr. Baker. Following his service in the Navy, Bill Baker had a long career as a banker, and also earned a law degree. He died in Nashville in 2014. He was survived by his wife of 72 years, Ruth Huddleston Baker, his daughter, Emily, two grandchildren, and two great-grandchildren.

BGA in 1939

View from football field

Battle Ground Academy will soon complete its 50th year. In the dormitories are boys from 13 states and three foreign countries—Venezuela, Mexico, and Cuba. Professor J.E. Poindexter lives on the first floor of the dormitory. He has charge of assisting students who need help in the evenings. On the second floor are Prof. Gaston Buford and Coach Nance Jordan, who see that all goes well in their section.

In order to house boarding students, Mr. Briggs is developing the "master and ten" system, which has long been successfully used in the East and in England. He has located two pretty houses on the campus. They are the property of the school, and are used as cottage dormitories. The younger boys are housed in *Greystone,* where Prof. and Mrs. Glenn Eddington supervise nine students. *Westover* is a bungalow occupied by eleven students, with Prof. W.T. Robinson in charge. The infirmary is located in part of a rented house occupied by Claiborne English and his family. Ample quarters are maintained to care for boys when a minor illness occurs. Mr. Briggs lives close by, and is on the scene at a moment's notice when he is needed.

The bell sounds every morning at 6:50, and each boy hits the floor. When the breakfast bell rings at 7:15, they are fully dressed and ready for inspection. If a tie is forgotten or a shoe is unlaced, the culprit receives demerits. A daily schedule is strictly followed. After breakfast, the boys get their rooms ready for inspection. They must be spick-and-span, or demerits might be issued. Classes are held from 8:15 until 3 o'clock, with lunch at 12:30. From 3:30 until 5:30, athletics or other recreation takes place. The evening meal is at six o'clock, and each student must come neatly dressed and wearing coats. The coats must not be omitted, even in warm weather. Table culture is not neglected. The boys come from homes that have trained them well in this art, and they are not allowed to become careless. They often leave BGA more impressed with the importance of table manners than they had been on arrival. After dinner, the study hours are from 7:15 until 9:15. Those who are well up on their schoolwork can study in their rooms, and a study room is provided for those who need assistance.

In each room are two single beds, and in nearly every one is a radio brought from home by the boys. The walls are decorated by the students, according to their tastes. One, whose father is a commander in the naval reserve, has pictures of ships on his wall and on the ceiling. There are also pictures of mothers and fathers, and framed photographs of pretty faces—who may or may not be relatives—give a homelike air to the rooms. In the corridor of the first floor of the main building, are photographs of ball teams and such celebrities as Carl Hinkle, Pete Gracey, Josh Cody, Stein Stone, and others, who are BGA alumni, and have made names for themselves in the world of athletics.

Boys are not allowed to go off the grounds except at designated periods, and they must check out when they leave, and check back in when they come back. No laxness is tolerated, and the teacher in charge knows where to locate them at all times. Except for seniors, who also have Sunday nights off, no student is allowed to leave the dormitory at night except on Friday. Church attendance is compulsory, but Sunday School is optional, and each boy goes to the church of his choice. If their work is up to standard, students are allowed to go home on weekends, twice before and twice after the Christmas holidays.

On May 26, 1939, A class of 32 young men will graduate, and can enter any college in the country with the certificate they will receive on that day.

This edited article was written by Miss Jane Owen, and appeared in the Review-Appeal on April 20, 1939.

Proctor System, 1940

The proctors are a carefully-selected group of boys whose main duties are to maintain order in the dormitories, and to help enforce the rules by setting a good example for the rest of the school. This relieves the teachers of considerable responsibility, and helps train boys to hold positions of trust and responsibility. Proctors are morally bound to do their duty in enforcing the rules of the school. Although it is oftentimes hard to penalize one's friend, the proctors should not be lax in upholding their responsibilities. They need the cooperation of the other students to not place them in positions that might cause hard feelings between them and their fellow students. The proctors receive privileges in recognition of their services. They have two extra nights out each month, freedom of the halls at all times, and 10:30 light permission. On the first Monday of each month, the proctors have a meeting under the direction of Professors Briggs, Eddington, and Buford. At this time, assistant proctors are chosen for the next month are chosen. Boys whose behavior and attitude qualify them for the job will, in time, become proctors. But proctors who are lax will be immediately replaced.

By John Hoskins, The Cannonball (1940)

George Briggs, Marble Champion

George Briggs playing marbles

This year, Professor Briggs again challenged BGA's champion marble shooter to a match. Sixteen of the school's crack shots entered the competition. Playing time was to last an hour, and each entrant was allowed ten marbles. Whoever was ahead at the end of the hour was acclaimed to be the winner. In the finals, Gary Smith gave Lee Mackey more than a run for his money. Lee Mackey finally won a hard-fought battle, and the students pinned all their hopes on him to beat Professor Briggs. Mr. Briggs had said that if he lost, he would give the whole school a big ice cream feast. He was unable to compete last year on account of a bad knee, but he came back as strong as ever to retain his title. He has never been defeated in the school tournament. Mackey pulled ahead several times, and it took the "old master" over two hours to defeat the courageous student. In the past few years, this event has been shown in newsreels all over the country. It has always been considered one of the main attractions of the year. It will probably continue as long as there are boys with enough courage to challenge the "Old Man."

By Philip Wanzer, The Cannonball (1940)

World War Two

Battle Ground Academy has many traditions and customs that will not be broken unless the most extraordinary circumstances demand it. Ever since our founding, there has never been a step taken toward coercing a student into taking military training. But now the situation is different. The school has decided to give as much aid as possible to the war effort. No sooner had war been declared than Professor Briggs announced that Battle Ground would do its part toward preparing to meet the aggressor. Under the leadership of expert militarists, the boys of BGA have been instructed in the fundamentals of marching, assembling rifles, and executing commands. They have responded well. It is a familiar sight to see an older student explaining some detail to the younger boys. If the response of our boys is typical of the youth of America, we cannot help but win this war.

The Cannonball (1942)

Van Montague, Class of 1943

I was born in 1922. My father died of pneumonia when I was about two months old, and my mother already had three other children less than eight years old. I was raised in Ripley, in West Tennessee, before the Second World War. The Depression was a tough time. A hard time. I was a couple of years behind when I started Ripley High School in 1939. I turned seventeen halfway through my freshman year. My buddies were out getting drunk, but I couldn't afford to drink. I tried to stay out of trouble because I knew what my mother was going through – raising children with no husband and no welfare. And I didn't want to smoke and drink, because I played football and baseball. I wanted to be an athlete.

Bubba and Bill Kirkpatrick were friends of mine, but I mostly hung out with Bubba. I only went to school about half the time. When Bubba was around, he didn't go to school at all. Bubba was really smart. He ended up building and flying his own helicopter. His father was Lucilius Kirkpatrick. He was usually away from home on business, so Bubba had even less parental guidance than I did. During the summer we'd stay out all night. I didn't really have much to go home to. We'd sleep at Bubba and Bill's grandfather's house.

The Kirkpatricks were kin to Dr. Robert Hutchinson, who was raised in Ripley and later moved to Franklin. A year or two earlier, Dr. Hutchison had suggested to Mr. Kirkpatrick that he send Bubba and Bill to Franklin, to go to BGA. Bubba had been sent home the year before for breaking windows. His bill for breakage was more than his tuition, but they were both going back in the fall of 1940. Mr. Kirkpatrick was rich, and he said if I wanted to go to BGA, he'd pay for me to go, too. Later on, I found out that tuition for the year, plus room and board, was $950.

Van Montague (on left)

I knew that my mother had a lot on her, but I wasn't sure what I should do. I'd never been more than 40 miles from Ripley. I'd ridden a bicycle to Jackson, but that was as far east as I'd ever been. I wasn't sure about going 200 miles to a school I'd never seen. So I went to Dr. James Sullivan, who was the preacher at the First Baptist Church in Ripley. He knew that I hadn't been going to school very much. He thought I should go ahead. He said that I'd get a good education. With that advice, I went to my mother and told her I had an opportunity to go to Battle Ground Academy. She was tickled to death. That would leave her with one less mouth to feed.

So that fall I left Ripley with Bubba and Bill in their father's limousine. It was driven by a black chauffer, but he didn't drive us straight to Franklin. We hadn't brought along any suitcases or clothes or anything, so he drove us to Nashville, and we went shopping at Davitt's, which was a men's and boys clothing store. After we got a big stack of new clothes, the chauffeur drove us down to Franklin. That was the first time I saw the BGA campus.

I'd come from a modern-looking high school, and I was disappointed. I didn't say anything, but the buildings looked like they were pretty much played out. I started to wonder what kind of education I'd get at BGA. But I really liked George Briggs, the headmaster. He seemed to know what he was doing. He'd played football and semi-pro baseball, and because I played sports, I felt like he understood me. He knew the advantages of playing competitive sports. When you get knocked down, you get back up. He would talk about how sports could make you a better person, and influence your drive and your will to win.

Mr. Briggs knew about life, and about straightening boys out. The local boys were pretty good guys. Some had grown up on farms, and had good parents. But BGA had a lot of boarders who were problem kids. Some of the boys weren't worth a damn. Some had too much money, and other ones had parents who weren't around a lot of the time. They weren't criminals, but they were halfway down the drain. Some guys didn't like Mr. Briggs. The way he got to the root of things could be on the rough side.

He was really good at reading kids. At understanding them. He could tell if they were going in the wrong direction. He could also see the good qualities they had. He knew what boys liked. He had a lot of personal contact with students. He would let boys be boys. There was a fight every once in a while, and he'd let them go at it. He'd let them wade through it themselves, and before you knew it, they'd be the best of friends. I saw so many boys that were right on the edge when they got to BGA, but by the time they left, they were pretty solid characters.

I lived in *Westover*. It was a house owned by the school, and it was across the road from the football field. My roommate was Zeke Grayson, who was from Alabama. He was a big guy. He was 6'4" and he weighed around 250 pounds. We weren't supposed to drink any alcohol, but every morning before breakfast, Zeke had a habit of drinking a beer. We lived in an upstairs room. My bed was over by a window, and Zeke's bed was next to a wall.

When he discovered that the wall was hollow, Zeke knocked a hole in it, and then he hung up a calendar – it had a picture of a pinup girl – over the hole. Then he put a case of beer in the basement, and lowered some long strings down through the hole. He tied the strings to the beer bottles, and he'd pull the bottles up one by one. After he had his beer, he'd just drop the bottle inside the hollow wall. John Bragg remodeled the house about 30 years later, and when the wall was torn out, there were beer bottles all over the place.

I played football under Turney Ford for three years. He'd been a top player at Vanderbilt. He was a little bit like George Briggs. He had lots of integrity, and he didn't curse at his players. He didn't drive us too hard, but we wanted to play hard for him. Back in those days, we didn't have face masks. If your nose got broken, you'd come out of the game, but there wasn't a doctor to look at you and tell you to rest for a couple of weeks. Coach Ford would straighten the nose out the best he could, and when you quit bleeding, you'd go back in.

I was a running back. My first year at BGA, we had a home game against Father Ryan, a high school from Nashville. I got tackled pretty early in the game, and while I was in the pile, one of the Ryan players jabbed me in the mouth with his fingers. A little later on, he tried to bite me in the leg, and he grabbed me in a part of my body where I didn't want to be grabbed. Between plays, when we were in our huddle, I looked across at him. He was crossing himself. We didn't have many Catholics in Ripley, and I asked Zeke Grayson, who was playing tackle, what in the hell the guy was doing. Zeke said, "He's praying." I just said, "Well he's crazy. And the next time he does anything to me, I'm going to kill him." But Zeke said he'd take care of it, and he did.

There were some good teachers at BGA. Glenn Eddington was a mathematician. He always had a pen and pencil set that he kept in the front pocket of his shirt. He'd had the same pen and pencil since he graduated from college. Mr. Briggs used to kid him about it. He'd say, "Something is *wrong* with that man. He's had that set for 10 or 15 years, and he still hasn't lost them. Something is wrong with somebody who can keep an eye on a pen and a pencil for that long."

J.B. Akin came to BGA when I was a senior. The only time he coached me was my last year of baseball. He was a good man. He was the sort of person that parents wanted their sons to be around. Each boarding student got an allowance of $2 a week, and Mr. Akin was the one who handed it out. I can still see him sitting there on Friday nights, pulling money out of a cigar box and handing it out – two dollars at a time.

Corner Drugstore (David Gentry on right, behind counter)

There was a soda fountain at the drugstore at Five Points, and we'd go down there and sit at the counter, and have a soda. One day I walking down there with my friend, Cecil Oliver. I'd noticed that there was a big room upstairs, and Cecil told me that Daly Thompson's wife taught girls to dance up there. So we walked over and went upstairs. There were 15 or 20 little girls dancing, but when I looked across the room I said, "Geez. *Who is that girl?*"

When I came to BGA I wasn't much of a ladies man, but the girl had a classic face. Not just cute. Beautiful. She had black, shoulder-length hair and an olive complexion. Cecil knew her, and I asked him to introduce us. We went over, and the closer I got, the more beautiful she was. Her name was Jane McCall. She looked at me with her big brown eyes, and she smiled. Her father was a local businessman named Tom McCall, who owned McCall Electric Company. Jane was 13 years old, and she was his only child. From the way she looked at me, I could tell that she thought I was alright.

But nothing happened for a long time. I was involved in sports, and we only got to go out one night a week. But if you didn't make good enough grades, you had to be back at school by 8 or 9 o'clock, so there wasn't much chance to have a girlfriend. Something like a year went by, but on the day of the attack on Pearl Harbor, Jane showed up on the BGA campus with an older girl who was seeing some boy at the school. It was the first time we'd been together since we met, and we hit it off right away.

VAN MONTAGUE, CLASS OF 1943

Jane McCall

The boarding students had night study hall during the week. If you made good grades, you could study in your room. But if you didn't, you'd be in study hall for two hours, and a teacher would be down in front to make sure everybody behaved. The bell would ring at about 9 o'clock, and then we had 45 minutes before lights out.

When I was a senior, I was going out with Jane, but boarding students were only allowed to go off campus for one night on the weekend. Well Jane only lived five or six blocks away on Lewisburg Avenue. I figured that 45 minutes was enough time for me to slip away and run to her house, and see her for a few minutes. Then I would run back and be in my room before Mr. Akin, or some other teacher, came by to make sure I was where I was supposed to be. There's no telling how many times I did that, but I only got caught one time. I ended up getting something like 75 demerits for that, but it was worth it.

I served off my demerits, and graduated from Battle Ground Academy in the Spring of 1943. I was twenty years old, and Jane was about to start high school at Ward Belmont, a school for girls in Nashville. I went into the Navy, and I was a Seabee. My unit was sent to the Pacific. We were attached to the 5th Marine Division. It was mostly older guys – electricians, plumbers, and pipe fitters. And we lost a lot of bulldozer operators when they were shot off their machines. We were at places like Saipan, Tinian, and Iwo Jima, and among other things, we built airfields.

I got out to the Pacific before I realized the situation I was in. There I was, 10,000 miles from home, and I could be killed at any time. Jane wrote to me every day, and I wrote her when I could. I had her picture with me everywhere I went. All I could do was look at it and hope I'd get back home. I served in the Pacific for two years, and I had plenty of time to think. I kept thinking about what George Briggs had done for me, and for so many other boys. He got us to do things we would never have done except for him. I wanted to talk to him and tell him that, but he died before I could. I never even wrote to him. I never got to thank him for what he did for me. Things were really tough out there. There was a lot of death.

When I came home in February, 1946, I enrolled at the University of Tennessee, where Jane was a freshman. We got married in that August. I had been pretty good-sized when I played at BGA, and I'd thought about playing college football. But when I got back, I only weighed 129 pounds. Football was over for me. After two years at UT, Jane and I moved to Memphis. We wanted to get out on our own. We didn't have a car or any insurance at first. I was a merchandize manager for a department store, and Jane was a secretary.

We were living in Memphis when our daughter, Becky, was born in 1951. Our son, Thomas, was born there in 1954. He was a healthy, good-looking kid, but when he was about two-and-a-half he got sick with polio encephalitis. He was in a coma for almost six months before he died. Jane was with him at the hospital the whole time. Later that year, we moved back to Franklin, where our second daughter, Leila, was born in 1959. We built a house on Hillsboro Road, and after working for a few years at McCall Electric with my father-in-law, I eventually took over the business.

I married the girl I was crazy about. Jane and I have been together for 66 years, and we've been very blessed. We have two great daughters who never gave us any problems. We could afford to live the way we wanted, and we're still physically active. I took up tennis, and one time I was state champion in the 75 and older bracket.

Van Montague

There's not a whole lot to look forward to at my age, and I spend a good bit of time looking back. I think about growing up in Ripley, and the two years I served in the Pacific. And I think about what a big part BGA, and George Briggs, played in my life. The only class I had with him was Bible. But what I learned about loyalty and integrity didn't come from his lectures, or from the assignments he gave. He taught by example. That was the beauty of what he did. Mr. Briggs taught me, and a lot of other boys, how to live with other people. He taught us how to take care of ourselves. I believe he had something to do with me being able to survive the war. I'd never known my father, and because my mother never remarried, George Briggs ended up being pretty much like a father to me. Coming to BGA was responsible for so much that happened in my life.

The information in this narrative came from an interview that took place on July 13, 2012, and from additional research. Van Bettis Montague died in 2016 at the age of 93. He was survived by Jane, his wife of 70 years, two daughters, one grandchild, and three great-grandchildren.

A Snow Day in 1943

The recent blizzard that left Battle Ground Academy snowed in for several days produced developments which have seldom been seen before. Some of the more childish members of the school decided to see what skiing is like. Duffield produced barrel staves in some mysterious manner. The fact that the barrel behind Professor Briggs' house is missing is, we think, purely coincidental. The first skiing party in the history of Williamson County was organized, and Brown Cannon, who introduced a new technique, was declared champion. Eugene Abercrombie ran a close second, and the local hospital reports that he is doing as well as can be expected.

The Cannonball (1943)

Bob Short, Class of 1944

Here's how I came to BGA. I was from Como, Mississippi, which is about 50 miles south of Memphis. But in the summer of 1942, I was a junior counselor at a camp outside of Memphis. One day I was told that a man was there to see me. I went over to see what he wanted, and he said his name was George Briggs. Then he stuck out his hand and said, "Welcome to Battle Ground Academy." I'd never heard of BGA, and I didn't know what he was talking about. I said, "What's that?"

It turned out that my father had enrolled me without telling me. It also turned out that I was kin to Mr. Briggs. And later on, I found out that my father had gone to BGA back in the early 1900s. Well, there was no arguing with my father, and when the time came, I got on a train in Memphis and headed to Nashville. When I got there, I changed trains and came to Franklin. Mr. J.B. Akin met me at the depot. He was a good man.

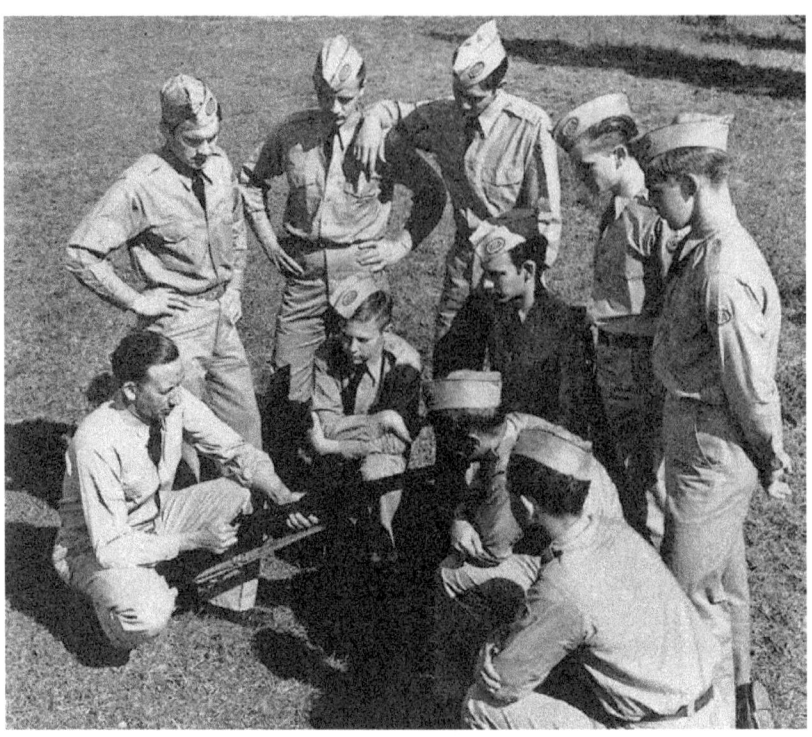

J.B. Akin instructing BGA Cadets

My first year at BGA, I was a junior. I didn't know a soul. And BGA was entirely different from the schools I'd gone to in Mississippi. There were only about 120 students. There were around 60 who lived in the dormitory, and the rest were day students. We ate down in the basement of the dormitory. The food was alright, but when the day students didn't hide their lunch, a sandwich might disappear.

Dining Hall circa 1940

My best friend was Jesse Colton. I played football, and the next spring I was on the tennis team. I liked BGA. We came up with different things to do. One time, when it snowed, we went to a hill that was back behind the school. We thought we'd try to ski. There were some barrel staves, and we nailed our shoes through the staves. Then we bent the nail back, and slid down that hill. It was fine the first day, but on the second day, somebody got tangled up in a hog wire fence.

Glenn Eddington lived next to George Briggs' house. He taught Math, and he was all business. He was a nice man, but I don't remember many smiles. I have a lot of memories of Mr. Briggs. He used to challenge students to play marbles. I think the deal was that if anybody could beat him, they'd get out of school. They'd have a holiday, but I don't think anybody ever beat him. He wasn't a tall man, and because he had a round stomach, I kind of identified him with Santa Claus. He taught History and Bible. He was a great instructor. Although he was strict, I don't recall him ever being unkind or rude—even though I was one of the worst-motivated students who ever attended BGA. Mr. Briggs would line the class up according to who made the best grades. The best student would be in the front, and I would always be the pigtail.

Mr. Briggs wanted the class to respond to whatever he said. If he said the wall was white, you were supposed to say, "Yes sir!" And one day he said, "That's as crazy as the Swiss having a Navy." And the rest of the class said, "Yes sir!" But I said, "No, sir." He said, "Short, do you have any idea where Switzerland is?" I said, "I think I do." He asked me a question. "What seaport do they have?" I told him, "They don't have one." He just looked at me. "But you're saying they have a Navy?" I said, "Yes sir." He said, "Well, how strongly do you believe that?" World War II was going on, and I was pretty sure I'd read that Switzerland had a small navy. I said, "I believe it enough to bet 20 points on each one of my final exams." He said, "You're on."

It was one of the greatest lessons I ever learned. I had to back up what I said. So for several Saturday mornings, I'd take the Interurban bus from Franklin to Nashville, and get off at Peabody College, and go to the library. The librarian was very nice to me, and would point me in the direction of the newspapers or wherever I was looking for information. I finally found it in a newspaper. Switzerland had two boats—I'm pretty sure they were both destroyers—docked in Geneva. I couldn't wait to take the proof back to Mr. Briggs. It wasn't long after that when Mr. Briggs died. He died in 1944, and the whole student body walked from BGA to Mount Hope Cemetery, which was on the north side of Franklin.

I guess I gained some independence at Battle Ground. Proving that Mr. Briggs was wrong, and I was right, certainly gave me some confidence. I guess I thought there might be something buried in me that was worthwhile.

The information in this narrative was taken from an interview conducted around 2013. Robert Mord Short died at the age of 93 in Sewanee, Tennessee. After earning a law degree from the University of Mississippi, he was a practicing attorney for several decades. He took up art when he was in his mid-60s, and became an accomplished painter. His art combined literature, poetry, and philosophy, and his work was exhibited as far away as New York City. He said, "I hope to get people to stop and look for a moment, and get them to think through the combination of narration and symbolism. I want them to go away with a new perspective on life, and on art."

Mama Haynes

In the main dormitory is the housemother, Mrs. R.E. Haynes. She came to BGA last fall, after the resignation of Mrs. Florence Wilson. Her gentle disposition, her sweet face framed in an abundance of gray hair, her engaging smile, and an adaptability for dealing with boys, coupled with her business ability and knowledge of dietary standards, make her an ideal person for the position she fills.

The love of her boys, who carry their joys and sorrows to her, amounts to adoration. She not only supervises the dormitory, the dining room is also her responsibility. She serves 69 hungry boys three times a day, which amounts to nearly 1500 meals a week. She plans meals, orders food, and sees to it that nourishing and well-balanced menus are prepared in an appetizing manner. She purchases the fresh food through Franklin merchants, and the wholesale items from local salesmen.

When boys get sick, Mrs. Haynes prepares their food with particular care, seeing that each one gets his favorite dishes. After a long day in class and playing on teams, husky boys always find a filling, satisfying evening meal waiting for them. On Thursday evenings and Sundays, the boys know they will get ice cream—not a dainty serving, but a bowl piled high and plenty of it. Mrs. Haynes has her quarters on the first floor of the dormitory. The home-like touches include gifts from "her boys"—pots of lovely Easter flowers that are blooming in her window.

The social side of life is not neglected, and banquets are great events. Halloween is looked forward to, because the boys take their girlfriends, and Mrs. Haynes spares no pains in making it a success. During ball seasons, Mrs. Haynes provides the teams with whatever the coach orders on game days, and she often feeds the visiting team as well. The football banquet is also highly anticipated, but the biggest gala of the year is the dance in the gymnasium with an orchestra that knows how to really play swing music.

To see Mrs. Haynes with her large contingent of boys is an inspiring picture. They enjoy a good joke at her expense, and like to include her in their pranks. There is only one thing she balks at. She says, "I feed them and love them, but I leave the discipline to the instructors."

This edited article, which was supplemented by additional research, was written by Miss Jane Owen, and appeared in the Review-Appeal on April 20, 1939, as part of an article titled "Battle Ground Academy." Mrs. Richard Edgar (Emma) Haynes died in Franklin in 1965 at the age of 83. She was the daughter of Confederate veteran, James Council Wooten, of the 48th Tennessee Infantry, whose unit had only been a few miles away when the Battle of Franklin took place. Immediately afterward, on his way to fight in the Battle of Nashville, he passed through the field of battle. Emma was born in 1881, and married a prominent local attorney in Columbia in 1909. Mama Haynes was widowed in 1937, and she was preceded in death by her only child, James, who had graduated from BGA in 1929. Her pallbearers included Ralph Naylor, Jonas Coverdale, J.B. Akin, Carl Smithson, Paul Redick, Ralph Brown, John Bragg, and Dr. Harry Guffee.

John Green, Class of 1945

I was born in Franklin in 1927. My father went to BGA, and my brother went to BGA. My aunt, who was my mother's sister, was BGA's librarian. She was married to George Briggs, the headmaster. I was expected to go there.

Mr. Briggs was a small man. He taught Bible, and he was a good teacher. There's a lot in the Bible about climbing mountains. He would put a chair on top of his desk, and then climb up and sit in the chair to illustrate what he was trying to teach us. There were times when he had to be patient. There was a boy in his class named David Haney. We were upstairs in the schoolroom, and the Professor was going through his lesson. David wasn't paying attention, and Mr. Briggs finally said, "David, do you see that bear in the door?" David got up out of his chair, walked over next to Mr. Briggs, and looked at the door. Then he said, "Yes sir. I see him." Then Mr. Briggs said, "What color is he, David?" David said, "He's black." Well, Professor Briggs threw his books in the air and stormed out and left the room. He couldn't stand it.

Mr. Briggs would go out and recruit students, and he recruited four or five boys from Cuba. Jose Palacio was one of them. We would have the Cuban boys to our house for Christmas dinner. The other guys in the dorm were gone, and they didn't have anywhere else to go. At one meal, Professor Briggs was there, and we were all at the table. Jose held up his hand, and Professor Briggs said, "What do you want to say, Jose?" Jose said, "I want beer." Of course, my mother didn't have any beer, you know. Professor Briggs was good to the students.

We had good teachers. Mr. Eddington was an excellent math teacher. When you were in his class, he taught you the mathematics you needed to know. He always had chalk on his hands, and used a handkerchief to wipe off the chalk. He had a lot of energy. Mr. Briggs was my uncle, but I don't know that I ever had a talk with him. About anything. Students always talked about how he played marbles. I played marbles, too. The place we played was under a big sugar maple. There was a dirt area right next to the dormitory. It was just off Everbright Avenue.

Sometimes there wasn't enough heat, and we wore ear muffs in Study Hall. And it could be freezing cold in the gymnasium. A fire would have to be built in a potbelly stove in the corner. And there was another problem. The backboard was on the wall, and when you went in for a shot, you could hit the wall. The gym was the locker room for football, and the players had to get in there and take their uniforms off, no matter how cold as it was.

Mr. Akin was a remarkable man. He was sort of intense. He seemed to have a lot on his mind. We learned physics and chemistry from him. He was a good teacher. The boys liked him, and he was nice to all the kids. He coached every varsity team. He just went from team, to team, to team. I'd go to the football games on Friday night, or the baseball games. I would sit in the stadium and watch, but I never enjoyed watching other guys play, I wanted to be playing myself. I would usually stay to the half and then go on home. There were some big ole boys that played ball. For most of my time at BGA, I wasn't strong enough or big enough, but when I was a senior, I finally made the baseball team. That was one thing I could do.

I've never been big. I've been known as Little Johnny Green all my life. Some boys gave me a hard time back then, but there were others I didn't have a problem with. I had a lot of homework. Being small, sometimes they would steal mine. Particularly my Latin. My dad could read Latin as well as he could read English, and he would help me with my Latin. I would go to school with my Latin homework. I was small, and there were one or two guys who would tie me to the wall and copy my Latin lesson. Being Little Johnny Green, I never liked school dances. I only went because I was supposed to go.

The war had an impact at BGA. Wooden guns were issued to the students, and we had to have a uniform, a hat, and a blue uniform, We would parade around on the football field. For one reason or another, the teachers at BGA weren't able to serve in the war. The army would've turned them down, but a great many of their students went straight into the military. Bobby Akin and I both grew up in Franklin. For a while, we only lived three or four houses apart. He and I were friends. We'd gone to grammar school together, and we were seatmates at BGA when we were freshmen. He joined the army during his junior year. Bobby was killed in action in Europe during that same year—on the week before Christmas.

Cadet training

Almost every guy in my class intended to join either the Army or the Navy right after they left BGA. With Bobby being killed, my dad said I should try the Navy. Sometime before that, Mr. Akin had brought a color chart to physics class. He tested the whole class. Everybody else made 100, but I made a mistake every time. He said, "Son, did you know you were colorblind?" I didn't.

When I went to the Federal Building in Nashville to try and enlist in the Navy, the old chief said, "We can't take you in the Navy, you're colorblind." But my dad had some connection with him. He said, "You need boys mighty bad, don't you?" He said, "We sure do." Then Dad said, "Well, take him." I tried to get into radar later on, but I couldn't see the screens properly.

I joined the Navy while I was still in BGA, but they gave me time to graduate. My grandfather was Walter Roberts, and he established an award which was given to the most outstanding student in the Senior Class. But the criteria must have changed over the years, because when I was a senior, I won the Roberts Watch. We graduated on a Saturday morning, and I left on Monday morning. I got on a train in Nashville and went to the Great Lakes Naval Station in Illinois. That's where I went through bootcamp.

I was going to be sent to the Philippines, but the atomic bomb was dropped, and the war ended before I got there. We were in what was called an "OGU," which stood for Outgoing Unit. We were put on a train, and we traveled west in boxcars with sliding doors on each side. They were five bunks high. If you wanted to look outside, you had to roll the door back and hold on so you didn't fall out. It was a trainload of boys. It took us four days to get to California, and we had sauerkraut every meal.

We got to California, and there was a terrible storm out in the Pacific at the time. We were going to board a ship, but the dock was rocking, and I was seasick before we even got on the ship. Instead of taking a direct route to the Philippines, the ship took us north to try and get around this storm, and it took us three or four weeks to get there. The water was really angry. We were just going up and down, and we were all seasick. I was in the Philippines for nearly a year.

John Green, circa 1945

In the beginning, my job was to repair the landing craft. I would have to get under them and scrape off the barnacles and repair the hulls. Later on I was put in charge of a few Filipino workers. One time I was stationed on an island where Japanese soldiers were still fighting in the jungle. Even though the war was over, they would sneak in at night and kill soldiers who were standing guard. One time a Marine on guard duty threatened to shoot me, and another time I almost went up in a plane to do some spraying, but I had been assigned to kitchen duty. The plane crashed, and the pilot was killed. When I was on my way home, we almost hit a mine that would've probably sunk our ship.

Vanderbilt started two weeks after I got back. I hadn't had enough time to change clothes, but my dad said, "Go on down there." That shouldn't have happened. I should have had at least three months to get my feet back on the ground. I went to engineering school and I got through, but I had to work hard.

I went into the insurance business in Franklin, and I was a scout leader for 50 or 60 years. I've got about 125 Boy Scouts. I've had plenty of help, but it takes a lot to keep a program that big going. Over the years I've had nearly 150 Eagle Scouts. When I was a boy, I'd spent a lot of time playing in and around the Harpeth River. I'd swim and fish, and look for arrowheads. I'd go back to Fort Granger, which was a Union fort right beside the river, and I found a few Civil War bullets.

One time I went there with some of my Boy Scouts. We were going to hunt arrowheads, and the owner of the farm put us in a wagon behind his tractor and took us to where I wanted to go. He said, "I'll just ride y'all over there. I'm going that way." So we went over to this field, and a little boy named Jimmy jumped off the wagon. As soon as he hit the ground, he looked down, and there was a beautiful arrowhead. He said, "Mr. Green, you put that there, didn't you?" I told him the truth. That I'd never been there before."

Glenn Eddington

Glenn Eddington was born in Nashville in 1905, but came to Franklin at an early age to live with his grandfather, Will Harvey, on Liberty Road. Glenn went to school at Triune, where he made his home with his aunt, Mrs. E.L. Pettus. His first year as a student in Franklin was under Miss Mary Lee Gray, a teacher widely known for her strictness. When he failed fifth-grade geography in his first term, his tears had no effect on her. By the time he reached high school, his grades had stabilized, and he was among the best students in his class. He also acquired a winning way and an endearing smile. His favorite subject was mathematics. His performance inspired one of his teachers, and he became an example to the class.

After school hours, he worked in North Brothers Drug Store as a porter, a delivery boy, a soda jerker, and wherever else he was needed. He graduated from high school in 1921, and went to work at the drugstore full-time for the next year. He longed for a college education, and through his own efforts and with the assistance of a kinswoman, he entered Davidson College, where he received his degree in 1926. He returned to Franklin, and while getting his Master's degree at Peabody College, he taught half-days at Battle Ground Academy.

He has been on the faculty at BGA for 12 years, and teaches plane and solid geometry, and trigonometry. Students call him Mr. Eddington to his face, but when his back is turned, they call him "Old Thirty-Minute Eddington." It was a name he received after he caught a group of boys engaged in some misdemeanor. They expected to receive demerits that would result in five or six hours of hard work, but being new to the job, he only dealt out a half-hour of time. His students claim that he never adds to or takes from the grades he gives them, and they know they deserve what they receive. Not one of his former students has ever failed mathematics in college.

Eddington has taught students from every state south of the Ohio River, as well as from Canada and Cuba. Hundreds of boys have come under the influence of Glenn Eddington. He is loved by his students, and is a highly respected member of the Franklin community. He is an elder in the local Presbyterian Church, and teaches a men's Bible class. His hobbies are photography and playing checkers. The first six weeks of his vacation are spent teaching summer school, and the rest of the time is devoted to looking for new places from which to obtain boys to come to BGA.

This edited article was written by Miss Jane Owen, and appeared in the Review-Appeal on January 6, 1938.

Bobby Gentry, Class of 1946

We were poor people and we had a big family – five boys and three girls. My brother Jimmy and I slept in the same bed until he went into the army. That's how close we were as children. My brother older Dan, who people called Shotgun, had gone to BGA because somebody paid his way. He graduated in 1940. Well, my dad had died back when I was 10 years old. In 1941, Mr. Briggs, the headmaster at Battle Ground, came by to see my mother. He thought I might want to go to BGA.

He said, "I'm going to let Bobby work. We don't have athletic scholarships, but people are helped sometimes in Franklin. They pay tuition for several of our students." And he looked at me. "I want you at BGA. One of your friends, Gordon McDaniel, is coming. He's going to bring milk from the country to help pay his tuition, and you're going to be working. This summer you're going to do a little painting and that sort of thing. And when school starts, I want you to work in the building." I think the tuition was $125. I decided to go, and I was excited about it.

I was crazy about Mr. Briggs. I felt like he was my Daddy. One time we were playing Castle Heights in baseball. I hit a foul ball, and I just stood there and watched it. He raised Cain because I didn't run it out. Things like that meant a lot.

Mr. Briggs was really good at shooting marbles. He could shoot marbles like he was shooting pool. Mr. Briggs didn't shoot the way most people shot. He shot country-fingered. He could get one marble to spin, and make it curve around and get to another marble. We would supposedly get a holiday if anybody could beat him. I was a pretty good marble shot. I used to go downtown to the courthouse with my friends. I told my mother I wasn't playing for keeps, but I was. I shot against Mr. Briggs when I was a sophomore. He died that year, but I couldn't beat him.

I was not much of a student, but BGA was the greatest thing that ever happened to me. There were two reasons. The first was that it was all boys. When we were in school, we didn't have anything on our minds but school. We didn't worry about talking to girls, or having a girlfriend. The other reason BGA was good for me was Saturday school. Every Friday at assembly, the headmaster read out a list of demerits. If you had to serve time, or if you failed any subject for that week, then you had to come to Saturday school. One teacher came in each Saturday to handle the whole group. The other teachers had left their assignments, and whoever was in charge made sure you did the work. It was real simple. If you passed every week, then you were going to pass every month. And if you passed every month, you were going to make it.

Study Hall circa 1940

We had eight periods – four classes and four study halls. My mother was uneducated, and my brother Jimmy couldn't help me. He was only 18 months older than I was, and he didn't like school anyhow. So because there wasn't anybody at home to help me with my school work, I did a lot of it at BGA. There were only eight of us in the eighth grade, and one of my classmates, Robin Courtney, was one of the smartest guys, and one of the greatest people, I ever knew.

For eighth grade, ninth grade, and part of my sophomore year, I swept out the study hall every afternoon. I swept the two rooms that were up there, then I swept down the steps and cleaned up the two rooms downstairs. But I didn't clean up the library or the restroom. A black man we called Uncle Henry was the janitor. He was friendly with everybody. We talked to him whenever we got the chance.

Mr. Briggs died when I was a sophomore. And at an assembly toward the end of my sophomore year, Mr. Eddington said, "I want to see Bobby Gentry in the library." Well, that scared me to death. So after assembly, we went in the library and sat down. He talked sort of fast. "Bobby, I don't believe in you being the only person working in front of the other students. I just oppose that." That scared me even more. Then he said, "All I'm going to say is this. You've been a good boy. You're not the best student here, but you deserve to graduate, so you'll always get to go to school here. And don't thank me. Just do something for somebody else." Then he left, and that was it.

I loved Glenn Eddington. He taught me math in the eighth grade and in all four years of high school. Without him, I don't think I would've ever ended up being a math teacher. He was a great person, but I was afraid of him. Not that he hit me. I just knew if I didn't do what I was supposed to do, I'd be in trouble.

I can see him now with his high top, patent leather shoes on. Every test he ever gave, he'd have a piece of paper. He'd unfold it and write whatever he'd written on the board – neat as it could be. Sometimes he talked to me about shooting pool, and how much geometry was in it. I don't know anybody that didn't think a lot of him.

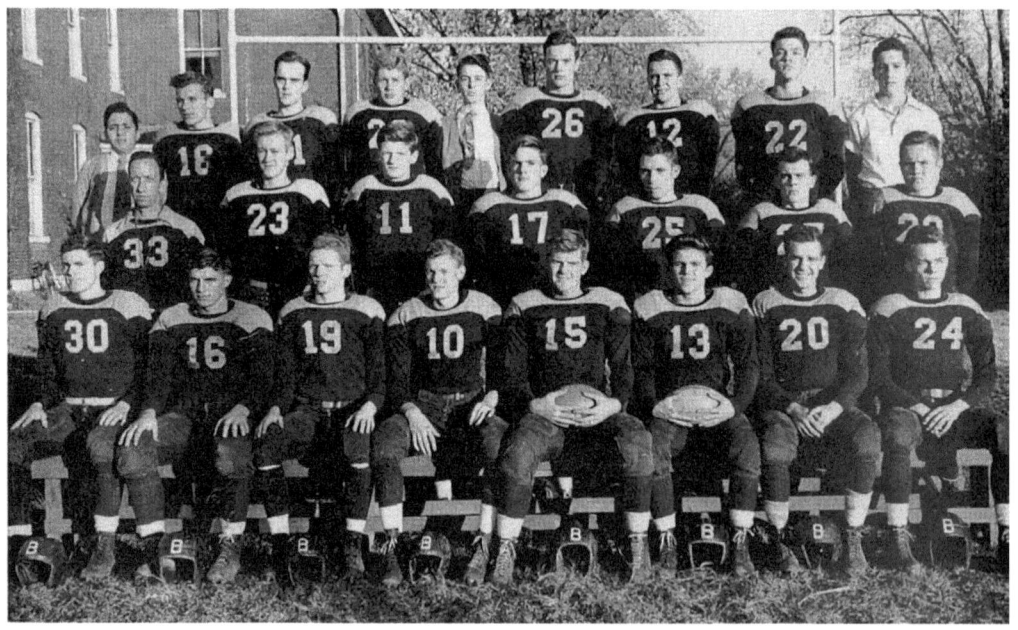

1945 football team (Bobby Gentry #15)

In the 1941 and 1942 seasons, in my eighth grade and freshman years, my football coach was Turney Ford. He had been a great player at Vanderbilt. That first year we were playing Baxter Seminary. Coach Ford said, "Bobby, you're going to play tonight." I said, "Well, I didn't think I could." Then Mr. Briggs came down out of the stands. He said, "You can't do that. He's going to lose a year of eligibility if you put him in." Turney Ford ended up joining the army. My coach in the 1943 season was Ira Jones, but he only stayed a year. Mr. J.B. Akin, who had been coaching the B team, was the coach for my junior and senior years.

Mr. Akin was not a football man, but he was a good disciplinarian. He knew how to handle boys, and he got the best out of his players. Mr. Akin didn't try to fire us up before a game. He just had a way about him. He wasn't ever mean – never fussed much. We believed in him. Mr. Akin got a book on how to run the Split-T, and he taught us how to run it. So we had something nobody else had. None of the other teams had ever heard of the Split-T, and we beat everybody we played. Bettis Montague was our tailback, Bill Ross was fullback, and I was the center. Gordon McDaniel – the one who brought the milk to school – was a great player. When I was a senior, I was about 5'11", and I weighed around 195. Duncan School was our big rival. We'd play them at Vanderbilt – at Dudley Field.

Back then, the school didn't have anything, but Mr. Akin really knew how to pinch pennies. He bought Vanderbilt's old uniforms and their used shoulder pads. He probably got the uniforms for 50 cents apiece. I wore the same shoulder pads that a great player named Dick Plasman had worn at Vanderbilt back in the 1930s.

When I first came to BGA, we didn't have any lights. We played our home games in the afternoon. Not many people came to see the games. The only people who would be there were the students. But before my senior year, Mr. Akin took me up to Portland, Tennessee because they were getting rid of their old lights. I think they might have given us the lights, and we loaded them up and brought them to Franklin.

Mr. Akin got poles from somebody, and my brother Dan asked some telephone company people to bring them to BGA. I helped dig the holes, and Mr. Akin and some volunteers got the poles set and the lights put in. Franklin Power Light hooked up the electricity, and when I was a senior we had night games.

When teams I was on played away games, we went all over the place. In baseball, when Mr. Akin was coaching, we traveled in a flat bed truck. He usually had a tarp in there, and we'd lay on it. We went to Castle Heights, in Lebanon, in the back of that truck. We'd go to football games in a closed-up van. I think Mr. Akin borrowed the truck and the van from Mr. C.C. Brown, who lived on Columbia Avenue. When I was a freshman, we played a game at McCallie.

That was a great trip. I had hardly ever been out of Franklin. To get to ride a bus all the way to Chattanooga was a real experience

The school had plenty of other needs. We were playing a basketball game one night, and while the game was going on, Spencer Holt fell through the floor. The basketball goals were on opposite walls of our gym, and there was one little room at one the end of the gym. That was our dressing room. And when the city of Nashville was giving away some used bleachers and school desks, Mr. Akin took me to Nashville to get them. They were beautiful wooden desks, and I was the one who cleaned them. Mr. Akin saved BGA a lot of money back then, and that money helped save BGA.

People didn't realize some of what Mr. Akin did to get students. There were times when BGA was barely scraping by, and the school needed all the students it could get. So it started taking boys from Nashville that were having trouble. Some of them had gone to MBA, and maybe they hadn't done any good. Mr. Akin would talk to their the parents. He would say, "You can come to BGA, but only if you board for the first year. If you do well, you can come back the next year as a day student." That mattered because boarding students paid more than day students.

World War II started, and when I was a freshman or sophomore, students would write letters to soldiers who had gone to BGA. We'd write a note to whoever we wanted, and mail it to them. Several BGA boys died in World War II. Junior Hill. Jack Reynolds. Bobby Akin. And my brother, David, died in 1944. I was in class and one of our neighbors, a lady, came and got me. She told me something had happened. We lived in Franklin, and I walked home.

When I went to BGA, we had the Greers and Platos. That was an especially big thing then, because the school was so small. The students met in assembly on the first day of school. They had a list of all the new students, and they chose them publicly. I became a Greer. The biggest competition was the tug-of-war. Mr. Eddington worked with the Greers, and taught us to heave-ho. If we could get that rhythm, it didn't make a difference how big or strong the other side was. They were going in the water. And the Greers won when he was helping us.

The tug-of-war was a great thing. We'd go to town and get the rope right in front of Franklin Elementary School, then we carried it down Main Street to the Franklin Theatre. If the movie was playing, they turned it off. We'd go up on the stage and do a cheer, and then we'd leave. After that we walked down around the square and all the way to the bridge, and there would be a mob there.

1944 Tug-of-War

We would've already chosen which side of the Harpeth River we'd be on. We usually had a coach who made sure we did the heave-ho together. Once we started pulling, it seemed like it lasted forever, but it only took a few minutes. I only missed one of them – the one that was right after my brother was killed. There were other contests between the Greers and Platos. The basketball games and track meets were exciting, and we also had a big debate.

There were times during the school year when BGA students would hang out at the Gilco, which was a little hamburger joint near Willow Plunge. And during the summer, BGA students from Franklin would spend time at Willow Plunge.

Old Mr. Claiborne Kinnard and his brother, Brown Kinnard, bought mules and a scoop, and they dug a big pond where a spring would fill it up. At first it was a place where their sons could be with their friends. Then they decided to make it commercial. Mr. Kinnard put in another pond, and there was a narrow strip of land between them. After that, he covered the bottoms and the sides of the pools with some kind of plaster. It never leaked, but you could chip off the plaster if you weren't careful. The spring water ran right into the pools. That's why the water was so cold. We were probably the only pool in the country that had fresh water. It was a great place. Parents could bring their children out there and leave them. They didn't have to worry about them.

I started working at Willow Plunge when I was 12 years old. I worked there most of my life, and after I grew up, I managed it for two years. The Kinnards owned it, and they were great people. On Sundays we might have 2000 people, but you better not bring any beer. We didn't allow anything like that. When I was about 13, I was picking up paper and cleaning up the hill. Mrs. Kinnard said, "Come here a minute, Bobby. There's a couple over on the hill, and a man over there keeps kissing the woman he's with. Go tell them we don't allow that." So I had to go over and say, "Sir, we don't allow that. Don't be doing that." And they quit.

Willow Plunge

Russell Brothers, who was a rich MBA boy, would try to get into Willow Plunge without paying. He was trying to save the 75 cents it cost to get in. Just to see if he could do it. I had him arrested one time. The last year I was the manager, I was a deputy sheriff and I could arrest people myself. I picked up some Father Ryan boys that got in the trunk of a car and tried to sneak in. There were two cars of them, and that made about eight of them trying to get in free. I carried them to jail, and they were scared to death. Then I brought them back out, and they called their parents. I also caught one of the Gayden boys. His father was a famous doctor in Nashville, and I made the boy call his daddy.

When my brother Jimmy became head coach at BGA in 1966, he wanted me to come help him. He had never coached the line before, but I'd been working with the line ever since I started coaching. I'd coached with Jimmy for seven years at Franklin, and then I coached with Tommy Owen at MBA. I took a pretty good pay cut, but I wanted to go home and have my son go to school at BGA. That 1966 state championship team was a good bunch. Harry Ford and Don Denbo. And Steve Robinson, George Silvey, and Jack Milam – among many others.

The first year Jimmy and I coached together at BGA, I remember seeing him hit Don Denbo. We were scrimmaging at football camp. Don had the sweat pouring off him, and he kept acting like he could hardly make it. He'd say, "I'm dying." After he did that four or five times, Jim opened up his hand and hit Don in the belly. I thought it would knock him down. We scrimmaged for another hour, but Don never said another word. Old Don Denbo was something else. I think a lot of him. He was a great player. He was so quick. He couldn't run, but he had that quick step.

The only time I ever remember popping somebody, two of our linemen were talking in Geometry class. I walked down the aisle while I was still talking, and I smacked them both in the back. I nearly knocked them on the floor, but my hand was open. They were alright.

Daly Thompson was old school. In 1966 Jimmy and I were getting ready to play at MUS. We were outside his classroom, and we must've been talking too loud. Mr. Thompson came out and said, "Bobby, you and Jimmy need to get on down the hallway. You're making too much noise." There we were, big time coaches, but we got ourselves back down to faculty area as fast as we could.

When I came back to BGA to teach, the Greers and Platos were still being chosen publicly. By then I thought that was awful. If a boy was a sissy or a cripple, he got picked last. I went to Mr. Akin. "Is there any way we can stop this?" When I told him what I was talking about, he said, "You know, I never thought of that." So from then on, the officers of the Greers and Platos would get together in private and divide the new students.

In the late 1960s, two teachers were living in the dormitory, and they came into see Mr. Akin one day. They said, "Mr. Akin, our room has centipedes crawling all over it." And he said, "They aren't poisonous. They won't do anything." He didn't want to spend any money on something like that.

Some of the old timers that played back when I played have said we could've beaten modern high school teams. Our 1944 BGA team was undefeated, but we would've gotten killed if we played a good high school team today. Back then, a big college lineman would weigh 220. These days high school linemen can weigh 300 pounds. I believe some of the high school teams I've helped coach would've killed the University of Tennessee's championship team in 1950. When I first coached, the quarterbacks called the plays. But it's not a boys' game anymore, it's a coaches game.

When I became head of the Math Department at BGA, Mr. Eddington found out about it. He wrote me the nicest letter, and it included something I hadn't known. He became the headmaster after Mr. Briggs died. He said, "Bobby, I didn't tell many people why I quit. I did it because I didn't have the personality to be the head of a school. I didn't enjoy shaking hands with people and welcoming them, and all that. It just wasn't me. I couldn't talk to people and sell them on the school. That's what I was pushed to do, and so I just left." Mr. Eddington was who he was. He meant so much to me as a man. And as a teacher.

The information in this narrative came from an interview that took place on December 27, 2012. Bobby Gentry died in 2020 at the age of 92. He was survived by his wife of 69 years, Peggy Sweeney Gentry, a daughter, three grandchildren, and four great-grandchildren.

Ralph Brown, Class of 1949

    I went to six different schools before I came to BGA. My father was in the military, and our family moved from Norfolk, Virginia to High Point, North Carolina, then to Birmingham, Alabama, and on to Jackson, Mississippi, before we finally moved back to Birmingham. When it came to school, I put athletics way ahead of academics. All I wanted to know was what I needed to do in class to be eligible to play ball.

    My sister was an honor student at William and Mary. At some point she said, "Ralph, there are other things to read besides the Sporting News." I said, "Really? Like what?" She said, "Like a book. Maybe something by Alexandre Dumas," I probably said something like, "Who does he play for?" My parents had been told that I had some intellectual ability, and they started looking for a boarding school. At first I thought I might be going to McCallie, but one of my closest friends had gone off to BGA. He'd been up here for a year, and I saw quite a change in him when he got back.

I was about to be a senior, and J.B. Akin and Glenn Eddington came down and interviewed me at my house. It didn't take them long to sell me on BGA. If I'd stayed in Birmingham, I would've been a senior, but I repeated my junior year and entered BGA in 1947. Mr. Akin didn't just become my mentor, he was like a second father.

I could write a book about J.B. Akin. He graduated from BGA in 1926, and he made the Dean's List at the University of Tennessee. When he graduated in 1930, he was accepted to medical school, but he was from Burwood, out in the country. His family didn't have any money, and he decided to become a teacher. He would've been a great surgeon or a great pediatrician, but in what was a great break for BGA, he went into education.

He took a job as a teacher and coach at Ashland City High School for about $75 a month, but the time came when they couldn't pay him for three months, and he came back home. He ended up being the principal out at Burwood Elementary, and he taught and coached at Franklin High School before he came to BGA.

I remember the first day I came to BGA. I had on a white T-shirt with the name of my old school, Woodlawn High School, written in gold and white. Mr. Akin asked for volunteers to help move old stoves out of the dormitory. So my first day was doing manual labor. On the second day, Pat Wade, the Latin teacher, was on duty. He wanted volunteers to go down to Franklin High School, which was just down the road, to play in a donkey basketball game.

I went and had a great time. I ran back to the campus, but it was about 11:15 when I checked in. Mr. Wade said, "Ralph, you're late. You were due here at 11 o'clock. You'll serve five hours for the first three minutes, and one hour for each additional minute." I said, "That's not fair, Mr. Wade. I was representing the school playing donkey basketball." He said, "Do you want another five hours?" I said, "No, sir." I went on up to bed, and I thought I'd better get on the ball.

There were six teachers and around 135 students in school, and around 70 of them were boarding students. Tuition for day students was $125, and it cost $875 a year to board. I lived in the old dormitory. The real spirit of the school started in the dormitory, but we had a great group of boys from Franklin. There was something different about them. I wasn't real sure what it was, but it was something I had been searching for.

When I came to BGA in 1947, Emma Wooten Haynes – Mama Haynes – was the house mother in the dormitory. She was from a very prominent family, but the Depression had wiped them out. All the boys loved her. She was a magnetic lady. It was like having a mother on the scene. She was a nurse and a counselor, especially for the younger kids. Mama Haynes had a small bathroom and a little bedroom in the old dormitory, and I guess that sort of helped maintain some order.

In those days there was not only the two-story dormitory, there were borders living in houses across Everbright Avenue from the school. Students occupied about half of each house, and a faculty family lived in the other half. One house was called *Greystone*, the next one was Mr. Akin's house, *Midway*, and then there was *Westover*. Mr. Eddington lived on Battle Avenue, and he also had four boarding students. He walked through every morning on his way to school.

Old Dormitory

I wasn't eligible to play on the varsity football team in 1947. I was on the B-team, which was coached by Mr. Naylor. About halfway through the year, Mr. Akin and Mr. Eddington let me know that I would eligible to be on the varsity from then on. BGA was in the Mid-South Association, which allowed post-graduates to play. Even though I wasn't a post-graduate, I would be almost 19 when I was a senior, and that was pretty much the same as being a post-grad. That was one of the big turning points in my life. Around the same time, the light began to flicker a little bit. I started thinking there might be something to this education thing.

The BGA faculty was as good as it was anywhere. They wanted to develop each student – academically and spiritually – into a total person. Gaston Buford was an English teacher. He had fought in the war, and he was a pretty deep thinker. Mr. Eddington was probably the best math teacher in the history of the school. He taught five math classes while serving as headmaster. He always wore a three-piece suit, and a belt buckle that had Battle Ground Academy on it. He'd wipe the board with the sleeve of his coat, and he knew all of the theorems by heart. He was a commanding figure, but with all his additional responsibilities, and he wasn't always a strong headmaster.

Sometimes, after we had exams, we might get a holiday. Mr. Eddington would sit up on he stage and say, "You know, it's a real pretty day. Why don't we all just come back tomorrow." When that happened, the dormitory boys would run out of study hall, and it would be a war going down the steps.

During my senior year, I lived in *Midway*. I played football that year, and along with being the punter, I played some end and defensive back. Notre Dame High School in Chattanooga was one of our big rivals. They had beaten BGA in Chattanooga the year before, and when I was a senior, they came to our place. The night before the game, the whole school marched down to the square and burned Notre Dames star fullback in effigy. We beat them 28 to 20.

1948 Team (Ralph Brown, number 49)

Mr. Akin had the ability to discern each individual's weaknesses and strengths. We always wanted to please him. Whatever he said was it. We never saw him get unraveled during the games. He would invariably pick out something in the game, and then make the right adjustment. Later that season, we played down at Lawrenceburg. Ex-GIs were eligible back then, and they had a tailback who was a veteran. We were behind at the half, and it was the first time I ever heard Mr. Akin get on one of his players.

Tommy Robinson was a great boy. He was a 225-pound tackle, and we called him Butch. He was a farm boy, and we were in the locker room at halftime. Mr. Akin said something like, "Tommy, I know a couple of farmers who were talking about you. They said you were sort of lazy. They said you didn't do much, and you didn't have much spark. I'm beginning to believe they were telling me the truth." It worked. Tommy wore Lawrenceburg out during the second half.

But with about 30 seconds left in the game, we were only leading 16 to 14, and I was punting from the back of our end zone. I got the kick away, and their star player, Howard Rau, brought it all the way back to our three or four yard line. I was the last guy in his way. I got knocked down by a couple of blockers, but I was able to get up and make the tackle. When I ran over to Mr. Akin, I said, "Coach, that one was for the fans. We just wanted to give them a thrill." He looked at me like he wanted to say, "You're a nut."

In 1947, BGA had lost 2-0 to McCallie in the Mid-South baseball championship. And in 1948, when I was a junior, we lost the championship to Baylor 2-1 in 10 innings. In 1949 most of our team was back, and we said, "Dad gummit, we know we're the best team."

1949 Team (Ralph Brown, front row, right)

I was one of four or five boys that Mr. Akin talked to a lot. We'd come to the chemistry lab, and he would pick our brains. It was pretty informal. It was like he just wanted to talk, and a lot of the time it was about sports. Baseball might have been his least favorite sport.

Frank Giles was going to be our catcher. He was 6'2" and 185, and he was a talented athlete. Gerald "Momma" Johnson, one of the greatest athletes BGA ever produced, was one of our best players. Gerald didn't mind saying what he thought, and one day he and Mr. Akin were talking in the lab. He asked Gerald what he thought about the team, but I didn't know what Gerald said until later. "We might have a problem at catcher."

BGA Bus, 1947

The next day at practice. Coach Akin wandered out to me in center field. I thought he wanted me to pitch batting practice. But he said, "Ralph, have you ever caught before?" I said I hadn't, but that I was willing to try it. It turned out that I loved playing catcher. I had a good arm, and I loved the grit and the work of playing that position. Well, we ended up beating McCallie two games out of three, and we won the Mid-South championship. I ended up being named the team's MVP.

We didn't worry about how our uniforms looked, or whether we'd get trophies. We just wanted to win. Anywhere we went – Castle Heights, Columbia Military Academy, McCallie, Baylor – we'd show up on the BGA bus. And we had that feeling that we were the best team. It was like, "Buddy, we're here. And you're about to have your hands full." We had bonded together, and we had great team spirit.

Mr. Akin would go around the dormitory at least once a week and ask the boarders about their academics. He'd come to my room, and say, "Do you need any help, son?" I don't care whether it was science or language or math or chemistry or physics, he would always say something that would help me. He had a way about him, and we just loved him. I never saw a better all-around teacher than J.B. Akin.

I went to Wake Forest because of Coach Peahead Walker. He was from Birmingham, and along with being the head football coach at Wake Forest, he was a scout for the New York Yankees. He watched me play in the summer baseball league, and invited me to come to school at Wake. I thought I might play football. I could kick pretty well and catch pretty well, but I probably wasn't big enough for the type of three-yards-and-a-cloud-of-dust offense they ran. I wasn't really gung-ho about football, so I just stuck with baseball.

By the time I got to Wake Forest, I was turned on to learning. I never cut a class. And that's where I met Helen. My roommate and I coached our fraternity team, and in four years, nobody ever beat us. We were something like 34-0. I played handball with a couple of the Wake Forest football coaches, and I went to some of their practices. Baseball was still my biggest interest, but I was always curious about the inner workings of football, and the strategic part of the game.

I married Helen in 1953, right around the time I was getting out of Wake Forest. I was 22 years old and she was 18. Then I got a call from J.B. Akin. He wanted to know if I would consider coming back to BGA to teach and coach. I had never dreamed that I'd ever go back to BGA. But Mr. Akin had seen me come to BGA as a weak student, and watched me progress.

When I was a junior I'd taken Bible, which was taught by Mr. Akin. I did well in that course, and that helped us get closer. When I was a senior, I dated his oldest daughter, and having him as my baseball and football coach helped us get to know each other even more. I didn't know until later on that the whole time I was at Wake Forest, he was keeping up with how I was doing. There were two or three other guys that played for him and had been good students. I wondered why he was offering me a job and not them.

Mr. Coverdale said he would pay me $240 a month, plus room and board, and that he'd pay me for 11 months. That included working at Camp Hy-Lake for two months in the summer, which turned out to be a great experience. So figuring in room and board, I was making about $400 a month. That was enough. Back then it was pretty good pay. I don't remember any of the teachers worrying about money.

There was a lot of difference between the way BGA was when I was a student and the way it was when I came back to teach. Back in the 1940s, the students hadn't been materialistically inclined. We wore old, hand-me-down uniforms from Vanderbilt, and we thought that was great. But around 1955, that began to change. Not just at BGA, but everywhere. Then there were letter jackets and all these fancy trophies. Sometimes they were too big to fit in a trophy case, but that was the trend.

And there wasn't a lot of maintenance back when I was a student. The buildings needed to be painted, but we didn't care. It didn't make any difference if a door was lopsided. The school was clean, and we had desks and books. It was what happened inside the buildings that mattered.

We had a faculty meeting once a month. In every meeting, we'd begin with the boys whose last names started with the letter A. We kept going until we'd talked about every student. Sometimes the meetings would last three or four hours. In the end we'd get down to the 10 or 15 kids that really needed some help, and we'd try to figure out which teachers could help them. We worried about the kids we were teaching.

We'd ask all our teachers if they were doing anything with a particular kid. We tried to find a way to get them going. We weren't always successful, but I'd say we were way up in the 90th percentile, and the boy would usually come around. A boy who had been a yes-sir, no-sir type of kid in seventh and eighth grade, might get off-track in ninth grade. We'd say that the sap was rising, or that he was going up Fool's Hill. I loved working with boys that were really struggling.

At first I was Mr. Akin's assistant coach, but he let me do almost everything I wanted to do. He had a great analytical mind. During games, he would see where we needed to change our game plan. He didn't give pre-game talks to get everybody fired up. His teams were well-prepared, and he would just say a few things before a game. Coach Akin had great stability. When he walked into a room, he had everybody's attention. Daly Thompson, Glenn Eddington, Paul Redick, and Jonas Coverdale were like that, too. For several years, he was the only coach at BGA. He did a great job of putting the right guys in the right position.

There were times when Mr. Akin would tell me about when he was a student at BGA, back in the 1920s. He would talk about Sam Fleming and Stewart Campbell, who had been a couple of years ahead of him. He said Albert Jordan was the best lineman he'd ever seen at BGA. Albert was a big, strong farm boy. Both Tennessee and Alabama offered to provide his father with two farm hands to replace Albert if his father would let him leave the farm, but Mr. Jordan wouldn't do it. Mr. Akin thought Albert would have been an All-American in college, and I've heard the same thing from lots of other people.

I was crazy about Daly Thompson. He'd come to BGA around 1909. He had big shoulders, and one day we were talking football. When I asked him what position he played, he said, "I was the other tackle." I asked him what he meant, and he said, "Well, Josh Cody was *the* tackle." Josh Cody, who was a legend at Vanderbilt and ended up in the National Football Hall of Fame, was the other tackle. After

Mr. Thompson went to Vanderbilt, he came back to teach at BGA before he went off to World War One. Later on, he was principal at Franklin High School for around 25 years.

There were times when Mr. Thompson had to administer discipline. Each teacher did that in his own way. One day, he and I were in the back of a study hall, and students were studying for exams. He was grading Latin papers, and an eighth grader down front started cutting up. Mr. Thompson said, "Son, people want to study. You need to be quiet.' After a couple of minutes, the boy started misbehaving again. Mr. Thompson said, "Ralph, would you mind holding my book?"

I can still see him walking slowly down to the front of the study hall. He took the boy by the ear, and said, "Son, didn't you hear me the first time?" Then he cranked him all the way down to the floor. When he finally let him up, he said, "If you don't want to work, just sit there and be quiet. But I advise you start studying." After that, he walked back up the aisle and took the book like nothing had happened. His disciplinary methods were unorthodox, but they worked for him. Today, he'd get put in jail.

Daly Thompson

Ralph Naylor was another veteran teacher. He had married George Briggs' daughter, Sarah Ewing, and he was a wonderful guy. He was very talented. He had a pilot's license, he could play two or three musical instruments, and he was the best dancer on the faculty. He ended up with all the odd jobs. He'd run the popcorn concessions and take up tickets at ball games. He'd drive the BGA bus, and sometimes he coached B-team football or basketball. He taught a variety of subjects. Ralph didn't have a dynamic personality. He spoke in a monotone and had a dry sense of humor, but he was really a fine fellow.

Carl Smithson was one of my great friends. He loved football, and I'd take him scouting with me. He was a foot soldier in the Battle of the Bulge. He was strong. He could hit a guy in the shoulder with his forearm, and knock him halfway across the room. He taught math through repetition. My seventh and eighth grade math classes were on the other side of the wall from his classroom, and we were good friends. I'd say, "For God's sake, Carl, you went over the same problem at least 15 times. Don't you think they got it by the sixth or seventh time?" He'd just laugh.

Carl was a good person. He was a farm boy from out in Williamson County. He played football, and one time he said, "I would walk to Franklin High School, and walk back home at the end of the day. People offered to give me a ride, but I wouldn't take it. I didn't want to be indebted to them." Carl had the kid's interests at heart, and when those kids came back from college, they'd shake his hand. "Mr. Smithson, thank you. I didn't have a bit of trouble with math in college." And John Bragg was head of the English department. He didn't talk about it, but John was a decorated veteran in the Pacific theater during World War II. John had a lot of energy.

Jonas Coverdale

When Jonas Coverdale came in 1950, BGA was probably at its lowest point. The school didn't have any money, and something had to be done. There was no endowment. If there was a crisis, men like Sam Fleming had to come up with what was needed. The board decided they needed to change leadership, and Major Coverdale and Paul Redick were recruited from Castle Heights Military Academy. Coverdale had a law degree, but because he didn't have a degree in education, he was the president, and Paul became the headmaster.

By 1960, the school was flourishing. I give Mr. Coverdale a lot of the credit for that. By then there were more day students from Nashville. They outnumbered the dormitory students. Camp Hy-Lake really helped us. Every summer 200 kids spent eight weeks at Hy-Lake. That brought in the bulk of the boys from Nashville. Five or six of us who taught at BGA worked at Hy-Lake, and every year we'd pick up boys that would've otherwise gone to MBA.

Jonas Coverdale had been captain-elect of the Vanderbilt basketball team when he was a senior, but he was declared ineligible because he had played a game on an unsanctioned team. Coverdale taught one or two classes. He had a lot of business sense, and he had a great way with people. He was a man's man, and the students really respected him.

Paul Redick had been an outstanding field goal and extra point kicker at Cumberland College. I remember seeing him kick the ball out on our field at BGA. He was a natural. He was the headmaster and taught US History, and he was Coverdale's lieutenant. He was a disciplinarian. He frightened some of the kids, but he had their interests at heart. J.B. Akin was the other part of that threesome, and they made a great team.

One time a couple of board members said, "If you ever get tired of coaching, you ought to think about becoming an administrator." I said, "I've already thought about it. I don't want any part of it." All that responsibility could consume you. I just wanted to teach and coach, and work with kids.

Before I took over as head coach, I'd had six years of experience coaching the freshman football and basketball teams. Back then, I'd go down at two o'clock and coach the freshmen till 3:30, then go over and do whatever Mr. Akin wanted me to do with the varsity. We'd be through at six o'clock. I was confident that I'd end up being the head coach. I had some offers from other schools. There was some talk about me going to Oak Ridge, but J.B. said what he always said. "Just be patient, son." That was good enough for me. I knew it would eventually work out.

My first year as head coach was 1959. I didn't feel a lot of pressure. Mr. Akin had been getting me ready to be a head coach for three or four years. Tommy Everhart was going to be our fullback. He was strong and athletic, and he weighed about 210. But five days before we went up to Hy-Lake for football camp, Tommy's girlfriend invited him to go with her family to Florida. He said he'd be two or three days late coming to Hy-Lake. I told him he had a choice to make. Football camp or Florida. He decided to go to Florida, and he didn't play for us.

That was a blow, but Charlie Trabue moved to fullback, and everything worked out. The boys put in a lot of hard work at Hy-Lake. We had seniors like Tom Fiveash, Harry Guffee, and Buddy Benedict, and a good group of younger players. Bobby Morel was a fourteen-year-old freshman, and I put him in a cabin with Fiveash, who was captain of the team. Fiveash thought Bobby was too young to be there, but after a couple of days, he came to me and said, "Coach, you've got to do something about Morel. Every practice, he runs down the hill hollering, "Bull in the Ring! Bull in the Ring!"

We tried to run the Double Wing T, but in the end it just didn't click. Our first three games were close, but we lost them all and the fourth game was a tie. It was my fault. As soon as I adjusted to the players I had, we started to come together. We won a couple of games, and then we had a road game at Tullahoma. They were unbeaten and averaging about 37 points a game, and it looked like they were headed for the Clinic Bowl. Bobby Morel was only 5'7" and he weighed about 170, but he started at defensive end. Early in the game, he crashed in and hit their big fullback so hard you could hear it all over that stadium. It set the tone for the rest of the game, and we beat Tullahoma by two touchdowns.

The next week we played at home against another unbeaten team, Franklin County. A committee had come up from Pulaski to invite Franklin County to play in the Butter Bowl. They had a halfback named Bub Wilkinson, who was probably the best running back in Middle Tennessee. They were backed up near their own endzone, and Morel roared in and hit Bub in the thigh with his helmet. Bobby was knocked out for four or five minutes, and Wilkinson was down with a leg injury. They couldn't stop Duke Shackleford's passing, and we beat them 41-20. We ended up getting invited to the Butter Bowl instead of Franklin County. After that we won two more games, and tied Manchester in the bowl to end the season. I give that 1959 team a lot of credit for putting us in position for what our program would accomplish over the next two years.

When the 1960 season came around, we had a lot of good players coming back. They had worked hard in the off-season, and they followed the training rules. Drugs weren't around much back then, and they weren't mentioned when I talked to the boys about the rules. "Some of you might have had a beer or two somewhere along the way. And I'm not dumb enough to think that none of you have ever smoked. I hope you'll never do those things. If you sacrifice, you will perform. But if you can't sacrifice for our team for the next four months, you'll get us beat in a crisis. So if you do those things, you're gone." Something else that sticks in my mind is the lack of profanity. Somebody might curse if he got stepped on, but there was very little cussing on the football field.

They were a tough group, and they were smart. I told them they that if they learned to play for each other, they could do something that was really significant. I was trying to do one of the hardest things a coach can do. Teach a player to pull as hard for his teammates as he pulls for himself. I told them they would never reach their full potential unless they wanted to win for the other guys on the team. That's what it took.

Back when *I* played, we used our shoulders to tackle. But early in my coaching career, players started tackling by putting their faces and head into the runner's body. We had less speed collectively, and there were fewer injuries than there are today. But overall, during my years at BGA, I didn't see much difference when it came to the level of contact there was. Collectively, the guys from 60 or 70 years ago might've been more rugged than they are today. Maybe a little tougher and more dedicated, but they were not more talented. High school football players eventually became a lot faster.

We were up at Hy-Lake for two weeks. We practiced three times a day, and we concentrated on conditioning and fundamentals. Blocking, tackling, and ball handling. Simple, basic stuff. We'd run our plays 70 or 80 times. We practiced them until the boys really had a feel for it. Sometimes we ran our players into the ground with drills.

Charlie Fowler was a big, strong junior from Hendersonville. He was likable and smart, but he was a little lazy. My line coach was Spencer Holt, and both he and I saw how much potential Charlie had. It was hot on the first day of practice, and before long, Charlie lay down in the grass. He was moaning and quivering, and I was so worried about him that I had him taken to the hospital in Sparta. They didn't find anything wrong with him, but I had our team doctor, Harry Guffee, come up to Hy-Lake from Franklin. Harry was at practice the next day, and Charlie did the same thing.

Dr. Guffee went down and examined him. He came over and said, "Nothing's wrong with him. He won't even miss a meal." Two or three players took Charlie up under some trees, and left him in the shade. He was sweating profusely, and there was dirt and mud all over him. Sure enough, that night at dinner he put away plenty of food. But he never had to be carried off the field again.

Our quarterback, Duke Shackleford, was a junior. He had come to BGA two years earlier. One day Mr. Akin and I were pulling up weeds around the circle between the two dorms. A man and his gangly, skinny kid drove up. It was Burton Shackleford, who played baseball and football at Vanderbilt, and his son, Duke. Duke was about 6'1" and probably weighed about 135. Mr. Akin showed them around the campus, and Mr. Shackleford finally asked if there were any available scholarships.

We had five scholarships, but they were only for farm boys whose families couldn't afford for them to come to BGA. The Shacklefords drove away, and we assumed that Duke would end up going to Columbia Military Academy, which had more scholarships. A week later, Mr. Akin and I were doing yardwork in the circle again, and Duke and his father drove up. Duke got out of the car and he was grinning. Mr. Shackleford said that Duke wanted to take the entrance test.

Duke experienced Daly Thompson right after he came to BGA. Years later, Duke said, "Coach, you nearly lost me on my third day of school in ninth grade. I was out behind the new addition, and I was cussing this boy down on the tennis court. All of a sudden, Wham. I was knocked up against the wall of the building so hard that I think my eyes were crossed. I turned around and Mr. Thompson said, 'Hmm, son, we don't use language like that here. You understand?'" Duke went to his dorm room and broke down crying. He called his family down in Mount Pleasant, and said, "I'm coming home." But when he explained what had happened, he was told, "You're not going anywhere. It was your fault, and you're going to stay there and suffer the consequences."

I coached Duke when he was a freshman, and the next year I thought he was getting a little too big for his britches. One day in practice I decided to teach him to respect his offensive line. Without Duke knowing about it, I told the line not to block Gary Anderson and Bobby Morel. Duke dropped back, and as soon as he turned around, Bobby grabbed him and drove him through a hedge, across an alley, and into a vegetable garden behind a house on Battle Avenue. When Duke came back, he said, "Coach, I get the message." We never had any trouble after that.

Duke Shackleford

Duke's greatest asset was his speed. He was the fastest guy in our backfield. And he had a great arm. When he was in ninth grade he could to roll out to the left or the right, and throw the ball 50 or 60 yards. Very few high school quarterbacks could do that. Bobby Morel was raised on a dairy farm. He was very humble, and he loved to play football. Most guys liked football, but Bobby loved it. He didn't have a lot of speed, but he had great instincts and mobility. He also had more staying power than any player I ever saw. And he was as relentless in practice as he was in games.

I'd gotten to know Charlie Trabue when he was a camper at Hy-Lake. He went to grammar school at Parmer, and I promised him that I'd come to see him play before he started high school. He had a basketball game at MBA, which was where he was destined to go the next year. Even though some people thought it was brazen of me to show up there, I didn't see anything wrong with going. So I watched Charlie play. I could see that although his upper body hadn't really developed, he had the strongest legs of anybody else on the court. I also saw how smart he was, and how much he hustled. And he had some athletic heritage. His grandfather, Big Ed Hamilton, had gone to BGA around the turn of the century – back when it was known as the Mooney School. He went on to become the most legendary athlete in Vanderbilt history. Instead of going to MBA, Charlie ended up coming to BGA, and he started at quarterback on the varsity as a sophomore.

Paul Guffee was a warrior on the field. He struck like a rattler, and he was very smart and very consistent. His father, our team doctor, had been an outstanding football player at BGA, and later on he was team captain at Vanderbilt. Larry Brown was 5'9" if you stretched him, and he might've weighed 160. Larry didn't say a whole lot, but he was a vicious tackler. Outside of Pedro Paz in the mid-1950s, he was the best open field tackler I'd seen at BGA. I don't remember him ever missing a tackle. He was smart and athletic. He was a gymnast and a diver, and he had been the state pole vault champion when he was a junior. Whitehall Morrison was the best punter in the state, and he played safety and flanker. Whitey wasn't that fast, but he was smooth. He ran great routes, and he had great hands.

I always wanted to get the best eleven players on the field. That didn't mean the eleven most talented guys. It meant the best eleven that could function together as a unit. I would tell them that running plays was like playing music. It's got to blend. It's got to have the right tone. Players had to work in unison, and the guys I had were willing to work together. We had hardly any injuries. In two years we only had a couple of boys miss two or three games.

We had three tough games to start off our season. Carthage was one of the top teams in Middle Tennessee, but we got by them 21-13. Then we beat Murfreesboro Central 12-0 in a downpour. The next week we were playing at Columbia. We were behind at halftime, but we scored four second-half touchdowns and won 34-14. We kept getting better, and after we won our next three games, we had another big challenge when we played at Franklin County. I had gotten wind of what their coach had said to his players. He said they were going to break Charlie Trabue. The coach told his kids that Charles was from an upper crust family, and that he couldn't take getting hit.

1960 Offense

1960 Defense

In the game against Franklin County, the score was tied and we had a first down on their three or four yard line. Charlie carried the ball three times in a row and scored. They had four boys that ended up playing in the Southeastern Conference. They turned Charlie upside down once, but he ran hard and he was tough. We won, and when I shook hands with the other coach, he said, "Ralph, I thought we knew how to beat you. We thought we could break your fullback – beat him down. But at halftime, two or three of my guys said, 'Coach, we're trying to break him, but he just keeps coming.'" I can't say that I ever took a timid boy and made him tough. Being tough is something a guy is born with.

And during that game, something funny happened that involved Paul Redick and Dr. Guffee. Harry and I would both chew tobacco during the games. Paul and Harry were close friends, and one day Paul said he needed to talk to us. He tried to be tactful, but somebody had complained that chewing tobacco was uncouth.

About three days earlier, the Clinic Bowl committee had called me and said, "Coach, if you beat or tie Franklin County, you're in our bowl." There was a huge crowd when we got to Winchester. They had a heck of a team, and in the second quarter somebody said, "Coach Brown, Mr. Redick wants you." He was over behind a light pole, and I went over during a time out. He was nervous. He just said, "Give me a chew of that tobacco," and I started laughing.

I never had any doubts about Charlie Trabue, but I wasn't sure how Charlie Fowler would turn out. Fowler was a junior, and he had never started a game the whole season. Charlie was a great boy. He was 6'2" and even though he weighed 225, he moved like a panther. I knew he could play, but he was inconsistent. He had what it took physically, but he didn't really like football. Guys like Bobby Morel and Gary Anderson loved football, but Fowler didn't. And Gary, who was rugged and tough, had a mean streak that Charlie Fowler didn't have.

I used to pace up and down the sidelines. It helped me think. I don't know why I did it, but in a game toward the end of the season I said, "Fowler, come up here." I asked him what he did on a couple of particular plays, and he told me. He was walking with me, and he finally asked if I was going to put him in. I said, "No, I'm not putting you in. You're the best-looking athlete in the whole stadium, but I just want all these people to look at you and wonder why you aren't getting to play. Now go sit down." That might've been the only time I used humiliation to motivate one of my players.

We blew out the last two teams we played, and finished the regular season at 10-0. We were going to play Isaac Litton High School in the Clinic Bowl on Thanksgiving Day. Because BGA was a small school, the Clinic Bowl officials hadn't expected us to sell many tickets. They told me the record for the most money a school had raised from ticket sales was just under $3000. When I said I'd be shocked if we sold less than $10,000 worth of tickets, they said they'd be thrilled if we made it to $5000. John Bragg headed up ticket sales, and we put up a painting of a wooden thermometer that showed how much we had sold. We updated it every day at Assembly, and we ended up selling $15,300 worth of tickets. The whole school was proud of all the tickets we sold, and that sort of fused into the football team.

Isaac Litton had a huge center named John Comer who weighed around 250. Joe Torrence, our middle guard, might've weighed 185. Litton also had Billy Tomlinson, an All-Southern left halfback, and I was worried about him bolting up the middle behind Comer. Joe would've given it everything he had, but both Spencer Holt and I thought he was too small to take on Comer. Charlie Fowler was big enough and talented enough to do what we needed, but he had never played middle guard, and we only had 10 days to get him ready.

I had a friend with the Philadelphia Eagles, and he showed me a defense that keyed on the halfbacks.

It fit our players really well. We called it the Eagle Defense, and we ended up using it about 80% of the time in the Clinic Bowl. The Isaac Litton team arrived at the stadium in a chartered Greyhound bus. When we showed up in our school bus, the announcer, Larry Munson, said, "There's the BGA team and, *My God*, the coach is driving the bus." He didn't know that I was also the one who taped my players' ankles. There were around 32,000 people at Vanderbilt waiting to see the game.

Litton had something like seven major-college prospects, and they had the reputation of trying to physically intimidate teams at the beginning of the game. I warned our guys about that. I wanted us to be mentally and physically ready, and to play with a controlled fanaticism. Before the game I told Fowler, "I'm going to keep an eye on you. And if you let down one time, you're coming out." Litton was favored to beat us by a six points, but I thought if we were really sharp, if we did what we were supposed to do, we had a chance to win by a touchdown. When I walked on the field before the game, I felt like I was a foot off the ground.

I hadn't expected us to be flawless on offense and defense and in our kicking game. I hadn't expected that we'd be two touchdowns ahead at halftime. I thought about opening up our passing game, but I wanted to avoid mistakes, and so we just stuck with our game plan.

Litton had only been shut out one time over the past several seasons, but they never got past our 30 yard line. Although Bert Phillips was boy of average size and average talent, he had a lot of heart. He was usually our number three guard, but he started in the Clinic Bowl. One of our other guards had been disrespectful to a faculty member earlier in the week, and that cost him his start. During the game, Bert threw an open-field block that injured Litton's star running back, Billy Tomlinson. The whole stadium seemed to go *Wooo* at the same time. That helped set the tone for the game, and so did Whitey Morrison. One of his punts went 67 yards in the air. Trabue, Guffee, Brown, Fowler, and several others led the way, and it was an outstanding team effort. Just about everything in the game went right.

After we beat Litton 13-0, their coach said, "Thank God for the final horn. I tried to tell my players what they were in for." Several college scouts asked me, "What about number 98? Where has Fowler been all year?" Charlie went berserk in that game.

We lost a lot of great boys to graduation, but players like Duke Shackleford, Charlie Fowler, Alvin Ford, Johnny Jewell, Sid Tompkins, and Bobby Morel were back for the 1961 season. We had won 11 games in a row, and hadn't lost a game since the third game of the 1959 season. We started the season 8-0, and ran our winning streak to 19 in a row, but then we lost to Bradley County in front of a big crowd at Vanderbilt. We bounced back with a tough win at Springfield, and closed out our season by going back to the Clinic Bowl and beating Father Ryan 18-6 in the rain.

By then, Charlie Trabue and Paul Guffee were playing on the freshman team at Vanderbilt, Larry Brown was playing freshman ball at North Carolina State, and Joe Torrence and Bill Redick were both playing at Centre College. The next year they were all varsity athletes, and Alvin Ford, Johnny Jewell, and Charlie Fowler were on the freshman team at Auburn.

After he graduated from BGA in 1963, Bobby Morel was a three-year starter at Tennessee. Trabue and Guffee both had distinguished careers at Vanderbilt, and Larry Brown became one of the leading cornerbacks in the Atlantic Coast Conference. Bill Redick had hardly played a down at BGA, but when he was a senior at Centre, he was an All-Conference defensive end. He was a late bloomer. He had heart and brains and desire when he was in high school, but his legs hadn't caught up with him yet. And Charlie Fowler just kept getting better. Only seven years after lying under a tree up at Hy-Lake in 1960, he was playing for the Miami Dolphins in the NFL.

Duke Shackleford could have probably played quarterback for any college team in the country, but he decided to play baseball. He pitched at Auburn, and after college he signed with the Yankees. But he developed bursitis in his shoulder, and went on to be a head football coach in high school, and an assistant coach in college.

I left BGA in 1962 and became the freshman coach at Vanderbilt. I came very close to being named head coach a few months later, but that didn't materialize, and I left coaching and had a long career in the insurance business.

Bill Redick, senior year

When a player dies, it's almost like almost losing a son. Bill Redick passed away a few days ago. I first knew Bill when he was 10 years old. He spent a lot of his life doing legal work. Fighting against the death penalty. Until I got to be eighty, I never thought about how long I'd live. Then I thought, man, the gap is getting pretty narrow. I better get as much done as I can. I haven't got much time left.

I could always sleep on the night before a game. But sometimes I would be so wound up after we played that I'd just lie there in bed. I'd finally get up and walk across Everbright Avenue. I'd walk down the middle of the field and listen to the popcorn bags blowing around, and think about how, four hours earlier, the place had been packed. There had been pandemonium and chaos, and then there was nothing. It was history. It was over.

When I graduated in 1949, the last thing my class did together was walk down and stand around the flagpole. Some of us were choked up, but we sang the alma mater. I felt like I was losing part of my heart. I loved the school. I choke up almost every time I come to graduation. And becoming a teacher, having something that gave me purpose, was wonderful. The most fulfilling part of teaching, and of coaching, was seeing a boy reach his potential. Coming to BGA was one of the best things that ever happened to me.

This narrative was taken from interviews conducted on February 10, 2012, October 5, 2012, and July 22, 2016, and from unrecorded conversations the editor had with Coach Brown over the years. He died in 2017 at the age of 86. Ralph Brown was preceded in death by his wife, Helen, and their son, Mike, and was survived by their son, Wink.

Henry Brown

From the early 1920s until the late 1940s, one of the most noted figures at Battle Ground Academy was William Henry Brown, who was called Uncle Henry. He was the subject of several brief articles in the school newspaper, the Cannonball. In 1937, an unnamed student wrote the following.

"Where did Uncle Henry live, and what did he do before he came to BGA? We asked him the other day, and "the sixth member of the faculty" told us some facts about himself. He was born out in the country, and had farmed all his life until he moved to Franklin. In his prime, he was a crack shot with the old double-barreled shotgun he still has. He never went hunting without bringing back two or three rabbits. He says, "Fried rabbit cooked good and done is the best meat there is." He left the farm and came to Franklin in 1921. He worked under Mr. Peoples for four years, and has worked for Mr. Briggs for the last 12 years. "I've been working here for so long that some boys who were here when I started are married and have children of their own." Uncle Henry leaves home at four o'clock every morning, and gets to the campus at 4:30. He puts in a full day's work, and says, "The boys serving off time are mighty helpful." Despite the myriad duties he has at the school, Uncle Henry finds time to preach practically every Sunday. Mr. Briggs says, "He is the most nearly perfect Christian I know."

Another article was written five years later by Milton Lea, valedictorian of the Class of 1943.

"One morning in 1872, in the village of Flat Creek, Tennessee, Henry Brown was born in one of the smaller houses in the community. At the age of 16 he took up residence on the farm of Dr. Arnold in Thompson Station. After wrestling with the soil for eight years, Henry left and spent about the next eleven years traveling around the country and working on various farms. But instead of spending the rest of his life working as a farm hand, he found religion. When he came to Franklin, he learned that Mr. Peoples, the headmaster of an academy on the outskirts of town, was in need of a handyman to maintain the grounds of the institution. He got the job, and was put in charge of the upkeep of the school. By the time Professor Peoples left BGA a year or two later, the man called Uncle Henry by the students had endeared himself to boys and teachers alike."

The veneration with which he was held was reflected in a 1946 issue of the Cannonball. Anyone wanting information about Battle Ground Academy should talk to William Henry Brown, who is better known as "Uncle Henry." He is an established spoke in the wheel that makes up BGA. He came 25 years ago, when Professor Greer Peoples was headmaster. George Briggs became headmaster four years later. Uncle Henry was born at Flat Creek, Tennessee, which is in Marshall County. That same year, his family moved to Williamson County. In 1911, he began preaching. From then until he went to work for Mr. Peoples, he was the pastor at the Church of God in the section of Franklin known as Hard Bargain. Uncle Henry has continued to preach during the past 25 years, though not as a regular pastor. Even though he is in his mid-seventies, he can be seen from early morning until late afternoon, on the campus or in one of the buildings, doing one of his many jobs. Work keeps him busy from fall to spring. Uncle Henry says, "During 25 years at BGA, not a single boy or teacher has said one short word to me."

What follows is an article written by the editor in 2025.

"Henry Brown, who became known as "Uncle Henry" in the BGA community, was born in the Flat Creek neighborhood of northern Marshall County, just south of Williamson County, on October 11, 1872. His mother, Caroline Brown, was the child of Amy Winstead, who had been born in Virginia. His father, Sam Perkins, was born in Tennessee, and was a decade younger than Caroline. Both the Perkins and Winstead families had been among the county's most substantial slaveholders, and Henry's maternal grandparents may well have been owned by those families. The records are not entirely clear, but it may be that Amy was connected to the family of Samuel Winstead, whose 1845 will provided for the eventual liberation of his slaves."

When Caroline was born around 1850, Amy Winstead, who likely had other children, was in her early forties. Slavery came to an end, and in September 1865, Amy married Sam Perkins in Williamson County. They were living separately in 1870, but they were only two houses away from each other. Their homes were close to the northern part of Marshall County, where their grandson, William Henry Brown, would be born two years later. By the end of the decade, Caroline's family was back in Williamson County. In 1880, she and eight-year-old Henry, along with her 13-year-old son Alfonso and her 75-year-old mother Amy, were living near the Mount Carmel community. The census was taken that year, and Henry's grandmother and mother were listed as being black. But both Henry and Alfonso were described as mulatto, suggesting that their father may have either been white, or of mixed racial heritage.

Henry completed six years of school, and he likely did farm work while he was receiving his education. Around 1888, he moved several miles west and became a tenant farmer near Thompson's Station. In 1892, when he was twenty, he married Sallie Presley. Their first child, Mollie, who would grow up to become a teacher, was born the following year. They remained in the same area, and four more children were born before the turn of the century. Some years later, Henry moved his family south to a farm in northwest Maury County, where Sallie had the last of their eight children in 1910. A few years after that, the family joined the mass migration of black people who were leaving the Jim Crow South. When America entered World War One in 1917, the Browns were living in Detroit, where Henry worked as a porter.

Although several of their older children remained in Detroit, Henry, Sallie, and their four youngest children moved back to Tennessee. In 1920, they were apparently living on the old McGavock farm, Carnton, just west of Franklin on Lewisburg Pike. The next year, at the age of 49, Henry was hired by Professor R.G. Peoples as the custodian of Battle Ground Academy. For a number of years, he worked eleven hours a day, at the same time he served as the pastor of the Church of God in Franklin. He soon purchased a comfortable home at 230 Natchez Street in Franklin. His mother Caroline was living there at the time of her death in 1927. By 1930 their children had moved away, and Henry and Sallie used their home to provide lodging for black students who came to town from rural areas to attend the Franklin Training School, which was just down the street.

Henry Brown's work at BGA continued into his late seventies, but his health was declining, and he finally retired in 1948. Following Sallie's death in 1951, Henry moved to Detroit, where two of his daughters and three of his sons were living. He died there in 1962, at the age of 90, survived by all eight of his children, 12 grandchildren, and 12 great-grandchildren.

Walter Reed Capps, Class of 1950

My hometown was Waverly, Tennessee. A young man from Waverly named Petey Lucas had gone to BGA in the late 1930s. Petey had gone on to play football at Alabama, and he was very successful in the grain business. At some point, he told my mother, "I think you ought to send Walter Reed off to BGA. It would be good for him." There weren't any real opportunities in Waverly back then. I recognized that even when I was a child. So it was his influence that started me on the path that led me to BGA.

I left for BGA one Sunday afternoon in the late summer of 1945. My mother and dad drove me from Waverly to Franklin. In those days, it was about a three-hour drive. When we got to BGA, they stopped in front of what was called *Greystone*, the old house where Mr. Eddington and his family lived.

I was going into the eighth grade, and a portion of that house was set aside for the grammar school boys who were boarding students.

Mother took me inside and made up my bed, and after she hung up my clothes in the closet, we walked back outside. My father was waiting in the car. She gave me a big hug and kiss, and off they drove. I had never known anything but Waverly. I was familiar with everything at home, but all of a sudden, I was in a different world. I had no idea what to do or say. When they were driving off, I thought of some cats we had left out on Blue Creek Road. I knew how they felt.

I went inside the house, and in one of the rooms at the back there was a guy named Tom. He said, "I should be a senior, but I'm in the eighth grade. My father's had me at about 12 prep schools, and three weeks from now I won't be here." The more I listened to him, the more I thought I had made a big mistake.

Hazing was semi-allowed, and I thought it was about to happen to me. There were two or three older guys who felt like they had a right to embarrass and humiliate you. One thing they did was give you what they called "a question mark." You'd bend over—or be bent over—and they'd put a coat hanger against your butt. Then they'd take a big book and...*wham*. They would hit you so hard that it would leave what looked like a question mark on your rear end. It hadn't happened to me yet, but a time or two it almost had. But there was a senior at BGA named Dicky McKeel, who was also from Waverly. He was a star on the basketball team, and I told him I needed some help. So Dicky came over and gave a little talk to the guys I was worried about. After that, life suddenly got a lot better.

Life went on, and I adjusted, but after 9th grade, I talked mother and daddy into letting me go back to Waverly. That was the year that my athletic ability started coming to me. I had an extremely good year in football at Waverly, and one of the teachers at BGA, P.H. Wade, came to Waverly and ate lunch with my father. He wanted to talk to me about coming back to BGA. They met in the cafeteria at the bus station, and while they were in there having lunch, the entire roof fell in on them and knocked out Mr. Wade.

I went back to BGA my junior year. I believe there were only six teachers for the whole school, and I still marvel at how competent and talented they were. Mr. Eddington was the best teacher I ever had at explaining math, and telling you how to apply what you knew. But he was different from the other professors. He was a little less accessible. There was an air of mystery about him.

Mr. Buford had an unusual talent for communicating with young boys. He worked with me psychologically and athletically, and brought out the best in me. I was a young boy living in the dormitory, and I felt like he was watching out for me. Mr. Buford did a lot to help me bridge the gap of being away from my parents. He helped me improve myself, and he just seemed interested in me. I respected him a lot.

BGA didn't have a competitive track team, but we had track meets between the Greers and the Platos. I was a Plato. Two of the events I thought I could do fairly well in were the broad jump and the high jump. I didn't expect to get any attention, but Mr. Buford would come out in the afternoons and give me some instruction. I was in four tug-of-wars, and I never went in the river. It was just a coincidence, but the only time the Platos lost was the year I was gone.

Greer-Plato track meet, 1949

Mr. and Mrs. Naylor lived across the street from the school in the house called *Midway*. They lived on one side of the house, and Bud Pointer, Frank Giles, and I lived down the hall. I believe Mr. and Mrs. Naylor were newly married. One of them would be taking a shower, and every now and then Bud would run down to the basement and cut off the water. And sometimes before bedtime we'd go out and sit on those stone steps that were down by Columbia Pike. When we'd see a car coming, four or five of us would go over on the east side of Columbia Pike, and the rest of us would stay on the west side, where the steps were. Then we'd all act like we were holding a rope. We'd be straining and pulling, and if the car screeched to a stop, we would all scatter.

By the time I came back to BGA, Mr. Akin was living in *Greystone* with his wife and two daughters. He was the head coach for the football, basketball, and baseball teams. He didn't try to fire us up before games, but because of the respect we had for him, we really wanted to please him. Mr. Akin had personality and character, and the right amount of friendliness for the boys he taught and coached. Whether you were a player or a student, you didn't question his integrity, or his willingness to give of himself. We all knew we had to give him everything we had.

Greystone

BGA played in the Mid-South Conference. The other schools included Castle Heights, Columbia Military Academy, Georgia Military Academy, Baylor, McCallie, and Sewanee Military Academy. The league was an athletic association for prep schools. Several of those schools, including Castle Heights, heavily recruited post-graduates for athletic participation. Guys who had made All-State, or who were really good players, were recruited, and the prep school would give them scholarships. So we were playing a lot of freshman and junior college-level competition. Even though BGA didn't do as much of that as the other schools, there was a period of time in my junior year when our football team was tied with Castle Heights on top of the Mid-South Conference. And that same year, we won the championship in basketball and baseball. BGA was like David and the other prep schools were more like Goliath, and David would go out and beat them all the time.

There were some great athletes on our football team in the fall of 1948. The team was roughly half day boys, and half dormitory boys. A few of the dorm boys were rebellious, but just about everybody we had were winners. I guess that came from the way they were raised, and from their nature. They were respectful of their elders and their teachers. Our best player was probably Gerald Johnson. Later on he had the nickname, Mama, and he was a legend in Franklin. He was an unbelievable athlete. He also had a great wit, and being around him was a lot of fun.

I played on the right side of the defensive line, and Bob Crenshaw, who was very talented, played next to me. We always said that we didn't have to worry about the other side of the defensive line. Butch Robinson played left tackle. Big Butch was 6'4" and he weighed about 225. That was real big for that day, and he had pretty good speed. And we had Gerald over there, too. When he tackled somebody, you'd hear it all the way across the field. He hit the way you're supposed to hit. Gerald and Butch were both placed on the All Mid-South first team. But they had lots of help. Jack Schmitt was 6'4" and weighed about 220, and he probably ran the 100-yard dash in 11 seconds. And we had guys like Tyler Berry, Jim Barney, and Ralph Brown.

Every other Thursday night, 10 or 12 guys who graduated from BGA around the same time get together. Gerald Johnson has been dead for three or four years, but he's there with us in spirit every time. We'll talk about his sense of humor, his personality, and his talent. It was a different way of life. I graduated a long time ago, but from time to time, I'll see a certain quality in another person. Maybe it'll be a quiet ambition and a level of humility, and I'll wonder if he went to BGA. In my opinion, BGA stands out as a haven.

The information in this narrative came from an interview that took place on October 5, 2012, and from corroborating research.

Gale Pewitt, Class of 1950

In 1944, Mr. Glenn Eddington came out to where we lived on Franklin Road – where the Clearview Baptist Church is located now. He was making a sales call. He told my parents that BGA was the place where I should go to high school. My father had worked on some shop programs at Franklin High School, and after seeing what was going on there, he and my mother were easily convinced. My older brother, Dudley, went to BGA that fall, and I went in 1946.

Tuition at the time was $125 a year, but if a family had two students, it was $100 a pupil. But money was tight. We had a 10-acre tobacco base, and we milked 24 cows. There were two tenant families living on our place, working the tobacco. They also did some truck farming. So my mother recruited the wife of one of the tenant farmers – and my brother and me – to can tomatoes and beans. My mother made a deal with BGA to barter the tomatoes and beans for tuition.

My father had done lots of different things. For a time, he had a filling station on Franklin Road, near Brentwood. But it was the Depression, and customers' unpaid bills kept building up. People owned property, but they had very little money and they ran up big gasoline bills. By 1937, he was fed up with trying to collect money, and he sold out. We moved to a 100-acre farm in the western part of Williamson County, but that didn't work either. He also taught at an automotive school in Nashville, and he worked in a program for military veterans in Franklin.

Milking cows was good money. The price for the milk was pretty high, but the problem with cows is that it meant working seven days a week – all year long. You didn't take vacations. Working with my father and brother, raising tobacco and milking, was a great experience, but I didn't appreciate it at the time.

I came to BGA in the ninth grade, and I remember my first day of school. My friends told me to get to study hall early and get a good seat, because you'd be in that seat for the whole year. If you tried to get too far back, the upperclassmen would throw you out. Then it would be too late to get a good seat, and you'd have to sit down in the front, close to the stage. So I got there early, and got a good seat. The next day, Mr. Eddington was up on the stage, and he looked at me. He said, "Gale, my nephew couldn't be here yesterday. I'm going to ask you to move down front and give him your seat. He's a sophomore, so he's ahead of you." But I said, "Mr. Eddington, do things work that way?" Somewhere along the way I'd learned that if you don't speak up for yourself, it just gets worse. He ended up getting another guy, Billy Jordan, to move down to the front. I was seatmates with Bob Harlin, and he would be my seatmate for the next four years.

Study Hall Desks (with double seats)

BGA had a competitive spirit, and during the first week of school, you either became a Greer or a Plato. I was a Plato. Even now, if I think of a guy, I can remember whether he was a Plato or a Greer. But there was a negative to that way of choosing. Bob Hutchison, who ended up being the valedictorian of our class, told me what he remembered about that process. "I was the next to last person chosen. The last guy was in a wheelchair. You can't understand, or maybe you can, the humiliation I felt."

I usually got to school by catching the Interurban bus that went between Nashville and Franklin on Franklin Road. There were a couple of guys from BGA who took the same bus. It was no problem to flag the bus down. It would drop us off at the square, and rain or shine we'd walk to school, which was about a mile away.

Mr. Eddington's classroom was in Room One. It was on the first floor, on the southeast corner of the building. He was a superb teacher, and I had him four years. He taught first and second year Algebra, and then Trigonometry, College Algebra, and Plane Geometry. He had a six-foot slide rule over his blackboard. He taught me a lot about solving equations.

One day we were talking about parentheses, and he went over and raised the window. He leaned out and yelled, "Parentheses scream, do me first!" If you're trying to solve an equation and don't do them first, you usually won't get the right answer. Ever since then, when I see a parenthesis, I think, "Do me first." Sometimes he would include history in what he was teaching. He'd say, "Today we're going to talk about measuring the circumference of the earth." He'd tell us about some Greek calculating the circumference of the earth, and the distance to the sun. He gave plenty of homework, but at the time we took four courses and we had four study halls. If you concentrated and made use of those periods, the homework was minimal. Mr. Eddington treated me very fairly. Between my junior and senior year, he chose me for Boy's State Representative. We had a good professor-student relationship.

I think I was a sophomore when I came home and my dad said, "I sold the herd. You boys aren't dependable anymore, and I can't do it by myself." I liked some of the cows more than others, but they weren't like pets.

J.B. Akin made a big impression on me. I have never known a man that I admire as much as I admired him. He respected everybody, even the ones that I thought were total losers. I had him in General Science and then in Physics and in Chemistry. My first year, when I was taking Bible, we had a chapter on Old Testament history. One thing we did was trapping. It was competitive. You had an hour to study and get all the trivia that might be asked. When we were studying Nebuchadnezzar, Mr. Akin said, "Nebuchadnezzar got up one morning and put on his shoes. Spell that with four letters." I didn't know what in the world he was talking about. Before long he said, "Pass your papers." Of course, it was a trick question. It only took four letters to spell T-H-A-T.

Mr. Akin was in charge when he was coaching. Everybody always listened to him. His practices were drill, drill, drill. I played football for four years, but I was not a real athlete. My senior year, Mr. Eddington said he wanted me to be a cheerleader. I had been hoping to play some football, but I stayed on the B-team. The class ahead of me, the 1949 class, had played in the new gym and won the Mid-South Conference championship in basketball and baseball, and I think they were runners-up in football. But they had all graduated, and here we were. We had a small class – 28 guys or something like that, but I was still just a cheerleader. Then the two first string guards got caught smoking by Mr. Akin. He kicked them off the team, and after that we had a couple of injuries. At the end of the season, I dressed out and got to play in a lot of games. That's how bad things were in football.

I also played some basketball. I was small, but I scored a few points. We had Frank Giles and Jerry

Bennett and Jimmy Odom, and we won a few games. We went to McCallie and Baylor. I'd never traveled much, and I enjoyed going to other places.

And there was the tug-of-war. I stayed dry all four years. I'd lay that to Mr. Akin. There was no talk ahead of time. We didn't meet, and we didn't discuss anything. But when we got down there with the rope in our hands, Mr. Akin would get everyone's attention. He'd say, "Boys, you have got to work together. I'm going to call the rhythm and y'all pull." I thought that all of the Greers would go in the water. But I found out that Jerry Bennett, a guy in my class who was a Greer, had seen that the Greers were losing, and he'd just run back to town. If we had known that, we would've chased him down and thrown him in the river.

I had Ralph Naylor for U.S. History. I liked Mr. Naylor, but he didn't hold the attention of the students as well as most of the other teachers. When Mr. Naylor was the study hall proctor, the students liked to irritate him. One time the bell rang, and everybody jerked up the seats of their desks in unison. It made a really loud noise. Mr. Akin was teaching in a room next to the study hall, and he came through the door and ran down the steps. He thought the boiler had blown up. When he found out what happened, he gave everyone in the study hall five hours. I served my time over at Mrs. Briggs' doing yard work.

At BGA we had monthly dances. There was a discussion for a couple of years about whether to have flowers for the girls at the dance. It was really a difference of opinion. One guy, Douglas Seward, was from Brentwood, and he made the statement that any girl who would go out with Nelson Griswold wasn't worth a flower. That got back to Nelson, and he challenged Douglas to a fight. It was going to be after school behind the old gym. A crowd gathered back there, and Nelson beat the tar out of Douglas. There wasn't a teacher in sight. I can't imagine that they didn't know what was going on.

Back then, there wasn't a dress code. And smoking in the restroom during class breaks was pretty evident. Smoking went on all the time. but I didn't see much of a drinking problem. There was a horse shoe pit at BGA. It was between the football stands and Everbright Avenue. Billy Isaacs and Tom Robinson could throw ringers three out of five times, and they'd take on anybody. If you had a B average, you didn't have to go to study hall. That was very useful. Bob Harlin, Phelps Montgomery, Dan Robertson, and I would meet outside and go over the Latin translation for the day.

At the time, BGA was in rough financial situation. I could see it. One time I went to see Mr. Akin in the chemistry lab. He was trying to repair a 35 cent chain pull socket. I worked at McCall Electric over the Christmas holidays when I was a freshman, and I knew what that item cost. But there he was, trying to repair it. Working at McCall Electric, I was the small appliance guy – the mixers and the hot plates, the irons, the toasters and all that – they would save them up for me to repair.

Old Gymnasium

The old gym was classic. The walls were out of bounds, and the edges of the balcony extended out over the court. There was a pot belly stove at one end, and at the other end, the backboard was against the wall. One time we were playing St. Andrews. They had a big Indian guy, a Native American, on their team. He jumped up and when he came down, he went through the floor. Gilbert Marshall, the maintenance guy, came out with his saw-horse. The crowd watched him make measurements and cut a piece of wood. After he nailed it in place, they finished the game. One time I was playing in the Greer-Plato basketball tournament. The Greers were one side of the balcony and the Platos were on the other side. When I was under their balcony, Jimmy Dawes Brown poured India ink on me.

There was a boiler in the old gym, but we never had any hot water. We didn't shower after practice. We'd just put on our clothes and go home. But we got the new gym in my junior year. McCall had the electrical contract, and I did some of the wiring electrical in the basement of the new gym.

When I got to BGA, I'd bring my lunch, but there were times when some boarding student would steal it. Well, the school finally decided they needed a lunch security system. Every morning, the lunches were collected from the day students. They were kept outside of Mr. Akin's room in a closet underneath the stairs, and at lunchtime they would get handed out again.

A lot of things would happen in study hall. Before football games, at Assembly, we would have pep rallies. They would call on different players to stand up and say something, and everybody would cheer. One time they got to Tom Robinson, a big guy who played tackle. Tom didn't have much to say anyway, and before he opened his mouth, Tommy Lance said, "Yay!" and started clapping his hands. So Big Tom just sat back down.

There were times when we had random holidays. Sometimes it would be on the Tuesday after the first monthly exams. We'd be at Assembly, and Mr. Eddington would say, "It sure is beautiful outside." After we stopped cheering, we'd be gone for the day. Or we might get a holiday after we won a big football game. At assemblies, Mr. Eddington would talk about the choices people make and how important they are. He'd talk about where you're going to college, what you'll do in your life, who you'd marry, the children you'd have – all sorts of choices in life.

Some of the dormitory boys were a pain. One of our teachers, Patrick Wade, called them reprobates. One day he gave a talk in Assembly. He said, "You know, if a guy rubs you the wrong way, you just look at him. If he does it again, you just sort of frown at him. If he keeps doing it, you tell him to stop. And if he still keeps doing it, pretty soon you're ready to knock his block off! That's the way I feel!" He was really under stress because of all the misbehavior of some of the boarders. That stuck with me.

Mr. Wade was a very competent English teacher, but English was not one of my better subjects. I'd never gotten a firm foundation in grammar when I was in elementary school. Composition was not my thing. One day we had to write a paragraph and turn it in. In the next class, Mr. Wade said, "Now, I want to give you boys an example of how *not* to write a paragraph." He started reading my paragraph, but he misread something and I corrected him. He said, "Gale, I wasn't going to tell who wrote this paragraph."

But I wrote "The Spectator," which was a column in our school newspaper, *the Cannonball*. It was anonymous, and not even the editor, Bob Harlin, knew who wrote it. One time Bob really got upset by something I wrote. His family owned Harlinsdale farm, where a lot of famous horses were bred and raised. I said something like, "The Harlinsdale Farm has a new world champion this year, and it's Midnight Mildred." Well, Bob was dating Mildred German, and he didn't like it. He tried to change it, but I went to Mr. Buford, the teacher who oversaw the paper, and quietly convinced him that what I wrote shouldn't be censored.

Gaston Buford taught me two years of English and two years of French. I liked him. He was very approachable, but I don't think he really enjoyed teaching because it was very easy to get him on another subject. One time we were talking about something and laughing, and I said, "We don't learn much French in here, but we sure do have a good time." Mr. Buford sort of cleared his throat and said, "Let's get back to work."

The night before the first day of my senior year, I was with Dan Roberts at a party, I said, "Dan, tomorrow I'm going to get to school at the break of dawn. I'm going to get the back seat on the left. That's going to be my seat." I got there around six o'clock the next morning, and Dan was in that seat! He'd spent the night sitting in that seat.

Going to Vanderbilt didn't involve taking tests or being interviewed. I just filled out an application and went. We bought the same textbooks we used in Mr. Eddington's Trigonometry and College Algebra classes at the Vanderbilt bookstore. Using the same books again, I felt pretty well-prepared in those subjects, and also in Chemistry and Physics.

Tuition at Vanderbilt was $175 a quarter, and it looked like paying it would be a real challenge. But I worked for Mr. Tom McCall. He was on the board of Williamson County Bank, and the bank had established a scholarship that paid $100 a quarter. Mr. McCall loaned me the rest of the money interest free. Mentors can make all the difference in the world. Working eight years with a bunch of adults at McCall Electric was a great experience for a young kid. Mr. McCall took to me. He told me, "Junior, if you tell me the truth, I'll take care of the rest." He knew I'd screw up, and I did. When I was working on the new BGA gym, I drilled all the way through a wall and broke a commode, and I had to go and tell him what I'd done.

At first I thought I'd be a dentist, but for some reason Organic Chemistry gave me problems. So I ended up going to see Dean Lewis at the Vanderbilt Engineering School. I told him I'd like to go into engineering. He said, "Well, what's your grade point average?" When I told him, he said, "We'd be glad to have you."

I graduated with a degree in electrical engineering. But then I heard about a fellowship in physics offered by the Atomic Energy Commission. I got the fellowship, and I spent nine months studying radiation physics. Then I had three months at Oak Ridge learning about the applications of radioactivity. After finishing up that year, the head of the program said there was a need for a radiation physicist at Carnegie Institute of Technology in Pittsburgh, and I got a PhD in nuclear physics from Carnegie Tech.

At Carnegie Tech I joined a group that built equipment to use on cyclotron experiments. We built bubble chambers where pictures were taken of ionizing particles going through a liquid. Then we worked in cryogenics, using liquid hydrogen at 20 degrees Kelvin temperature. Later on we got a helium chamber, which is four degrees Kelvin.

From Carnegie Tech I went to Argonne National Lab, and I was there for over 28 years. In that time, we built a bubble chamber with a superconducting magnet. Then, there was a new accelerator. We continued to do development work in superconductivity. It was the pioneer period of superconductivity, and the development work we did led to the MRI device. Later on I worked at Fermi Lab near Chicago. One of our major projects was supporting the Superconducting Super Collider that was ultimately built in Texas.

I was born with some gifts, but BGA – and especially Mr. Eddington and Mr. Akin – gave me the educational foundation to do what I did. I was especially well-prepared in math and physics and chemistry. And what I learned from being on teams at BGA taught me some valuable lessons. Team sports aren't like playing golf or tennis. During my career as a physicist, I worked on several large projects. By then I already knew that it's the team that wins, not one individual.

This interview took place on February 26, 2013. Dr. Gale Pewitt died in 2024 at the age of 91. He was survived by a son, two daughters, and numerous grandchildren and great-grandchildren.

Jonas Coverdale

Jonas Coverdale was called to BGA in 1950 to succeed Glenn Eddington as president of the school. At the time, he was head of the Junior School of Castle Heights Military Academy in Lebanon, Tennessee. I was one of the first teachers he hired after he came to BGA. Coverdale was born in Indiana, and moved with his family to Nashville as a child. He was a star basketball player at Hume-Fogg High School, and he went to Vanderbilt on a basketball scholarship in the early 1920s. He later graduated from Vanderbilt Law School, but instead of practicing law, he became an educator. After teaching for several years at Castle Heights, he became head of the Junior School.

In the early 1930s, Jonas Coverdale started a boys' summer camp at Quebeck, Tennessee, on the Caney Fork River. He built his camp from the ground up, and Camp Hy-Lake ultimately developed into one of the premier boys' camps in the country. It drew campers from all over the Southeast, but particularly from the Nashville area. He hired well-known coaches and educators from metropolitan areas throughout the region as counselors, and he paid them a commission for each camper they recruited. This technique quickly filled Hy-Lake camp with new campers.

When the BGA Board of Trustees offered Coverdale the position of president, he recognized that it would be a challenge to rebuild the school, but he saw that it would be a natural fit with his summer boys' camp. He could not only offer year-round employment to his teachers and to members of the Hy-Lake staff, the camp could serve as a feeder program for BGA. A number of outstanding student-athletes in the Nashville area who normally would have gone to Montgomery Bell Academy, Duncan School, or Peabody Demonstration School eventually came to BGA. The affiliation with Hy-Lake allowed BGA to end its enrollment problem.

As he had done with his staff at Camp Hy-Lake, Coverdale hired well-qualified young teachers at BGA, and worked them into the life of the school. He made his faculty feel they were important by giving them key responsibilities. Those who accepted these responsibilities were rewarded in some manner and were made to feel good about themselves. He knew how to bring out the best in both young people and adults.

One of Jonas Coverdale's strongest points was his fiscal management. He carefully watched his budget. Needed repairs were made, and facilities and athletic fields were remodeled for surprisingly little money. He hired men like Odis Stutts who could do carpentry, plumbing, electrical work, masonry, landscaping, and almost anything else the school needed. The buildings and grounds gradually began to look much better.

One of the things Coverdale did especially well was buy war surplus items for pennies on the dollar. Some students joked that BGA was beginning to look like a military operation. One of Coverdale's biggest projects was remodeling the old gymnasium. What became the lower floor included a dining hall and a lounge, and the upper floor became a dormitory with a teacher's apartment. He was also able to buy *Westover*, a home on the campus that belonged to the widow of George Briggs.

He was gradually able to improve the financial situation of his teachers. When Jonas Coverdale came to BGA, there was no hospitalization insurance to protect the school's employees, but it wasn't too long before teachers had group hospitalization insurance. In that period, private schools were not required to participate in the social security program on behalf of its employees, but members of the faculty were soon able to enter that program.

During the 1950s, Jonas Coverdale was carrying a tremendous work load. He was not only running BGA, he also had all the pressures of operating Camp Hy-Lake. I could tell that his energy level was falling and he looked ill. In 1958, he announced that he had developed heart problems, and that he was retiring from BGA at the end of the school year. Jonas Coverdale came along at the time the school needed him; and he performed beautifully.

This edited article was written by John Bragg. Jonas Coverdale died in 1978 at the age of 76. He was survived by his wife of 52 years, Gertrude, their two children, and their nine grandchildren.

Paul Redick

Paul Redick is a native of Benton County, Tennessee. He grew up in his father's store in Camden, a thriving town on the Tennessee River. When he was a boy, he spent as much time as he could fishing in the Tennessee River with other boys. His father gave him a regular job when he reached the age of 14, and he worked in the store after school and on Saturdays. He spent his last two years of high school driving an ice truck. Carrying 50 and 100-pound blocks of ice helped him get stronger. He was a member of Camden High School's football, basketball, and baseball teams, but he did not neglect his school work. His father would not allow him to play on a team unless his grades were good. He was a member of the Dramatic Club, and appeared in over 30 plays. But because of his mischievous attitude, he was never given a serious role. Two of his sisters had been valedictorians of their classes, and there was a family reputation to uphold. Redick, who was named "Most Mischievous" when he was a senior, graduated fifth in a class of 33, but his father, a former school teacher, was not impressed.

His grandfather had been an attorney, and intending to follow in his footsteps, Redick entered the University of Tennessee Junior College at Martin. He was on Martin's football, baseball, and boxing teams, and in order to help pay his tuition and expenses, he worked at the school as a custodian. With the Depression underway and money scarce, he found other jobs when he wasn't in school.

"In 1930, while I was a student in UT Junior College, I spent the summer with a college crew selling magazines. We visited 207 towns and traveled 7500 miles through Tennessee, Kentucky, Illinois, and Missouri. I was often tired and had sore feet. Before I could get out the words, 'I'm working my way through college,' a lot of doors were shut in my face."

After two years at Martin, he served as principal of the elementary school in Camden, and was the coach at Camden High School. Three years later, still intending to become a lawyer, he enrolled at Cumberland University in Lebanon.

"In the summer of 1933, I worked through the wheat harvest season in southeastern Kansas. I had two motives. To make money, and to be in shape to play football at Cumberland College. My first day in the field, I moved a shock of wheat, only to find a large snake curled up underneath it. It turned out that harmless snakes were kept to kill gophers, which were regarded as pests. Gophers dug holes, and sometimes horses or mules would break a leg by stepping in a hole. After I ran my pitchfork through the snake, I held it up for everybody to see. I thought I had really done something. Then the head boss came over and gave me a dressing down for killing his pet snake. The next morning, the local paper had the headline, 'Tenderfoot Kills Pet Snake.'"

In 1935 Paul Redick married Elizabeth Hays, a student at Cumberland from Huntsville, Alabama. Later that year, he received honorable mention—as an end—when the all-conference football team was named. Not long after coming to Lebanon, Paul Redick had met Jonas Coverdale, the headmaster of the junior school of Castle Heights Military Academy. A friendship developed, and Redick went to work at Camp Hy-Lake, Coverdale's summer camp for boys between Sparta and McMinnville. Their friendship strengthened, and Redick eventually dropped his intention to study law. Having decided to get his degree in education, he graduated in 1936 and joined Coverdale at Castle Heights as a coach and history teacher. He became assistant headmaster in 1940, and entered the Navy in 1943. But while in training at Great Lakes, Illinois, he was injured, leading to his honorable discharge in 1944. He continued to work with Coverdale at his summer camp, and a year after entering Peabody College in 1945, he earned his Master's degree.

Last August, headmaster Paul Redick came to Franklin from Castle Heights, where he taught for 14 years. He had been head of the history department, and director of intramural athletics. He will also be head of the history department at BGA, and will help J.B. Akin coach when necessary. He and Mrs. Redick, with their children Becky, 12, and Bill, 7, live on Battle Avenue near the school. For five years, Mr. Redick has been athletic director at Camp Hy-Lake. He and Mr. Coverdale have been closely associated, summer and winter, for 16 years, and during that time there has never been a disagreement or a short word between them. Redick has distinct opinions about the importance of education.

"The youth of today constitutes the citizen of tomorrow. The better he is trained morally, physically, and spiritually, the better the next generation will govern our country. I have worked with boys the greater part of my life. I think I have only found one boy who was without a redeeming trait. I looked long and diligently to see if there was one spark of human kindness in the boy, but I failed. He was playing ball one day, and there was the expression of a murderer in his snake-like eyes while he was tackling another boy. I knew right then that he was a square peg in a round hole. Soon he was no longer a member of the school. When he actually became a murderer later on, I knew we had been right in clearing a rotten apple out of the barrel for the good of the other students. But I am fully convinced that 99 percent of the boys in our country are good, red-blooded Americans. If they are wisely led early in their lives, they will make top citizens. I do not want to convey the impression that all bad boys should be barred from school. There is basically nothing wrong with American youth that intelligent guidance won't correct.

"I've described one boy who failed, so now I'll talk about a boy who made good. In 1930, when I was coaching in Camden, I met a 16-year-old boy who had left school in 6th grade. He reminded me of an alley rat, but I saw the prospects of a good athlete. I wanted to save him from the life he was leading, and I prevailed on him to return to school. I took him into my classroom, and gave him special work and attention. But it wasn't long before other pupils began to miss books and other belongings. I had my own idea about who was responsible for the loss. I appointed a committee to look into the matter, and I chose the new boy as chairman. Gradually, all of the missing books were returned. He came to my office later, and cried like a baby. He made a clean breast of it all, and asked for another chance. He got it, and eventually became a model student. He eventually graduated and was the president of his class. He served for four years in World War Two, and became a good citizen and a successful businessman. These two examples show that while most boys are not fundamentally bad, some cannot be changed once they have a running start on the downward road.

"I have worked with about 6,500 boys. I can't think of a better way to spend my life than having a hand in molding the characters of young men. I have never been thrown in with a finer group than the boys at BGA. They are cooperative, friendly, and good students. But they are as red-blooded as any boys I have known. They are ready for any prank, and are never so taken up with their own affairs that they can't help somebody else. Mr. Coverdale and I are highly pleased with our new set-up, and we are happy in our work."

Along with a great many other recreation and sports programs that have been installed at BGA is the new boxing class. This class is the forerunner of future teams that will be coached by Mr. Redick. Although they started late, this year's team quickly worked themselves into shape, and went to the Mid-South meet in Sweetwater, Tennessee. Three of our boys, Jimmy Patterson, Jimmy Hayes, and Alan Kirshner, all had hard luck when a draw determined their opponents. Patterson had to face a national champion, while the other two had to face previous Mid-South champions. Kirshner fought in the 132-pound division, Patterson in the 148-pound division, and Hayes in the 156-pound class.

They were all outclassed, but they were game, and they all lost creditably. They will all return next year, and will form the nucleus of future teams. Mr. Redick, who himself has boxed, brought the boys a long way in only three weeks. With Mr. Redick's assistance, boys may enter the class as freshmen, and in four years time become skillful boxers and ready for the fights.

All except the final paragraph of this edited article, which appeared in an issue of the 1951 Cannonball, was written by Miss Jane Owen in 1952. Paul Redick died in 2002 at the age of 91. He was survived by Becky, his wife of 66 years, two children, three grandchildren, and nine great-grandchildren.

Bunny Akin, Class of 1951

    I was born in 1933, the next to last of eight children. My mother and father parted ways when I was about four-years-old. He did farming out in the county, and I would only see him on Saturdays. Back then, everybody came to town on Saturday to get their groceries, or do whatever they were going to do. It was usually down on Main Street. As far as having a father figure, there wasn't one. Because my mother worked, when I did something wrong, my older brothers or sisters would discipline me. And they would spank a whole lot harder than my mama would have. So instead of parents, I had older brothers and sisters. They all worked, and contributed funds for the family to buy food and all.

    We lived in Franklin, but my Uncle Bob Jordan had a dairy farm out in the country. He worked all his little nephews morning and night. We were cheap labor. We would go out there during the summer and milk cows, put the milk in bottles, put caps on the bottles, and put the bottles in cases in a walk-in refrigerator. The next morning, we would take the milk from the night before and put it in his truck.

Then we would come to town—riding on the running board of his truck—and help him deliver his milk. I would take one side of the street, and one of my brothers would take the other side, and we'd go down the road delivering one bottle at a time.

My four older brothers went to BGA. We didn't have any money, but we able to go because we got scholarships. I believe it was called the Wall Scholarship. Mr. Coverdale took over before I was a senior. That's when they cut back on the size of the scholarships so more boys could come. Mr. J.B. Akin knew we didn't have the money, and he gave me a job that summer cutting grass. I would get paid by BGA and then use that money to pay my part of the tuition, which was $150. That summer, I bought a new pair of white Keds basketball shoes. After working about two weeks, they'd turned green.

The boys in our neighborhood played ball in a vacant lot on Fair Street. We'd just choose up sides and play. Then my brother, Bobby, organized our little neighborhood team. We played baseball or football. We'd challenge the boys out at Harlinsdale farm, and the Harlin boys would get a team up. At first it was just flag football, and later on we got into tackle. And Bobby also organized Boy Scout Troop 135. That was another neighborhood thing. All of us enjoyed anything that was outdoors.

Main Street in Franklin

Bobby had gone to BGA, but with so many good friends at Franklin High School, Jimmy Gentry being one of them, he left BGA and went to Franklin. He enlisted in the army, and after basic training, he was sent overseas. When I was in sixth grade, we were renting the house at 918 Fair Street. I was there when the policeman came up and gave a telegram to my mother. Bobby had been killed on December 14 during the Battle of the Bulge. He was 18 years old. It was awful. Just awful. That afternoon Bobby and Jimmy Gentry's older sister, Dorothy, brought a coconut cake to our family.

Their brother, David, had been killed just seven months earlier in Italy. Many, many people knew my brother because of all the things he did with kids and in the Boy Scouts. Bobby was buried in Margraten, Holland. When I was older, I hitchhiked through Europe. I went to the military cemetery and stood by his grave.

I started BGA in 1945, when I was in the seventh grade. Mr. Glenn Eddington was my headmaster. Every year he personally registered each student. One on one. You'd go in there, and he'd write out the schedule of the subjects you were going to take. I had him in Algebra One. Mr. Eddington was very precise and very smart. He didn't fool around. When it came to discipline, he wasn't harsh. He was just very straightforward. This is the way it should be, and this is the way it's going to be. This is what you did, but you should not have done it and here's why. You knew exactly where he stood, and you knew exactly how you needed to act.

He did his best to get his students to succeed. He was a motivator. During assemblies he would talk to us, and he gave wonderful devotionals. He loved to surprise us. Every now and then, if we won a big ballgame on Friday night or something like that, we might get a surprise. He'd be up there, and after our devotional – when we were getting ready to go to class – he'd say, "Let's just take the rest of the day off." He was a student-oriented headmaster. But I saw him get upset once. Something happened that he didn't like, and he drop-kicked a trashcan that was on the stage about 10 yards.

Back around 1950, times were hard. I sensed that the financial situation at BGA was very serious. Before my senior year, somebody from BGA went over to Castle Heights Military Academy and hired Jonas Coverdale and Paul Redick. They both came at the start of my senior year, and Mr. Eddington went off to teach in a college.

Ralph Naylor had come to BGA following World War II. He was married to Mr. Briggs' daughter. I believe he was an engineer or a pilot, or something like that. He was smart, but he never let us know it. And although he would say some of the funniest things, he would never smile. Sometimes he would be somewhere that you wouldn't expect him to be. He might be behind a door. He wasn't spying or anything, he'd just be there. But whatever the school asked him to do, he would do it. He was the school photographer, he coached teams, and he headed up the Cannonball. I liked him a lot.

Another teacher I really liked was Turney Ford. He had been an outstanding athlete at Vanderbilt. He was really the first person I'd ever seen who was sort of muscle-bound. I'd never seen anybody like that. He could do anything with a ball. He had been a coach at BGA before going into the military, and then he'd come back. I believe I had him in the seventh grade math class. He was a good math teacher, and he motivated the seventh graders to want to play football. He left BGA and eventually ended up at Carthage, where he won all kinds of championships.

John Bragg came to BGA my senior year. He was my senior English teacher. We always respected him very much. Whatever he said he was going to do, he did, and whatever advice he gave was good, sound advice. Part of taking Mr. Bragg's class was memorizing part of the Canterbury Tales, and I can still remember part of it.

I always thought that Mr. J.B. Akin was a lot smarter than he wanted people to know about. He was a good coach, but he had never played football. I don't know if he could throw a football across a room, but he bought this book and ended up knowing the game.

J.B. Akin in Science Class

Mr. Akin put in the Split-T, and none of the football coaches around here had ever heard of the Split-T. Then in basketball, he was the first to put in the 1-2-2 zone, and he won plenty of games using that. He was an innovator in this part of the country. He was analytical. He say, "This is what they do. And this is what we need to do to stop that." Or when we were running our 1-2-2 zone in basketball, he'd say, "Boys, they're going to shoot at this weak point right here, and it's your responsibility to get out there." He was not an excitable person. He sat on the bench in football and basketball, but he couldn't coach third base sitting down, so he had to stand up in baseball. We all liked him a lot.

I never saw him try to get anybody fired up. The closest he came might've been when we went down to play Columbia High School. We had five or six post graduates on our football team. They were guys who had already graduated from high school. They went to class every day with the rest of us, but they were just there to play ball. They could play against other private schools, but not against public schools. So we were pretty good when we played the private schools. One of the post grads was Darris McCord, who was an All-American at UT, and was eventually an NFL star with the Detroit Lions.

But none of those guys were allowed to play against Columbia. We should've cancelled that game, because every year Columbia was either state champions or runner-up. Before the game Mr. Akin said, "Boys, they put on their britches just like you do." But they beat us by four or five touchdowns. After the last game was over, some of the post graduates didn't come back to school.

When Mr. Coverdale and Mr. Redick showed up, there were some changes. They didn't know anybody, and we didn't know them. A lot of us objected to things that they were doing. But in the long run, they were doing the right things for the school. If they'd talked to the honor council, or let the senior class in on their plans, I think it would've been a smoother transition for them and for us, but I'm glad Mr. Coverdale came to the school. He was a good leader.

When Mr. Eddington was head of the school, he had also been a teacher. Mr. Coverdale was usually in his office, and we didn't see him very much. He didn't teach any classes. But Mr. Redick was hands-on. He was a teacher, and he presided over assemblies and things like that. He'd show us his muscles in class. I loved his history classes. He would tell stories that made the past come alive. When I was a student, I thought he was a great history teacher, but later on, when I worked for him, we were never close.

I walked or rode a bike to school every year until I was a senior. My friend, Tommy McCall, came in from Bethesda every morning to deliver milk to Franklin. He'd drive by my house, and I'd jump in the back of his truck and get a ride to school. We had a small senior class. Maybe 35 guys or something like that. They were mostly local boys, and a few dormitory boys. Mike Lavin, Jose Magyar, and Henry Mustelier had come to BGA all the way from Cuba. We called Don Blankenship "Moon Man," because he was always in outer space somewhere. Dudley Casey was smart and talented, and he was a good athlete, but he didn't really care about sports. "Tippy Toes" Jackson lived on 4th Avenue. His daddy was a Church of Christ preacher. Carol and William Jenkins were twins. Their parents owned the 5 & 10 cent store on Main Street. Ben Waller lived on Fair Street in Franklin. He was short, and very stocky. And very smart. We called him "Iron Man."

I spent five years at BGA, and I never got one demerit. I stayed in the background, but there were plenty of guys who didn't. They were always doing things like rolling marbles down from the back of study hall.

I hated to leave BGA. I didn't know what was going to happen after that. There were parties at the end of the year, and then we all said goodbye to each other. That summer I worked for a man named Calvin Fowler out on his farm on Old Hillsboro Road. At some point, Mr. Fowler asked me if I was going to college. I said, "Yes, sir. I'm going as soon as I can make enough money to go." He owned a couple of furniture stores in Chattanooga, and he offered me a job. So one day I caught the Greyhound bus to Chattanooga, and talked to the admissions director and got admitted to the University of Chattanooga. I stayed for two years, and then I joined the Army and went to Korea.

I was a private in the infantry. I was on the 38th parallel, and when I wasn't I living in a tent, I was in a foxhole on a mountain. We could see the enemy on the other side of the parallel. We would round up people from North Korea who were coming to the South to find jobs, then we'd bring them in for interrogation. But when I was in Korea, I had plenty of spare time on my hands. I would write to classmates like Earl Beasley, Ben Waller, and Tom McCall, among others. I'd write them and they'd write back. I'd ask how they were, and how BGA's ball teams were doing.

One night I was on guard duty. I didn't have anything to do, and I was listening in on a telephone call. I heard a sergeant say that some guys in our unit were being transferred to Hawaii. I made sure my name got on that list. I was so glad to get out of Korea. After I left the service, I came home to Franklin. And then I finished college at Middle Tennessee, and went to work at the Franklin Post Office.

I came to teach at BGA because one of the teachers had cancer. Mr. J.B. Akin came down to the post office while I was working and asked me if I could take the man's classes for three weeks while he was getting his treatments. I said, "Well, I'd have to check with the post master." He said that was okay, so I taught Biology and General Science for two-and-a-half months or so, and finished out the year. Then I was asked to teach on a regular basis, and I stayed for two more years. After that I would leave and teach at Ensworth and Oak Hill, and later on Mr. Akin asked me to come back to BGA again.

When I came back to teach at BGA in 1959, and it still seemed like the same place. That made it easy. There were more teachers and more students by then, but I felt very much at home. But I remember Mr. Akin saying the strangest thing one time. I think it was during the 1960 football season, and it took me a while to figure it out. We were really winning football games. Ralph Brown was the coach, and he was doing a wonderful job. He came into study hall, and sat down with a particular boy. And on that Friday night the boy played the best game he ever played. Ralph was a great motivator. But Mr. Akin said, "You can win too many ball games."

1952 Tug-of-War

When I think about my years at BGA, the first things that come to mind are Greers against Platos, athletics, and the unity of the students. BGA had wonderful school spirit. There were really good coaches who were there for the benefit of the boys as well as the school. BGA has meant a lot to me. It's an unforgettable place. There have been great scholars and great athletes. But I see BGA as taking boys – I'm saying boys, because the girls came after my time – that may have only been average when they first came. But somewhere along the line, BGA inspired them to do better. I've learned that the ones who eventually give back to the school are usually the guys that remember what that school did for them. They want to give something to help some other little guy who is just like they used to be.

The information in this narrative came from an interview that took place on October 4, 2012. William Burnett "Bunny" Akin died in Franklin in 2025 at the age of 92. He was survived by his wife, Carole, five children and step-children, and five grandchildren.

Leaving the Mid-South Athletic Association

It has been announced by Mr. Coverdale that BGA has decided to discontinue its affiliation with the Mid-South Athletic Association, and apply for admission into the TSSAA. Mr. Akin has had such a move in mind for several years, and it has been thoroughly discussed and considered by the entire faculty since the beginning of the school year. It is felt that affiliation with the TSSAA will have a benefit for the following reasons. 1) To stress the foremost academic training for BGA students. 2) For the school to develop its own athletic teams and players, rather than solicit star athletes from other schools. 3) To give the boys who are students at BGA—year after year—the opportunity to play on varsity teams, rather than be replaced by one-year students. 4) With a better opportunity to participate, students will have more incentive to participate in varsity sports. 5) There will be more interest in playing teams from nearby, rather than teams from far away. 6) To lower the expense of fielding teams. In last year's football season, BGA traveled as far north as Louisville, Kentucky, and as far south as Gainesville, Georgia, to play against teams in the Mid-South Association.

The Cannonball (1951)

Carl Smithson

Carl Smithson is the son of H.C. Smithson, a Williamson County farmer. His mother was the late Etta Poteete Smithson. The Smithsons and the Poteetes lived next door to each other on Cummins Street for years, and were close friends when their children married. Carl and his four sisters and two brothers were born on a farm on the Lewisburg Road. He remembers milking a large number of dairy cows, each morning and each night, with his brothers and sisters. He always had a serious turn of mind, and he longed for an education. Sometimes he would come across his mother when she was working in the kitchen. She would be praying that a way might open up for him to attend college. After both his mother and his sister, Mary, lost their lives in a fire that destroyed their newly-completed home, Carl was determined to leave no stone unturned to have her prayers fulfilled.

When his studies at Franklin High School were interrupted with a call to go into the service, Professor Daly Thompson advised Carl that he keep track of all the educational advantages he would have while he was in training. He took the advice, and received enough credits to entitle him to his high school diploma. He gives Mr. Thompson much credit for making his college work possible.

During World War Two, he served for 18 months in France and Germany as a master sergeant. After being released from the service, Carl entered Trevecca College, where he received his BA degree. While he was at Trevecca, he married Dorothy Williams, one of his classmates. But she died 18 months later, leaving him with a six-month-old daughter, Anne West Smithson.

He then received his Master's degree at Peabody College, where he is currently working on his PhD. He was called back into the service in August 1951, and when he came home, he married Valeria Sharpton. In 1952 their son, Robert Carl Smithson, was born. It was too late to secure a teaching position, and Carl went to work for a shoe company, where he was assigned to instruct men in the art of salesmanship. He enjoyed the job, but it was not what he had studied so hard for when he was in college.

It was with a great deal of pleasure that Carl recently accepted the offer of President Jonas Coverdale and Headmaster Paul Redick to join the faculty of Battle Ground Academy. Here he reconnected with Coach J.B. Akin, under whom he played football at Franklin High. Carl is blessed with a splendid physique, being over 5'10" and weighing 200 pounds. He has never known what it is to be sick, and is thankful for his good health.

Carl and Valeria are members of the Church of the Nazerene. They both love music and enjoy hearing musical programs on the radio. Carl likes to hunt, and he confines most of his reading to books on mathematics and child psychology. He believes in working hard and being persistent, because he feels that the path to reach a goal is not always a pleasant path. He says that the thing he has always hoped and worked and prayed for—teaching back home in Williamson County—has at last come true. He tries to live by his mother's favorite Scripture, "Whatsoever a man soeth, that shall he also reap."

This edited article was written by Jane Owen in 1952. Carl Smithson died in 1975 at the age of 53, and was survived by his son, Bob, and his daughter, Anne.

Tiger Grimes, Class of 1953

My father was a HAM radio operator and an electrical technician, and he owned a public address system. He had a very good voice, and Mr. Eddington got him to do the play-by-play at BGA football games. He probably made $5 or $10 a game. I was just 11 or 12 years old, and I would go with him on Friday afternoons to wire up the PA system. My father was Mr. Bob Sewell's first employee when he started Sewell Electric. At first, he did wiring and was a radio technician, and he also sold appliances in Mr. Sewell's store. Later on, he was a television technician. As far as I know, my family had the first television in Franklin. I think it was a Dumont. It had a fairly small screen, but people would come by just to see it.

One Saturday night at the end of August, there was a football game between alumni and the varsity. When Mr. Eddington came over after the game to pay my father, my father said, "I sure would like Billy to come to BGA. But I'm not sure that I can afford it." There were five kids in my family, and in the mid-1940s, the economy still hadn't come back after WWII. Mr. Eddington looked at me and said, "Young fella, come up to my house in the morning at nine o'clock, and I'll talk with you."

We lived down on 3rd Avenue, about a mile from BGA, and I rode to see him on my bike. I remember sitting with Mr. Eddington and his wife in their living room. They asked me a bunch of questions. I had been brought up to be respectful, and when Mr. Eddington stood up, he said, "Well, Mr. Grimes, I believe we can fit you in." He said, "I'll work out financial arrangements with your father." Then he arranged for me to get used school books. Around the time I started my sophomore year, we moved to Columbia Avenue, right behind the Briggs house. I lived there for the rest of my time at BGA. It was just a jump and a skip to school from there.

I came to BGA in eighth grade, and it was a very difficult transition. I had never taken any difficult courses, and I was suddenly taking Greek and Roman history. It was tough, and I had to study a lot. It didn't get any easier from there. I had to take Latin when I was a freshman. Back then, Latin was a prerequisite to get in colleges like Vanderbilt. And when I was a junior and senior, I took first and second year Spanish under Mr. Bragg. It was a difficult transition. I had courses like English grammar that I did pretty well in, but I had to study a lot. I was mostly a C+ student.

Mr. Eddington was the proctor for my final exam in first year Latin. We took the final exams in the study hall, and Mr. Eddington was up on the platform, sitting behind the desk. I was the only student left, and I remember Mr. Eddington looking at his watch and looking down at me. I needed a good grade on the exam to pass Latin for the year. He finally came down and sat next to me in one of those double seats. He said, "Now, what is the problem?" I said, "I'm having a difficult time translating this paragraph." He said, "We'll do the translation together, and you write it down." He'd say, "What does this say?" I would struggle with it, and he kept coaching me along. It took about 15 minutes, but I ended up translating that paragraph with Mr. Eddington, and I passed the exam.

One day Mr. Eddington was teaching a class, and he was talking about the Canadian Royal Mounted Police. He told us that their motto was, "We always get our man." A few days later, Mr. Eddington was looking for Uncle Henry, an older black man who looked after the buildings. Mr. Eddington picked out Phelps Montgomery, and said, "Go find Uncle Henry for me." Phelps took off, and he was gone for a really long time. He finally came back, and Mr. Eddington said, "What took you so long?" Phelps said, "Well, Uncle Henry was in Franklin. He went to town to get some supplies, so I went after him." Mr. Eddington said something like, "Why in the world did you do that?" And Phelps said, "I remembered that story you told us about the Royal Canadian Police, and I was determined to get my man."

Mr. Eddington was known for kicking waste baskets. If he caught you asleep, he'd pick up a wastebasket and walk over to whoever was asleep. Then he'd put it down, and when he kicked it, you'd wake up rather quickly. One time William Jenkins and I got into a fight, and Mr. Eddington saw us. He took us into his office, and after he gave us some advice, he made us shake hands. But we still had scowls on our faces, and Mr. Eddington said, "Y'all hug each other." So we hugged each other, and we both sort of smiled. Whatever had happened was forgotten, and we went back to being friends.

When Mr. Eddington stepped down, Mr. Jonas Coverdale took over in 1950. Mr. Coverdale was a businessman, and he helped restore the financial security of BGA. He and Mr. Redick came together from Castle Heights, and I really liked Mr. Redick. When I was playing football, he would pull me off to the side. I mostly played defensive end and linebacker, and he'd show me what I needed to do better.

When I was a senior, there was a picture in our annual that showed Mr. Redick and an arrow pointing to a cow. Somebody had drawn horns on the cow to make it look like a bull. Mr. Redick's nickname was "Bull." He didn't like the picture at all. Mr. Bragg was the annual advisor, and Mr. Redick wanted him to destroy all the annuals before they were handed out. I don't think the Bull nickname referred to BS. It was more like he was a bull in a china shop.

There were something like 112 students at BGA in my eighth grade year, and the enrollment increased after that. One thing that helped the school was when the Duncan School in Nashville closed down. A lot of Duncan students came to BGA.

Mr. Bragg was one of my favorite teachers. One day I was taking an exam, and I needed to borrow a pencil. I was looking over toward whoever was sitting next to me, and Mr. Bragg saw me. He said, "Mr. Grimes, please move over to one of those back rows by yourself." When I asked him why, he said, "Well, what were you doing?" I told him I needed something, and he said, "Well, what do you need?" I said, "Mr. Bragg, all I need is somebody to trust me." That disarmed him.

Another time, in Senior English, I had a Jew's Harp. When Mr. Bragg was writing on the board, I'd make a *boing* sound. I'm sure he knew who it was. I was the only one in that class who was that goofy. He finally caught me getting ready to do it again. He said, "Can you play that thing?" I told him I could, and he said, "Well, what can you play?" I said I could play *Turkey in the Straw*, and he said, "Well, play it." So everybody got to hear me play *Turkey in the Straw* on my Jew's Harp.

I was on the football team, and when I was about to be a sophomore, we went up to Camp Hy-Lake for pre-season camp. Mr. Coverdale had taken over, and we had some new players who looked old enough to vote. We stayed in cabins, and there were four boys to each cabin. I was sort of a loudmouth, and some of the post-grads started picking on me.

One night I heard some rustling outside our cabin, and I thought they were coming to do something to me. So I reached down and I grabbed one of my football shoes. A guy on the upper bunk saw me sitting on the side of my bunk, holding my shoe. He asked me what I was doing, and I said, "If any of those upperclassmen come in here and harass me, I'll hit him with this football shoe." Then the guy said, "Sick 'em, Tiger." It didn't take long for the story to get around, and the next day at football practice, everybody started calling me Tiger.

There were other changes when Mr. Coverdale and Mr. Redick came in. There was a lot more discipline than when Mr. Eddington had been in charge. But they explained why it was going to be that way, and we accepted it. The camaraderie was still there, and the academics didn't change.

J.B. Akin

Mr. Akin was our coach, and he was a great mentor. He was firm, but he was always fair. He was the one that had introduced the Split-T at BGA. One thing I remember is how he'd grab you around the waist when he was about to send you into a football game. He would be a little nervous. He'd walk, and sometimes run, up and down the sidelines, and tell you, "Hon, get in there and do something!" Even though he wasn't calm on the sidelines, when Mr. Akin got you in a huddle, he'd be very calm. He'd tell you what to do, and we did what he said. He also coached baseball and basketball. He studied the sports he coached.

And you couldn't have asked for a better guy than Mr. Akin to teach Bible class. I remember those classes. We'd have trapping. He'd ask, "Why didn't Moses put elephants on the ark?" Then he'd start at the head of the class. They'd say, "Elephants are too heavy," or something like that. He'd go down each row until somebody had the right answer. Somebody would finally say, "It's a trick question. Moses wasn't in the ark – it was Noah." When Mr. Akin asked a trapping question, you had to be your on p's and q's .

Mr. Naylor got his nickname, Goober, because he loved to eat peanuts. He was the advisor for the Beta Club. Students who made good-enough grades were in the Beta Club. They could go outside when the weather was nice, and they could study under a tree, or do whatever they wanted. My grades weren't that good, but I would sign in to the library, and then climb out the window and enjoy Beta Club privileges with my buddies. There's no telling how many times I got caught. Every time Mr. Naylor caught me, I'd get five demerits. But he was a nice guy, and good teacher. He was a man of many talents, and they asked him to do a lot. He would drive the school bus on football and basketball trips, and he also coached.

When I was a junior we had a teacher named Coleman Crockett. His nickname was "Prunes." He lived in the dormitory, which was above the cafeteria. Other than the three houses across the street, that was the only dormitory. Sometimes they had prunes for dinner. Most guys didn't eat prunes, but Mr. Crockett would end up eating all the prunes in the bowl at his table. So he got the nickname, "Prunes." One day Mr. Crockett walked into class, and there was a bowl of prunes on his desk. He was very proper and prim, and he said, "Is this a treat for me, or is it a practical joke?" When we all started laughing, he said, "Then I take it that this a practical joke."

Another time, one of the students erased the black board, and after he cracked the door open, he put the eraser on top of the door. When Mr. Crockett opened the door, the eraser fell down on his head. He had very dark hair, but it was almost white from all that chalk. He never said a word. He just started teaching his class.

Tiger Grimes

One time I mixed some chemicals together and made hydrogen sulfide. I put one end of a tube in a container, and after running the tube through one of my sleeves, I held the other end in my hand. I would walk around and when I opened up the tube, you could really smell that hydrogen sulfide. I eventually got caught. One day after lunch, I was roller-skating in the old gym when the bell rang. I went over to put my shoes on, but they weren't there. I decided that I'd just wear the skates to study hall. When I finally got upstairs and skated across study hall, Mr. Bragg saw me. "Grimes, 10 demerits. Skating in study hall." Years later, Mr. Bragg told me how much he enjoyed some of my antics.

When I was a senior, Tommy Helm was our quarterback, and we won our first four games. Stanley Gale was one of the guys who came to BGA after Duncan shut down. He was one of the hardest running guys I ever played with. Stanley had an unusual habit. He would drink coffee – a lot of coffee – right before our games. I guess it gave him an edge. He had a barrel chest, and he would almost be at maximum speed when he hit the line of scrimmage. Stanley would bust through the line, and sometimes it took a gang of guys to tackle him. He'd get up with his helmet on a little bit sideways, then he'd adjust his shoulder pads and the same thing would happen the next play. He was a really tough runner.

Billy Fey Gray was one of my other teammates. He was a great athlete. And Erwin McKee probably weighed 135 pounds. He played guard on both defense and offense. For his size he was the toughest lineman we had. Nib Pelot played halfback. He was bow-legged, but he was fast and quick, and so was Elbert Ashworth. We were a really good team until we started having injuries. Elbert and Tommy both got hurt, and Allen Kirshner took over at quarterback.

When we played Sewanee Military Academy, we lost 6-0. They scored their touchdown around me.

I was playing right defensive end, and the SMA quarterback was running to my side. He acted like he was going to throw a pass, and when I jumped up with my hands in the air, he went by me and ran 10 or 12 yards for a touchdown. Mr. Akin told me not to leave my feet. But he was so nice about it, I wanted to thank him. That's the kind of man he was.

Football games were a big part of our social lives back then. There wasn't a heck of a lot of other stuff to do. I vividly remember some of the pep rallies we had. We got to go outside, and we'd sit on the bleachers beside the football field, and players would get up and say something to try to fire everybody up. We'd have pep rallies, and big crowds, at basketball games, too.

Christmas Dance, 1952

When I was a senior, I was named "God's Gift to Women" in the yearbook. I'm not sure how that happened, but it could've been because I dated some nice looking girls. I had a big time at the dances. I was always willing to show off my dance skills. At least I thought I had dancing skills. Mary Ed Eggleston was the homecoming queen, and she dated Tommy Helm. I started dating Barbara Higgs the summer before my senior year. She was from Franklin, but she had moved to Nashville and gone to West High.

I graduated in May, 1953, and then I went to Tennessee Tech in Cookeville. Barbara and I briefly dated other people, but it wasn't long before we got back together. The next September, when I was starting my sophomore year at Tennessee Tech, a friend of mine drove Barbara and me to Canton, Mississippi, and we were secretly married. She was a senior at West, and it was almost Christmas before we finally told our parents.

Barbara had been elected Miss West High, but she felt compelled to let them know she was married, so she didn't get to represent the school in the Miss Nashville pageant. I ended up leaving Tennessee

Tech. I went to work for General Shoe Corporation, and trained to be an industrial engineer. I was moved to McMinnville, Tennessee, but late the next spring I told them I had to take a day off to go back to Nashville. I had to watch my wife graduate from high school.

I went to night school at UT Nashville for eight years, and I don't know how our lives could've turned out any better. We had three daughters and lived in Oklahoma for 21 years, and we moved back to Franklin in 1994. I had made a vow that when I came back, I was going to contact every one of my BGA classmates, and have a conversation with them. There were two guys in particular that we'd made fun of and beaten up a little bit. We thought we were macho guys. I'd been thinking about those two guys for years. We would joke around with them, but we probably hurt their feelings. I was going to apologize, but I had waited too late. They were both dead by then.

BGA had a great impact on my life and on my well-being. And I'll tell you what – BGA was a *great* school.

The information contained in this narrative came from an interview that took place on May 24, 2013.

David Wood, Class of 1954

My father lived in Southern Virginia. He was born shortly after the turn of the century, and he was one of seven children. He was the only one in his family to get a college degree. My mother was the daughter of an Italian immigrant, and she also got a college degree. In 1942, my parents moved to Waynesboro, Georgia, where the number one commodity was cotton. The high school curriculum had a lot of Home Economics, Industrial Arts, and Agriculture classes, and school closed for two weeks in the fall so the children could go out and pick cotton. There was no summer school in Waynesboro. There was no makeup work at all. If you flunked, you repeated. When I was in eighth grade, 30% of the students in my class were repeaters.

One day in the spring of 1950, my parents said, "We're going to send you to a boarding school." My dad had a map, and he used a compass to draw a circle with Waynesboro at the center. The circle only included places within a one-day drive from home. He located a bunch of private schools inside of the circle, and one of those schools was Battle Ground Academy.

We didn't know anybody who had heard of BGA or Franklin, Tennessee. My parents decided that we could afford the $750 a year it cost to board, and we picked BGA sight unseen. When it was time to leave home, I got in the car with my father, and we started driving. It was dark by the time we got to Franklin. We stayed at the Post Hotel, and the next morning he drove me to BGA. We put my trunk in my room, and after I met my roommate, Charles Shanlever, my dad headed back home.

When I walked onto the campus for the first time, I didn't know exactly what to expect. Along with meeting the students who lived in the dormitory, I'm sure that I met Coach Akin, Mr. Redick, and Mr. Coverdale. Mr. Akin had been there for some time, but Mr. Redick and Mr. Coverdale had just come from Castle Heights Military Academy.

Jonas Coverdale was getting ready to leave Castle Heights when he was offered the job at BGA. Camp Hy-Lake was booming, and he was just going to live off his income from the camp. But he had a gift for working with boys, and Dr. Hamilton Gayden, who was on the BGA board, talked Mr. Coverdale into coming to Franklin and running the school. My understanding is that he didn't take a salary for several years. The school couldn't afford to pay him. Mrs. Gertrude Coverdale told me about one of the first things she did after they came to BGA. The students at BGA were drinking out of jelly classes, and she went up to Hy-Lake and brought back glasses, plates and silverware from the camp.

The house mother for the dorm students, Mama Haynes, was a lovely lady. Her father had fought under Nathan Bedford Forrest in the Civil War. She and her husband had lived in Franklin, but he died of a heart attack back in the mid-1930s. She had a son who was a graduate of BGA, but he was in the Merchant Marine, and he was always traveling. She was a member of the Methodist Church, where George Briggs taught a Bible class. Mama Haynes had no money because of the Depression, and Mr. Briggs hired her to be the house mother at BGA. She moved into a little apartment in the dormitory. It had two rooms and a bath.

Mama Haynes took a shine to me. Later on, if I had an injury in sports, she'd call Dr. Nolan, and he would come down and see what he could do for me. As she got older, she became more of a figurehead. She had no income, and up until she died, Jonas Coverdale took care of her. He and Paul Redick would bring her up to Camp Hy-Lake in the summer so she wouldn't be alone, and so she'd have something to eat. Growing up, she had lived in a big house in Columbia, but she never complained about her status in life.

I didn't know it at the time, but when I got to BGA, it was in danger of closing. The school needed as many students as it could get, but the dormitory had several empty rooms. Two of the first-year teachers, Mr. Bragg and Mr. Jackson, lived in one of the rooms. They used the bathroom and showered down the hall in the same bathroom the boarding students used.

That was back around the time when BGA took anybody who had a pulse and a wallet, and not necessarily in that order. Several boys in the dormitory had jackets from the schools they attended before they came to BGA. In those days, it wasn't uncommon for a headmaster to get a phone call from a headmaster at another school. "I've got a boy I've got to get rid of. He's not a bad boy, he's just been bad for us. Would you give him a chance?" We had two boys with Darlington jackets, one boy from Baylor, and one from CMA.

The school had four buildings, including the new gym. The whole student body was about 100 boys. The academic building had five classrooms. The dining hall was in the basement of the dormitory. and the wood stove that had been installed when the dormitory was built in 1922 was still in use. But the stove came in handy the first winter I was there. There was a big blizzard at the end of January, 1951, and there was no electricity in Franklin for about 10 days. All the dormitory boys went down to the basement, and we gathered around the wood stove and tried to have some semblance of classes.

The sports program consisted of football and basketball and baseball. My first year might've been the final year that there were post graduates on BGA teams. Post graduates were students who had already graduated from high school. They hadn't gotten college football scholarships, so they would hang on for another year and try to get one. And a lot of them left as soon as football season was over, which was one of the reasons BGA got out of the Mid-South Conference. Once we stopped using post-grads, we couldn't compete with schools that still had them. It might have been Mr. Coverdale who decided that it wasn't fair for somebody to pay tuition and not get to play, because scholarship guys were always coming in.

When I came to BGA there was no music program, and there was no art program. There was a speech program under the leadership of an elderly lady named Mrs. Pryor Lillie, who lived near the school. She would teach us to give little speeches, and at some point we'd stand up and speak in front of the whole the student body.

David Wood in the Museum

I loved being at BGA. I made a lot of friends in the dormitory. I think we took four classes, and one of them was Bible, which was taught by J.B. Akin. We had John Bragg for English and for English history, and because he had spent six weeks in Mexico one summer, he also taught Spanish. There were several Cuban students at BGA, and they would have to correct Mr. Bragg from time to time. Thanks to Mr. Bragg, who was a Sewanee graduate, and Bruce Jackson, who was a Davidson graduate, I developed a love of English that I probably would not have gotten if I'd stayed in Waynesboro.

There were only seven teachers including Jonas Coverdale, but three of them were new. Mr. Coverdale had never taught English before, but somebody had to do it. With such a small faculty and student body, the students and the teachers got to know each other extremely well. It wouldn't have been like that back home. And at BGA, if you were having problems in class, the teachers would work with you at night and go over what you didn't understand.

A lot of the seniors didn't like Jonas Coverdale, who had replaced Glenn Eddington, but that didn't bother Mr. Coverdale, or his right-hand man, Paul Redick. They just said this is the way it's going to be, and that's the way it was.

People used to make fun of Mr. Coverdale because he bought surplus goods to use at BGA. He got desks and file cabinets, and whatever else he could find. A lot of things were olive drab or battleship gray, and he got an old city bus that people made fun of. And he ran a bus to bring boys from Nashville to Franklin. Along with teaching English, John Bragg drove the bus. One day he stopped at a red light, and he saw a tire rolling down the street. Then he realized that the tire had come off the back of the bus he was driving.

Jonas Coverdale eventually got the school going financially. One of the biggest factors in the survival of the school was the way he and Paul Redick were able to get so many of the boys who went to Camp Hy-Lake, to come to BGA. A lot of campers from Nashville would have gone to MBA, but after getting to know Coverdale and Redick, and several teachers over the summer, they decided to come to BGA.

And when Duncan School, which was in Nashville, closed in 1952, most of those boys came to BGA. There were 18 boys in my class when I was a sophomore. Two years later there were 36 seniors, and about half of them had come from Duncan. The student body went from about 100 boys when I was a freshman, to around 150 when I graduated. The school just kind of took off after Jonas Coverdale got there.

Paul Redick was a great number-two man for Jonas Coverdale. He was a guy you wanted on your side – if you could get him on your side. He liked athletics, and he liked athletes. He was a good man for keeping up with the day-to-day operations. He was a hard worker, and he was at school all the time. He was also a good teacher, and he told a lot of stories.

Along with their classroom duties, teachers drove the bus and had weekend duty supervising the boarding students. They also had night duty overseeing the study hall, and Saturday mornings they oversaw the boys who were serving off demerits.

Carl Smithson got the nickname, Goat, when he was playing football at Franklin High School. Carl was a good man and a good math teacher. His students would spend hours every night on their homework. I played one year of B-team football, and Carl Smithson was my coach. I liked him.

I had a math teacher my sophomore year named Coleman Crockett. One night at dinner, he made the mistake of picking up a big bowl of prunes, and putting almost all of them on his plate. From then on, his nickname was prunes. He would find prunes in his desk, and one day I was in his class, which was on the first floor. Somebody in an upstairs classroom tied a string around a prune, and kept dangling it in front of a window. I can see Mr. Crockett right now going over to look at it, and then taking off upstairs to try and catch the culprit.

Boys were more mischievous in those days. They pulled a lot of pranks that I don't think they would try today. If there was a teacher they could run off, they could spot him from 100 yards away. But nobody would've ever pulled a joke on a teacher like J.B. Akin or Jonas Coverdale. When I was a sophomore or a junior, John Bragg was the yearbook sponsor. Somebody had inserted a picture of a cow, and drawn an arrow pointing to Paul Redick, whose nickname was Bull. Paul was livid about it, but the yearbooks were gone and it was too late to do anything about it.

Coleman Crockett

Mr. Akin was a very quiet man. He spoke in grunts and single syllables a lot of the time. Maybe it was because his wife was so loquacious. He taught Bible, General Science, Chemistry, and Physics. He was also the football coach, the baseball coach, and the basketball coach. We loved him. If he said, "Go run through that wall," we'd say, "What part of the wall do you want us to hit? If anybody started to cut up in his class, he'd just look at whoever it was and snap his finger.

Ralph Naylor was a graduate of Emory and Henry College in Virginia. He had married the daughter of George I. Briggs, who had become BGA's headmaster in the mid-1920s. Mr. Briggs died in the 1940s, and most of us thought Mr. Naylor was there was because he was the son-in-law of the ex-headmaster. Ralph was a very bright guy, and he did all sorts of things that had to be done. He coached B-team football and basketball, because the school needed somebody to coach those teams. He was really just there to throw out the ball. Mr. Naylor did a lot for the school, but I don't know how happy he was. When I was a student, he taught the seventh and eighth graders. There weren't enough classrooms, and he'd sit down in front of the study hall and have his classes there.

We rode the bus to see away games, but the main reason we went was so we'd have something to do. It was a chance to get out of town. I remember when Ralph Naylor drove the bus to Centerville and turned it over. John Bragg and his wife, Jane, were on the bus, and Jane broke her arm. The bus was on its side, and the first thing Mr. Naylor did when he stood up was dust off his coat.

Ralph Naylor, teaching in Study Hall

My freshman year, I had John Bragg for English, and another year I had him for English history. He taught us a lot of poetry. He had us memorize passages, and we'd get up in class and recite them. I respected him because I could see how bright he was, and I respected his ability. He oversaw the yearbook and the school newspaper. I worked on the newspaper. We ran off the copies at night. Looking back, we included some things that we probably shouldn't have, but we included them anyway.

When we went to dinner in the dining hall, we were required to wear ties. I played athletics, and after practice I'd take a shower, and get to my dormitory room a little before six. To save a little time, I'd slip on a shirt with a tie that had already been tied, and I wore the same coat every night. The head cook was Cora Spencer. She and the other two cooks lived right around the corner. We'd see them walking together up Everbright Avenue in the morning, and then walking back home every afternoon. My first year at BGA, they did their cooking on an old woodstove. I liked to have a salad with my dinner, and each night, Cora would fix me a quarter-head of lettuce with some French dressing.

After dinner we either studied in our rooms or in study hall, depending on our grades. I would have about two hours of homework a night, so from about 9:15 until 10, I usually did whatever I wanted. My first year at BGA, the school got a TV set. It was in the dining hall. There usually wasn't anything showing, but they'd turn it on anyway. We'd just sit there and watch the test pattern. We got $2 a week for our allowance. As long as we hadn't gotten in some kind of trouble, we were allowed to go to town on Wednesday and on the weekend. We'd walk around Franklin, and get a Coke or have some ice cream.

The main attraction in downtown Franklin was the theater. There was a small restaurant on the square called West Point, and Tiger Grimes, who went to BGA, worked there as a short order cook. He would load us up with bacon and eggs and toast and sausage, and just charge us a quarter. Another restaurant on the square was the Red Grill. There was also a burger place called the Gilco next to the railroad on Lewisburg Pike. And the Globe was out on Columbia Pike. Sometimes after a ball game, a bunch of us would go over there and get a burger.

On Sunday mornings I went to the Methodist church, but on Sunday night, I'd go to the Presbyterian Church. They had more young people and better food. There were pool halls downtown, and even though we weren't supposed to go, we went anyway. There might be a few unsavory characters in there, but that's where we'd hang out sometimes. One of my BGA classmates was R.V. Kennedy. He had a big Oldsmobile 98 and a lot of money, and he lived his life in the fast lane. When I was a junior he took me to the Highway Pup, which was a beer joint in Nashville on Harding Road. That's where I had my first beer.

The dormitory had filled up, and when I was a senior, six other boys and I lived on one side of *Westover*, the faculty house where Mr. Bragg lived with his wife, Jane. Every now and then, he would come over and bum a cigarette. A lot of students and most of the teachers smoked back then. At night, after dinner was over, they'd light up a cigarette and smoke right there at the table.

David Wood and J.B. Akin

When I was a senior, the guy who was supposed to be captain got kicked out of school, and I ended up being captain of the basketball team. We never had any great teams, and Mr. Akin really didn't try to fire us up before a game. We just sat there and listened to him. There wasn't a lot of pressure to win. The way we looked at it, basketball was just something to do. Our biggest rivals were Franklin High School and MBA. Franklin was better than we were, and when we played them my last year, it wasn't much of a game. MBA had a terrible gym. You'd be dribbling, and the ball would hit a dead spot on the floor and it wouldn't bounce. We also played at places like Bethesda and Hampshire and Santa Fe. Those schools were all way out in the country.

The gym at Bethesda had a linoleum floor. Sometimes it was wet, and you'd slip and fall all over the place. The goals were so close to the wall that mattresses were tied up at each end of the court to keep players from getting hurt. There were times when a Bethesda player would get a rebound, and throw the ball down to a guy who had been hiding behind the mattress at the far end of the court.

Ralph Brown came to teach at BGA in my senior year. I was co-captain of his first baseball team at BGA. We didn't have a very good team, but Ralph was enthusiastic, and he taught us a lot. I remember when he took us down to a sporting goods store. We only had three or four bats, and I was proud to be given the responsibility of going down and picking out another bat.

David Wood, Michie Barber, and Ralph Brown

Along with athletics, we had things like declamation contests, talent shows, and minstrel shows. I remember being up on the stage of the Franklin Theater in blackface. Jimmy Tippins and I had worked up a skit that got a big laugh. He played a character named Mr. Interlocutor, and I was Mr. Bones. I asked him, "Mr. Interlocutor, what's the difference in mashed potatoes and pea green soup?" He said, "I don't know, Mr. Bones, what's the difference?" Then I said, "Well, anybody can mash potatoes."

The Greers and Platos had several competitions. There was the Greer-Plato basketball tournament, the Greer-Plato debate, a track meet, and the tug-of-war down across the river. The tug-of-war happened every spring. The Greers and the Platos would put the rope on our shoulders and walk up Columbia Avenue to town. We'd walk down Main Street, go through the theater, and march around the square. Then we'd flip a coin to see who would get the Nashville side. Whoever had that side usually won, because the slope wasn't as steep as it was on the Franklin side. I was a Greer, and when I was a freshman we were on the Franklin side and it only took about 12 seconds before we got pulled in. But we won the last three years, and one of those years we were on the Franklin side.

When there was a dance, most of us went stag, and everybody just danced with everybody else. We had dance cards, and before the music started, we would ask certain girls to dance with us during the no-break dances. There were certain dances when nobody could break in on you. The girls would write their names on your card, and your card would fill up. If you had a date, you'd try to save the last no-break for whoever your date happened to be.

Every spring the Junior-Senior Prom took place in the gym, but the school was so small, that sophomores and freshmen could go, too. When I was a senior, Mr. Bragg's sister-in-law was my date for the prom. The gym was as hot as it could be, but there were decorations and refreshments. There was a receiving line, and as soon as we walked in, we'd go down the line and introduce our dates to all the teachers.

Owen Bradley's orchestra played, and it was a big orchestra. 1954 was the year before Rock and Roll really caught on, so we danced to songs like *Little Things Mean a Lot* and *Hey There* and *I Apologize*. Unless it was a no-cut dance, other guys could tap you on the shoulder and cut in. After somebody cut in, you'd go over and wait in the stag line until you asked somebody else to dance. So even though you had a date with a girl, you both might dance with 20 different people in the course the evening, which lasted from 10 o'clock until around two in the morning.

I graduated from BGA in 1954. I went on to Davidson College, but I didn't lose my connection to Battle Ground Academy. I was a counselor at Hy-Lake for several summers after I started college, and I kept talking to Jonas Coverdale. I had been in ROTC at Davidson, and I planned to go into the Army as a second lieutenant after I graduated. But it was peacetime, and the Army had too many second lieutenants. I went to intelligence school for six months, and that was the extent of my military service.

I was about to marry Margie, and I needed a job. I spent the summer of 1959 at Hy-Lake. Mr. Coverdale had just retired from BGA, and Paul Redick was put in charge. The school finally called and said they had a job for me, and I was very grateful. I took my bride of 10 days, and moved into the same little two room apartment in the dorm where Mama Haynes had been living when I came as a freshman ten years earlier.

When Paul Redick became headmaster in 1959, he ruled with an iron hand. Sometimes we'd wonder, "How will we get away with something like that?" But if it was something that Paul wanted to do, that's what we did. One of the decisions he made was that the students could pick their advisers. Everybody wanted Jimmy French or Ralph Brown, or one of the other younger teachers like me. But nobody would choose Ralph Naylor, and Ralph was called out for that.

BGA was growing, and the year I was hired, four other new teachers were also hired – Bunny Akin, Johnny Bennett, Jimmy French, and Ernest McCord. I found out I was going to be teaching English and Algebra. Margie was teaching deaf students in Nashville. She had to get up at 5:30, then eat, get ready, and go to Nashville. I'd see her off, and get back in bed. Along with dorm duty, I also had to run the school store, which was in the basement of the dormitory. Cora, who had been so kind to me back when I was a student, was still the head cook, and I came up with a way for her to make a little extra money. I would buy these little chess pies she cooked, and students would buy them when they came to the store.

Jimmy French was supposed to help with dorm duty, but when he was busy courting Susan McKeand, I was on my own. The last bell would ring at 10 o'clock, but it would be 10:30 before I could get everybody quiet. I remembered John Bragg trying to creep down the hall when I was a student. Those old floors would creak, and we knew when he was coming. Sometimes it was 11 PM before I started grading papers. I only got a few hours sleep each night, and then I had to get up and do everything all over again. It was difficult. My first year, I made $2,700. They gave me a place to live and free meals, but the next year I got a $300 raise.

From time to time, Margie and I served as chaperones for class parties. My first year back, there was a junior class party at Gary Anderson's house on Old Hickory Boulevard. It was Charlie Trabue, Paul Guffee, Bill Redick and that bunch. We got there, and the only light on in the house was a little lamp in an aquarium. So I cut on the lights, and all the couples who'd been cuddling in the dark got up and found another dark room. We spent all night going through the house and cutting on lights. That was a fast group. They moved fast and they partied fast.

There was so much talent in that class. So many good athletes. For that bunch to beat an undefeated team from one of the largest schools in the state was unbelievable. The culture at BGA seemed to change after Ralph Brown became the head football coach. We were more successful than we'd ever been before, and nobody enjoyed it more than Paul Redick. He was just swept up by the whole thing. Big crowds came to the home games, and we'd take spirit buses to the games that were out of town. It was a lot of fun.

I enjoyed the two years I taught at BGA, but it wasn't the same as it had been back when I was a student. There was such an emphasis on athletics. That's just how things were, and I was ready to move on. John Beasley, who worked at Vanderbilt, lived in Franklin. He was a good friend of mine, and he said I should apply to be the assistant director of admissions at Vanderbilt. I didn't know anything about admissions, but I could double my salary. Cannon Mayes and Johnny Bennett were both leaving, and Paul Redick was very mad because I'd signed an employment contract. But I made the jump, and I never regretted the decision.

I never lost my love for BGA. One of the things that stayed with me was the affection I had for people I met there. One of those people was Daly Thompson. He had come to BGA and graduated in 1910. He went on to Vanderbilt, and then he came back and taught at BGA before going off to fight in World War One. He served in Europe, and he was the principal of Franklin High School for 25 years. He retired, and the year after I graduated, he came back and taught at BGA. I had known him from going to the Methodist Church in Franklin, but I got to know him a lot better when I came back to teach.

Mr. Thompson was a very good man. He was quiet and very religious. His wife, Ouida, talked all the time, and her nickname for him was Monkey. I guess it was because of his long arms and the way he moved. She'd say things like, "Monkey, will you pass me that plate?"

I used to sit and talk to Mr. Thompson. I have a distinct memory of what he told me about coming to BGA in 1909. He said, "The day I arrived at BGA from Pocahontas, Arkansas, a teacher was at the train station waiting to meet me. But the train was late. When I got off the train, he said, 'Are you Thompson?' I told him I was, and he said, 'Well, come back with me to the baggage car.' He was in a hurry, and when we got back there he said, 'Which trunk is yours?' We got the trunk and threw it on the back of the buckboard, and I climbed up and got in the seat. When we got to Columbia Avenue, he whipped the horse and we started going pretty fast. I was holding on, and I finally said, 'Why are we going so fast?' He said, 'Because we have a football game today at two o'clock, and you are playing right tackle.'"

But Mr. Thompson had never seen a football game. He said, "I played in the very first football game I ever saw." He played right tackle, and the left tackle was Josh Cody, who was one of the best players in the South. He said the other team would always run their plays at him to stay away from Josh Cody. I remember asking him who BGA played in those days. He said, "Well, it just depended on where the railroad went. There weren't many roads, so we had to take the train to wherever we were going to play." I really enjoyed the time I spent listening to him.

1909 Team (Daly Thompson front row, second from left)

I could've stayed in Waynesboro, Georgia, and still gone on to Davidson. Then I would've probably gotten a job at a bank or sold insurance, but I wouldn't have been happy. The teachers I met at BGA made me want to go into education. I loved teaching and coaching, and I loved the things I was able to do later on – from being the Director of Admissions at Vanderbilt, to being Headmaster at Harpeth Hall. Coming to Battle Ground Academy changed my life.

The information in this narrative came from an interview that took place in 2012, and from two subsequent conversations in 2025.

The BGA Museum

Battle Ground Academy's collection of museum items, some of which date back to the War of the Rebellion, are of interest to students of American history. The array of blood-stained boots, rifles, swords, uniforms, and bullets were given to BGA by Dr. H.A. Laws, who spent much of his life collecting and studying the relics. Many of the items were probably salvaged on our own campus after men lay writhing on the battlefield. (Note – Dr. Laws was born in 1850, and lived in Thompson Station, only a few miles south of the Franklin battlefield. He was fourteen when the battle took place, and it is highly plausible that he collected many of the artifacts in the collection from the part of the battlefield that later became the BGA campus. Dr. Laws died in 1929.) The Laws Museum is located in the BGA Library. The museum contains many items, including unusual relics of the Civil War. The collection was presented to the school by a former student, Dr. Hiram A. Laws. One of the most interesting objects is an old-fashioned snare drum, which was carried by Robert Graham of Saxapaw, North Carolina, during the War of 1812. Graham later gave the drum to his son, Thomas, who used it in Franklin to encourage enlistments in the Confederacy in 1861. Also in the museum, there is a Confederate soldier's uniform worn in the Civil War by Scipio Thompson. In the glass case, there is a photograph of Thompson wearing the uniform.

This information came from an article by Dale Porter in the 1940 Cannonball, and from a 1947 article in the Cannonball by an unidentified author.

Winder Campbell, Class of 1955

Going to Battle Ground Academy was a family tradition. My great-grandfather was Patrick Campbell. He and his brother Andrew came to Franklin and started the Campbell School in the 1850s. It was on West Main Street. They retired around the time Professor Peoples was starting BGA, and I think some of the Campbell students ended up going to BGA. So the Campbell School was sort of a predecessor to Battle Ground Academy, which was always the place I was going to go.

My father, Jim Campbell, who became a lawyer in Franklin, graduated from BGA in 1921, and my uncle, Stewart Campbell, graduated in 1924. George Briggs, who was my father's uncle, lived until I was six or seven. He was BGA's headmaster from 1925 until 1944. I remember sitting at the table and listening to his stories. He was a bright, energetic man. He had been the captain of several sports teams when he was younger, and he was great at recruiting boarding students. He traveled all over the southeast, and it was Mr. Briggs who went to Miami and started recruiting Cuban students to come to BGA. He developed a pipeline to Cuba. My parents adored him.

We lived over on Lewisburg Avenue, and I went to Franklin Elementary School, where my mother was a teacher. I went to BGA as a freshman, and I either walked or rode my bicycle there every day. There were plenty of Franklin boys at BGA who I'd known for most of my life. Most of the boys from Franklin were pretty well-behaved. We didn't smoke and carouse and drink, but some of the Nashville boys who came as freshmen had a wild streak. Some of them smoked and drank beer and ran around with girls, and the Franklin guys would look at them askance. Most of the Franklin boys had been raised the same way I was – in a sheltered environment. I could walk to school, or walk around town all night by myself, and I rode my bicycle all over the place.

When I started in the fall of 1951, Jonas Coverdale was the president, Paul Redick was headmaster, and J.B. Akin was the head football and basketball coach. Mr. Coverdale was pretty hands-off. As an administrator, that's what he needed to be. But Mr. Redick was in the middle of everything. Between the two of them, they took the school to another level. Mr. Redick coached the freshman football team. He was a hot-tempered guy, and everybody was sort of scared of him. He was very intense, but he was a good guy and a good coach. Just about everybody had a lot of respect for him.

Mr. Redick was very old-school when it came to football. He would have one-on-one drills, and he didn't care whether you were a lineman or a running back. I was a quarterback, but it didn't make any difference. I had to hit those big ole lineman. It was brutal, and we banged heads constantly. But most of his players loved him. Because of how intense our practices were, we felt like we were more prepared than the teams we played. I think our freshman team won most of our games.

When I got there, the school was already focusing on getting Nashville boys to come to BGA. Duncan School was in Nashville, and when it closed at the end of my freshman year, several Duncan students, including a great football player named Stanley Gale, came to school at BGA.

When he coached us as freshmen, Mr. Redick had been in our back pockets the whole time. But Coach Akin was much more detached. He would tell you how to do things, and then stand back to see if you did them. He was highly respected. He called everybody "Honey." When we practiced, he let Ralph Brown and Cannon Mays do most of the coaching. I was a junior when Coach Brown came back to teach and coach at BGA. He was just learning the ropes and starting to feel his wings, but he was a very inspirational coach. He would sit down with you, and explain how you could beat the man in front of you. He'd tell you that you could do whatever it was. He was just a terrific motivator. An amazing individual.

I'd gone to BGA games when I was back in grammar school. I remember sitting there and thinking, "I'll never be able to do this. I'll *never* be as big as those guys." But then I got to high school, and I was one of those guys. I really took it seriously. I was a quarterback on the freshman team, and Allen Kirshner was the quarterback when I was a sophomore. But Allen got hurt partway through the season, and I was sort of thrown into the position. I was the quarterback for the last half of my sophomore year, and for all my junior and senior years.

BGA was sort of old-fashioned. Coach Akin would go to Vanderbilt and get surplus uniforms and helmets from Vanderbilt, and then he'd paint them blue. I think we all wore leather helmets when I was a freshman, but after we got a little money in the budget, we shifted to plastic helmets. Mr. Akin also got some clear facemasks, which Vanderbilt was just getting in.

I was one of the first guys who didn't wear high-top football shoes. My dad took me to Nashville Sporting Goods, and I bought some low-cut Riddell football shoes. When I was a sophomore, we played a home game against Columbia High School, who ended up being the state champions that year. We were okay, but not that good, and they beat us 39-0. They had a big tackle named Jimmy Linville, who went on to play at Vanderbilt. One time he tackled me, and knocked me for a loop out in the middle of the field. All the fans went oooh and aaah. It would've made my highlight reel.

Sometimes there were dances in the gym after football games, but other dances were more formal. We had dance cards we'd fill out. Everybody wanted to be with certain girls for the slow dances. There were junior no-breaks and senior no-breaks, which meant that nobody could tap you on the shoulder and cut in. If you had a girlfriend, you'd really want to be with her during the slow dances. That was when you could snuggle up together and all that.

When I was a junior, our class had the responsibility of building the props, buying flowers, and decorating the gym for the Senior Prom. We were supposed to buy roses, but we didn't. We took some clippers, and three or four of us got in Bobby Cameron's jeep and started driving through some of the neighborhoods in Franklin. When we found a garden, we'd sneak in and clip branches off the rose bushes and put them in the jeep. A couple of times somebody came running out of the house. "What are you doing to my rose bushes? I'm calling the police!" We'd run to the jeep and speed off. One man got in his car and tried to chase us, but Bobby drove across a couple of yards and we got away. When we showed back up at the BGA gym, we had a jeep full of beautiful roses.

I was probably a senior when some of us decided that we were going to skip the first part of study hall, and then slip in through one of the back windows. Mr. Redick was keeping study hall. When we weren't there at roll call, we were pretty sure that he would go out looking for us. Our plan was to stand on each other's shoulders, climb through the back window, and slip into the back of the study hall. When Mr. Redick came back in, he might think we'd been there the whole time. Pedro Paz and Bill Cherry had already made it, but we were standing three or four guys high under the back window when Mr. Naylor caught us. We had to go see Mr. Redick, and we all got demerits. I got called into Mr. Redick's office a few times, and he scared me to death. I would be sweating blood the whole time. I would get a good talking to, but I never got paddled. But he was the man with the paddle, and if you were called into his office, you were usually in big trouble.

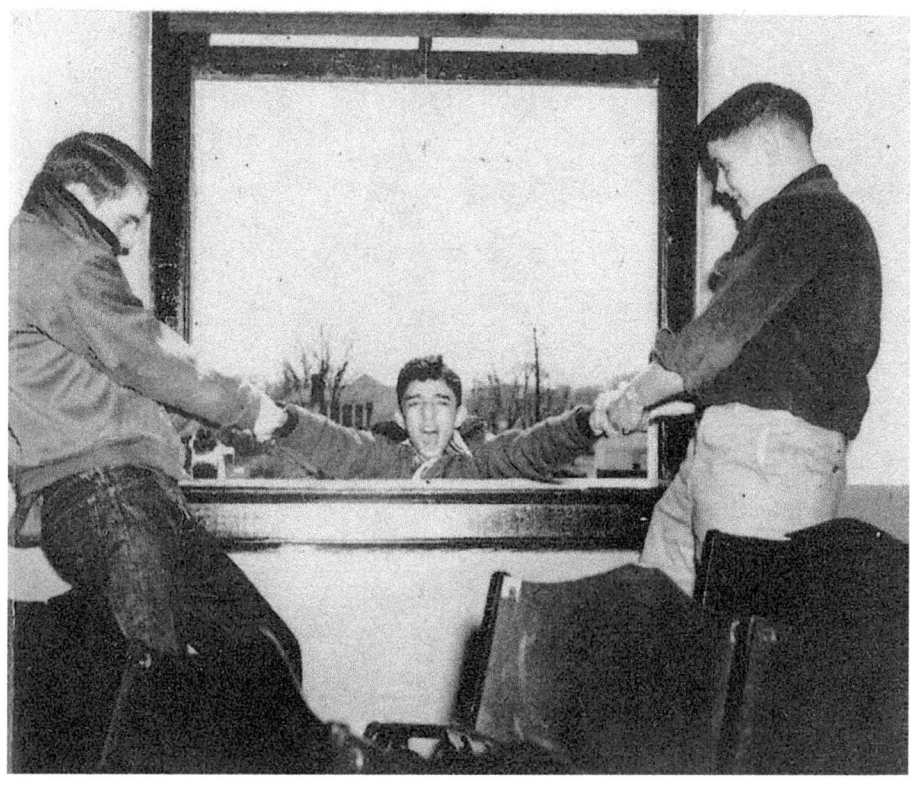

I sat at his table at lunch. There was a cook at BGA who everybody liked. She was jolly and friendly. But one day she wasn't there. When she showed up the next day, somebody said, "We all missed you yesterday." She said, "Well, yesterday I was having a baby."

Along with football, I also played basketball and baseball, but my best sport was football. I had always been pretty nervous, but as I got older, I got more confident. I started to calm down. I was a senior for the 1954 football season, and Stanley Gale and I were the captains of the team. We were really good that year.

We had a good line and some great running backs. Pedro Paz was a fireball, and he ran for a lot of touchdowns. He was a terrific athlete, and one of our hardest hitters. Tommy Brown and Stanley Gale also hit very hard. We had a big, very physical center named Walter Rasmussen. Bill Dotson and Ronald Ligon were our guards, Dob Johnson and Box Hawkins were our tackles, and Bill Herbert and Bill Cherry played end. Stanley Gale was the fullback, and Tommy Brown and Pedro Paz were our halfbacks. I was the quarterback. I tried to use my brain rather than my body, and I tried to avoid contact. I was not very intense. The other guys on the team made me look good.

Coach Akin would analyze the other team before each game. He'd say, "Boys, this is a pretty good team we're playing. They have a lot of bulldogs on their team. They've beaten some good teams, so you're probably in for a rough game. I want everybody to go out and play your best." Then he would give us a swat on the butt, and say, "Now get on out there." Sometimes he'd get excited during a game and grab you by the back of your shoulder pads. He'd say, "Now Honey, get in there and do this and do that."

Coach Akin would just tell me, "Get out there and run the team." He knew the game, but he would stand on the sideline and let me call the plays. I don't remember doing anything spectacular. I'd occasionally improvise, but I usually just called run right or run left, and pitch it to Stanley Gale. Stanley could make a long gain or a touchdown run out of almost any play we ran.

When we needed to pass, I'd say something to Bill Cherry like, "Go down the sideline and then cut across the middle." We ran so many running plays, that if I faked it to Stanley Gale, the whole defense would just converge on Stanley. Then I'd just drop back and flip it to Bill Cherry, who was usually wide open.

In those days, we'd take our uniforms home. We'd get them washed and all cleaned up, and bring them back in time for the next game. On the night of a game, I'd get to school at around six o'clock. The team would be down in the sweaty, stinky, old basement of the gym. While we were putting on our uniforms, we could hear noise coming from up near the field. BGA didn't have a band, but we had some guys with horns. It still excites me to think back to those times.

Most of the girls we knew would be up there. I remember walking off the field after the games. I was dating a girl in Nashville girl named Gretchen Gardner. Gretchen's little sister, Patsy, came to the games, too. She was two or three years younger than me, and she would always wave and yell "Hey, Winder! Hey, Winder!" I ended up marrying Patsy.

When I was a senior, we played a big game at Columbia and we won. It was a couple of nights before Halloween, and we rode back to BGA on our old rickety bus, still wearing our uniforms. We were sweaty and dirty, and after we got back to the gym, we took showers. By then it was 11 o'clock at night. Since it was almost Halloween, the downtown Franklin theater was playing *Frankenstein*, with Boris Karloff. The whole team went down there, and we got in for the late show. We stayed downtown pretty late that night.

Sometimes after a game there would be a party down at the Red Grill. The Red Grill was on the square. It was Franklin's one and only downtown restaurant, and there was party room up on the second floor. The girls would go down there and so would the boys, and we'd have dances upstairs. About half the guys didn't have girlfriends and half the girls didn't have boyfriends, and we'd mix and mingle at the Red Grill. Other times we would go to somebody's house, or we'd all go to the movie together.

We won our first eight games my senior year, and we were invited to play in the Tobacco Bowl in Hartsville. We had a meeting, and Coach Akin said, "Do you want to go to Hartsville, or do you want to wait and try for the Clinic Bowl?" The Clinic Bowl was a much bigger deal, and we declined the bid to the Tobacco Bowl. Our next-to-last game was down at Lawrenceburg.

In the Lawrenceburg game, we were behind. I told Pedro Paz, "I'm going to fake a handoff to you. Then I'll just put the ball on my hip and run a naked reverse the other way." Nobody else on our team knew we were going to do it. I ran for a touchdown, and that put us in position to come back and win the game. Coach Akin called me over and said, "Honey, that's the most wonderful play I've ever seen." But we lost the game, and we ended up kicking ourselves. We beat Hillsboro our last game, but even though our record was 9-1, we didn't go to a bowl game.

BGA had some great teachers. Carl Smithson came when I was a sophomore, and he taught math. I was terrible at math. Everybody referred to him as Goat, but not to his face. They'd say, "Oh, I've got to go to Goat Smithson's class." He didn't throw chalk at me or do a lot of the other stuff, but sometimes he'd grab me from behind and put his thumbs into my shoulder blades. I only made something like a C in math, but he was a good teacher and I always liked him. He also tried to teach me trigonometry, but I didn't understand it then and I don't understand it now. How I got out of his class without failing was a miracle.

Ralph Naylor had been at BGA for several years. Mr. Briggs, the former headmaster, married early in life, but he and his wife divorced. Then he married Susie Lee Roberts. Their daughter, Sarah Ewing Briggs, grew up and married Ralph Naylor. They lived right across from the campus. I always liked him, and he was a good teacher.

Ralph Naylor

John Bragg was a young English teacher just a few years out of Sewanee. He was very particular about the way he dressed. He wore a tweed coat, a button down collar, khaki pants, and white buck shoes. We were pretty amused by how preppy he was. Mr. Bragg was really big on the classics. We had to memorize passages from Chaucer and Shakespeare. He added a new dimension to BGA. He seemed like a new breed of teacher. He married his wife, Jane, when I was about halfway through BGA.

On Friday nights, if we didn't have anything else to do, Billy Cherry, Bob Cameron, Jerry Pollard, and I – and sometimes Mike Hudgins – liked to go up to Breezy Hill, which was out Columbia highway. We would pull off to the side of the road, and wait for cars to come speeding down the highway. We'd bought a big spotlight, and we would immediately pull out and catch the speeding car. Then we would cup our hands around our mouths and start making sounds like a siren. We made as much noise as we could, and when we shined our spotlight on them, they'd would pull off to the side of the road. Then we'd breeze on by and disappear down the road. We didn't want to get caught.

When the tug-of-war came around in the spring, the Platos and Greers would march from the campus all the way down Columbia Avenue into town. People would be cheering on the sidewalks, and we'd be yelling, "Plato, Plato!" or "Greer, Greer!" We'd walk past Earl's Fruit Stand to the bridge on Franklin Road over the river. Mr. Coverdale would lean over the middle of the bridge, and drop a handkerchief, and that was the signal to start pulling. It was really exciting. Girls would be there cheering, along with moms and dads and people from town.

1954 Tug-of-War

I was a Plato, and when I was a senior, I was in the front of our line. When we started losing, I got pulled off the bank. I was dangling off the rope and yelling, "Pull me back boys, pull me back!" But by then other guys were hanging off the rope, too, and it was too late. I finally just let go and dropped into the river. It wasn't long before everybody else piled into the river, too. I loved the tug-of-wars.

Tom Clarkson was our valedictorian, but I was somewhere between average to good as a student. I wanted to go to Vanderbilt, but I didn't know how I could afford to go. I grew up in a middle class family. My father wasn't wealthy, and my mother was a school teacher. I think it was Mr. Redick who convinced me to try for the NROTC scholarship at Vanderbilt. It was something I needed to do. BGA had prepared us pretty well to take tests. I went to Nashville and took the test, and I passed it and got the scholarship.

I didn't know what I was getting into. When I accepted the scholarship, I had to be sworn into the Navy. They said, "If you don't make it through Vanderbilt, then you're going right into the Navy as an enlisted man. You'll be swabbing the decks. But if you make it through school and graduate, you'll go in as an officer." I felt very fortunate that I got that opportunity, and I made it through.

My father died when I was in my second year at Vanderbilt, and my uncle Stewart Campbell, took me under his wing. When I got out of the Navy, Sam Fleming, who was president of the Third National Bank, offered me a job. I had known him my whole life, and I worked at Third National Bank for 42 years – almost my whole career.

When the George I. Briggs gymnasium was dedicated in 1948, my father gave the dedication speech. He talked about his Uncle George Briggs, and how happy he would've been to have the gym named after him. That gym was impressive. I was blown away by how beautiful it was. But by the time I got to BGA, I wasn't as impressed. I remember all the time I spent down in those sweaty locker rooms. Years later, I had an opportunity to go down there again. It still smelled like sweat and dirt and old uniforms. It's funny how smells can bring back old memories. If I could go back in time, I wouldn't change anything. One of the highlights of my life was going to BGA.

The information in this narrative came from an interview that took place on December 14, 2012, and from corroborating research.

Richard Ashworth, Class of 1957

When I started BGA, we lived on Columbia Avenue, at the corner of Strahl Street. We were just a block from the school, and I could see the Briggs house from my front yard. When BGA's headmaster, Professor George Briggs, had his stroke, I remember seeing a light in the corner room. My mother and daddy told me that's where Mr. Briggs was, and that he was probably dying. His widow, Mrs. Susie Briggs, was one of the finest women you could imagine.

My daddy raised eight children on a postman's salary, but six of his seven boys were able to go to BGA. I think the tuition was about $150 a year. He couldn't send us, and if it hadn't been for Mrs. Briggs, we would've never come to BGA. Mrs. Briggs' father, Walter Roberts, had endowed a scholarship fund, and she got us into BGA even though we didn't want to go at first. My oldest brother went to Franklin High School, and we went to all the Franklin High School games. I can remember my brothers arguing with my daddy. "We ain't going to BGA." But he said, "Oh yes you are."

Three of my brothers – Harold, who graduated in 1951, Donny who graduated in 1952, and Elbert who graduated in 1953 – were all able to go to BGA because of that scholarship. I graduated in 1957, and my brothers Charles and Bill graduated in 1958 and 1963. I remember J.B. Akin coming to our house in my junior or senior year. He was sitting in a big chair with his clipboard, figuring out a payment plan for my daddy to pay for Charles and I. By then, I think tuition was about $250 a year. I don't know if he had any help paying for us to go to BGA.

My freshman year, I had Mr. Akin in Bible class. He was a very good Bible teacher. We did a lot of what was called trapping. Mr. Akin would ask a Bible-related question to whoever was sitting on the left end of the front row. If he didn't know the answer, the guy in the next chair tried to answer the same question. Mr. Akin would go in order, seat by seat and row by row until somebody had the right answer. Whoever got it right would move to the seat on the front row, and everybody else would have to move down a seat. Whoever was in the first chair at the end of class, or at the end of the week, would get points added to his grade. I enjoyed Bible class a whole lot.

When I registered for my junior year, Mr. Akin told me I needed to take Physics. I said, "I don't know, Mr. Akin. It's got some math in it, and me and math don't get along." He called everybody Honey, and he said, "Oh Honey, you ain't no dummy." But I sure showed him. I failed Physics for the second semester. The next year, when Chemistry came around, he registered me again. I said, "Mr. Akin, I don't think I should take Chemistry." He said, "No son, I don't believe you should." He had a lot of wisdom. Mr. Akin was a great man, and he was probably more respected than any teacher in the school. Some teachers demanded respect, but Mr. Akin earned it. When you were in his class – maybe we'd be cutting up or talking – he'd say, "When you folks quit talking, then I'll talk." Boy, it would get quiet fast.

He loved basketball more than any of the other sports he coached. Every year, when football was over, he would say, "Well boys, it's time for round ball." He called it round ball. That was his favorite sport, and I guess football was next. I think he had less interest in baseball, because they didn't play many games.

A lot of people were afraid of Mr. Redick. He was a big man, and he was very much of a disciplinarian. He could get tough, but I think he was a very good guy. We had a boy named Willie B. Crouch in our class when I was a sophomore. One morning on the way to school, he caught a possum. He brought it inside, and he took it into Mr. Abe Hatcher's room, which was just off the study hall. He put it on the desk, put a trash can over it, and put some books on top. Well, Mr. Hatcher came in and picked up the trash can, and the next thing we knew, he was running out in the study hall, hollering, "Mr. Redick! Mr. Redick! There's a big rat in my room!"

Mr. Redick went in there, and picked up a yard stick. Then he hit the possum on the head, and picked it up by the tail and carried it outside. He was laughing and he said, "I guess this qualifies me as a big game hunter." He turned it loose, and we never heard another word about it. He didn't ask who did it. Nothing. We knew he was in charge, but he could go with the flow. And he was a great history teacher. One thing that I learned from Mr. Redick was to respect authority. He really preached on that. I came from a pretty disciplined family, but a lot of guys didn't.

I was the water boy for the football team, and the second week of the 1954 season, we were playing at Centerville. But the main team bus couldn't hold all the players, so being the water boy, I had to go on the next bus with some of the other players. We were going down Highway 100, and I was sitting in the back right-hand corner beside Mac Gayden. Somewhere on the way to Centerville, somebody yelled, "Don't hit that hot rod!" Some guy was turning into his driveway or something. Mr. Naylor was driving, and we went off down an embankment. The only thing I remember was flying through the air.

A few other guys got some bumps and bruises, but I think I was the only one who broke any bones. I broke a couple of bones in my hand. Mr. Bragg was sitting right behind Mr. Naylor, and his wife was sitting next to the window. Across from them was a big freshman wearing his football uniform. He had to hold onto the bar to keep from falling on Mr. Bragg and his wife. The guy would've crushed Mrs. Bragg against the window if he hadn't held on. Mr. Naylor was supposed to have stood up, taken off his coat and brushed it, and then said, "Oh my."

I was taken to the hospital in Centerville. After they set my hand and put a cast on it, Mr. Smithson showed up at the hospital. That's the kind of man that Carl Smithson was. A Cuban boy named Otto Galdo had a real bad headache, and they was afraid that he had a concussion. They kept saying, "Don't let him go to sleep." Anyway, the bus wreck destroyed my career as a water boy.

I lived in Franklin, and because I didn't have enough self-discipline to study at home, I'd go up to BGA at night and study. They had a two-hour study hall. Well, it was Halloween night, probably in my senior year, and I think we'd had a bonfire. Mr. Coverdale was in charge that night. There was a black man that lived down behind the school, and he had a goat. Mike Hudgins and somebody else, it might've been Britt Knox, went down and got the goat. They took it to Mr. Smithson's room, and tied it to the radiator. When he came in the next morning and saw the goat, he wasn't happy.

We heard later that what bothered him the most, was that Mr. Coverdale had discovered the goat the night before, and hadn't done anything about it. I got along with Mr. Smithson pretty well. He had gone to high school with my older brother, Bobby, at Franklin High School, so he took to me a little bit. Mr. Smithson was a disciplinarian, and he was a good math teacher. I didn't make good grades in his class, but I managed to get through.

Back then teachers had to do it all. I remember one day when we were playing basketball in the old gym. Mr. Naylor came in with his work clothes on, and he started doing some carpentry work. He kind of did it all. I never had Mr. Bragg in class. When I was a senior, he went back to McMinnville to work in his family's nursery.

Mr. Coverdale was president of the school, and if it hadn't been for Mr. Coverdale and Mr. Redick, the school would have probably gone under. They came to BGA from Castle Heights in 1950. With the way he handled things, with his financial abilities, he brought the school back. He brought it back, but he had to use a lot of cost-cutting measures. He bought army surplus stuff. And he also bought some old buses and had them fixed up, and painted,

In my freshman year there was a pep rally and a bonfire on the football field the night before we played Hillsboro. People wore things like pajamas and bathrobes and long underwear and wading boots. There were speeches from Coach Akin and Coach Brown, and cheers from the students, and then everybody walked over to Columbia Pike and marched to Franklin. When we went through the theater, they stopped the movie, and we stood on the stage and cheered. After that we went out onto Main Street and hung an effigy of Mr. Hillsboro on the Western Union sign. Then we went back to BGA.

Another time we went down to Mt. Pleasant on a Thursday night pulled off a big upset in football. The next morning there was an assembly right after we got to school. Either Mr. Coverdale or Mr. Redick said, "We're required to have school a certain number of days every year. We can't just turn school out." We'd been hoping for a surprise holiday, and we were disappointed. Then he said, "But there is a teacher's meeting today, and some of our teachers would really like to go." So we didn't have school that day. My brothers used to get surprise holidays three or four times a year. They'd go into school one day, and the headmaster would get up and say, "It's a beautiful day outside. Why don't we just take the day off?"

After the ball games, we would go to the Gilco. It was over on Lewisburg Pike by the railroad tracks. There's a beauty parlor there now. That's where everybody went. You could hardly get into the place, especially if BGA and Franklin both had home games the same night. It would be packed. It could be pandemonium in there. There was a jukebox, and I remember hearing Elvis and Carl Perkins songs. You could get a milkshake for something like a quarter, and a hamburger for a quarter or 35 cents.

Mike Hudgins was the class clown. He would've probably been considered the guy least likely to succeed. But he ended up succeeding in a very big way. He is one of the most kind-hearted, most charitable guys you'll ever want to meet in your life. A really, really good guy. Mike was quite a football player, and he was really a good baseball player, too. He got a baseball scholarship to Florida State.

DeBow Casey

Somebody else that was always getting into trouble was DeBow Casey. Bow was an outstanding basketball player, and we were on the tennis team together. I wasn't very good. When I was a junior, Mr. Guiton was the coach. The team only had five players, and because we needed six, I made the team. When we went up for a match with St. Andrew's, they had the Mid-South Conference champion. So Mr. Guiton decided to reverse our lineup. I played against their top player, and DeBow, who was our best player, went against their worst guy. But it didn't work. We all lost, and the guy I played just embarrassed me. I don't remember getting a single point. And to top it all off, Mr. Guiton got a speeding ticket on the way back.

I don't know that I would've thought Britt Knox would become a war hero, but he was always a leader. If he saw something he didn't like, he would speak up – and he would be pretty emphatic. Even when it came to something like putting chewing gum in the urinals. He played college football at the Citadel, and was in the Tangerine Bowl. But he wasn't even supposed to play football at BGA. He'd been in a real bad car wreck back when he was in the eighth grade, and he had severe head injuries. But he went ahead and played at BGA. He started at end, and was a good football player.

We had several classmates from Cuba, and the Cubans weren't allowed to speak Spanish when there were other students around. I remember Mr. Smithson getting on some of them one time for doing it, because he didn't know what they were saying.

We enjoyed the dances, because we'd get to be with the girls. A lot of Franklin girls had boyfriends at BGA, and some of the Franklin High School boys were jealous of guys from BGA. But the girls wanted to go to the dances, and we had more dances and social gatherings than the high school did.

I was a Greer. There were Greer-Plato basketball games and track meets and debates. But the competition would get really intense when we had the tug-of-war. I only got pulled into the river one time. It was in my sophomore year. We had it down by the bridge on Franklin Road. Whoever got the Nashville side almost always won because it was more level. The Franklin side was on a slope. I remember picking up the rope at the elementary school at Five Points, and the Greers and Platos would march down Main Street, go around the square, and then they'd flip the coin. Mr. Naylor was in charge of the Greers, and Mr. Akin was in charge of the Platos.

Even though we were on the side closest to Franklin when I was a freshman, we won. The next year, we got the Franklin side again, and we lost. But if you won, you better get out of there, because the other side was going to come get you and throw you in the water. That's probably as much hard work as you'd ever do in two or three minutes. When it was over, we'd be exhausted.

I didn't go to college. I had a career in banking. I went to work for First American Bank the January after I graduated. I worked there for eight years, and then I moved on to some other banks. I never made a whole lot of money.

The first reunion we had was 30 years after we graduated. It was like we'd gotten out of school on Friday, and we'd gotten together again the next night. It was like no time had passed. We had a lot of fun. When we were in school, it just seemed like, "God, I want to get out of here as quick as I can." But later on – after you're gone – man, you really miss it. You miss it. I can hardly put into words what

BGA has meant to me. I learned some great lessons about life when I was at BGA. I wouldn't take anything for the time I spent there. I love the school.

This interview took place on November 9, 2012. Richard Ashworth died near Nashville in 2023 at the age of 83. He had a long career as a banker, and was survived by a daughter and one grandchild.

Larry Stumb, Class of 1957

My father died when I was young. I was 10 years old when we moved to Hendersonville to live with my grandmother. Along with my mother and my grandmother, I lived in a house with my sister and my aunt, and a lady boarder also lived with us. But my mother wanted me to be around men. She was worried that I'd turn out to be a sissy, and she sent me to Hy-Lake Camp.

Back then, the population of Hendersonville was something like 300, and the school system wasn't very good. Instead of going to college, most students stayed home and worked on their farms. When I was about to start high school, my mother said, "I think you need to go to BGA and live in the dormitory." But I wanted to stay in Hendersonville, and I talked her out of it. I did the same thing when I was a sophomore. When I was a junior, she said, "Do you want to go to college?" When I told her I did, she said, "Then you really need to go to BGA. They can teach you how to study." Well, I already knew how to study, I just didn't want to. I would rather throw paper wads and annoy the teachers.

I'd gone to Camp Hy-Lake, so when I got to BGA in the fall of 1955, I already knew some of the other students. My roommates were Sam Hardy, who was from Clearwater, Florida, and Johnson Terry, who was from Leighton, Alabama. We didn't know each other. It was Saturday night, and we had just gone to bed. I was really homesick. I wanted to be with my buddies back in Hendersonville.

The next morning we woke up, and Sam Hardy got out of bed and put on his clothes. But Johnson Terry didn't get up. He was kind of staring, and his eyes were glazed. I was scared and we went and got the nurse. Her name was Mama Haynes, and she was really old. Johnson was in a diabetic coma. She gave him a glass of orange juice with some sugar in it, and he perked up.

After that, I adjusted pretty quickly. I wasn't much of an athlete, but the year before, I'd been a substitute on the basketball team at Hendersonville. There was a TSSAA rule that said you couldn't play athletics for a year after you transferred, so I didn't play on any teams during my junior year.

We stayed in *Westover*, which was a little two-story frame house next to the Redick's. Tom Guiton, who taught English and History, lived with his wife on one side of the bottom floor. Students had the other side on the bottom floor, and we had the whole upstairs. We were supposedly mature enough to live off the main campus, which was right across the street. When Britt Knox came and boarded briefly, some synergy got started. It wasn't long before we start thinking about what could we do for mischief.

Westover

When a big water fight finally erupted with toilet paper soaked with water and ink, Britt fired the first shot. Hervin Romney was coming in the front door, and Britt hit him with a wad of wet toilet paper. It was one of those things where the next person retaliated by doing something a little worse.

Then it became the downstairs guys against the upstairs guys. We weren't trying to destroy property, but that's what we did. We made the biggest mess you've ever seen. The Guitons weren't around, and when they got home, water was dripping down through the ceiling. We got all sorts of demerits, and I spent several weekends working off my time.

Staying on campus could be lonely. Franklin was a small town, and there wasn't much to do. I would walk to the pool hall or the movie theater on Saturdays, or walk to the Catholic Church on Sundays. That was about it, so I did a good bit of studying.

I hadn't played much football, but when we were seniors, a couple of my friends decided that they would try football. I was on the team, too, but I mostly just sat on the bench. J.B. Akin was our head coach. Ralph Brown had been coaching the freshman, and he helped Mr. Akin coach the varsity. He worked with us before the final game, and he really got us going. He was passionate.

Our last game was at Cohn, in West Nashville. They had a guy named Tommy Wells, who was really a good running back. He went on to play at Georgia Tech. Coach Brown gave us a pep talk, and he got us so fired up that we thought we could beat those guys. He said, "Our defense is going to stop those guys. We're calling it *The Rackin' Ass Defense.*" We were all fired up, and John Brown ran the opening kickoff back for a touchdown. Things went back and forth from there, and at the end of the game, Wells scored what looked like the winning touchdown. But there was a penalty and they called it back. The game ended up in a tie, and there were some angry fans from Cohn.

We had to change out of our uniforms in the restroom. Somehow or other, a couple of us got separated from the rest of the team. We were on our way to the bus when four guys came out of nowhere, and they were upset about the game. Cohn was in a pretty rough neighborhood. They kind of surrounded us, and one of them had a switchblade. We were frightened, and we didn't say a word. All of a sudden Mr. Akin walked up. I didn't even know he was around. He said, "Boys, I expect you better put up that knife and disperse." Mr. Akin was almost fifty. He wasn't as big as the guys with the knife, but they just backed up and walked away.

Mr. Coverdale was in charge of BGA. He was a gentle sort of man. I had a sense that no matter how upset he was, Mr. Coverdale wouldn't lose his temper. I don't believe he taught any classes. The 1950s were financially difficult, and I think Mr. Coverdale went around and raised money to keep the school going.

Mr. Redick wasn't as gentle as Mr. Coverdale. He would lose his temper, and I was afraid of him. But I remember the stories he told us in American History class. His grandfather had fought for the Confederacy in the Civil War. He remembered his grandfather sitting beside an old stove in a country store down in Big Sandy, Tennessee where he lived. One day another old man came into the store wearing a Union coat. Mr. Redick said, "My grandfather picked up a piece of stove wood and started after him, but somebody stopped him." He told us a lot of stories like that.

The teachers at BGA were such good role models, but I missed out on having John Bragg as a teacher. During my senior year, he took a leave of absence, and went back to McMinnville to work at his family business. But I sat at Mr. and Mrs. Bragg's table when I was a boarding student. We had to wear a tie to supper, and you can't imagine the outfits that people had on. Flannel shirts with ties that didn't match. We made it a point to look as bad as we could. Mr. Bragg was a perfect gentleman. He and Mrs. Bragg were mature, very gentle people, and I was afraid to misbehave. I never would've guessed that Mr. Bragg was a decorated World War II hero. He never mentioned it.

Mr. Smithson's nickname was Goat, and he didn't like it. At basketball games we had a cheer that went, "Go! Go! Go!" If Mr. Smithson was sitting down in front of us, we'd say, "Goat! Goat! Goat!" When he turned around, we'd go back to saying, 'Go! Go! Go!' And I think it was on the morning after one Halloween when something else happened. When Mr. Smithson opened his door, there was a goat in his classroom. And it had made a terrible mess. At first nobody knew who did it, but it turned out to be Mike Hudgins and Pedro Paz.

I remember how impressive the honor code was. We were told that if we saw somebody cheating on a test, to go and grab his paper. And that happened during an exam in my senior year. Several of us saw this guy cheating, and three of us stood up and went over to get his paper. Johnson Terry got there first. His face was red, and he grabbed the paper and took it up to whoever was monitoring the class. The guy who cheated didn't end up graduating.

There were a lot of characters in my class. In a way, we were all characters. One was DeBow Casey. We had unflattering nicknames for most people. Mine was "Scummy." Vance Akin was "Rat." Bill Anderson was "Sleepy." And Richard Ashworth was "Albino." His hair was almost white, and his skin looked like it didn't have any pigment. I was a Plato, and we lost both years I was in the tug-of-war. When we first started to pull, the rope would stretch and I thought we were winning. But then I found out that we were losing ground. Since we were on the losing side, everybody harassed us. It was fun.

Cannon Mayes

Britt Knox was another character. He was adventurous, and fearless in football, but I wouldn't have necessarily picked him out to do what he did later on. He had two tours in Vietnam as a helicopter pilot. He flew something like 200 missions under fire. And after he retired from the army, he went to Peru with the Corps of Engineers. He secured airfields in Peru to fight the drug trade. He had to have a driver, and travel around in an armored car. And Pedro Paz was an unusual guy. He came to BGA from Cuba when he was 12 or 13 years old. He stayed with the Coverdales for a while because the dormitory hadn't opened. Pedro was a very good all-around athlete. He could play anything.

Cannon Mayes coached and taught English. He was single, and he lived in the old dormitory. I remember going down to his room, and there was a really nice D-18 Martin guitar on his bed. I was learning to play, and I really wanted a guitar like that. It must've been during my junior year when there was a rock 'n roll show in Nashville.

The Coasters, the Drifters, Bo Diddley, Little Willie John, and Fats Domino were some of the performers, and I took a bus from Franklin. It was the best show I'd ever seen. Fats Domino was the headliner. At the end, he sat down at the piano, and I knew every song he sang. When I graduated from BGA, my grandmother, my mother, and my aunt all got together and paid $100 for a used Martin guitar. Later on I got a Martin D-18, just like the one Cannon Mayes had. I still play it all the time.

I never studied until I got to BGA. That enabled me to get into Vanderbilt. I might have eventually figured out how to study on my own, but I wouldn't have ever met guys who became lifetime friends. Those were great days. The class of 1957 meets for lunch on the first Friday of every month. Sometimes there'll be eight of us, and sometimes there'll be 15. I've been able to see my classmates in a different light from the way they were in high school. BGA was a tremendously positive experience for me.

The information in this narrative came from an interview that took place on October 26, 2012. Larry Stumb died in Nashville in 2021 at the age of 82. He was survived by his wife, four children, 14 grandchildren, and nine great-grandchildren.

J. B. Akin, 1957

The first coach in the state to use the Split-T formation was J.B. Akin, the popular head coach at Battle Ground Academy. He instituted this system in 1944, when he started coaching at BGA, and he is still using it. Oddly enough, Mr. Akin didn't play football in college. His first job after finishing the University of Tennessee in 1930 was coaching at the high school in Ashland City. He stayed there for five years. His father's store, M.F. Akin & Brother, was a landmark in Burwood for nearly a half-century, and when his father died, he stopped teaching in order to sell the store and wind up the estate. After teaching at Burwood and Franklin High School, he joined the faculty at BGA in 1942.

He went to BGA as a science teacher, but in 1943 he started coaching basketball and baseball. In 1944 Turney Ford, then the football coach at BGA, went into the service, and Akin became the football coach. In his first year, he turned out an undefeated team. Two of Coach Akin's players have gone on to become All-Americans in college. Bob Harris was an All-American in basketball at Oklahoma, and later played for the Boston Celtics. Darris McCord was an All-American in football at Tennessee, and plays for the Detroit Lions.

He and his wife, Katherine, have two daughters. Akin smiles and says, "Raising two girls in a boys' school has been a most interesting experience." Janice, the older of the two, finished college at Auburn, and is married and living in Mobile. Her sister, Polly, inherited her father's scientific mind. As a junior in high school, she did research for a physician at Vanderbilt, and excerpts from a paper she wrote were published in the Journal of the American Medical Association. She was later one of only three girls in the nation to win a scholarship to Duke University.

A number of J.B. Akin's former players are connected with sports. Bobby Gentry is now coaching at Sewanee Military Academy. Dick McKeel has a coaching position in North Carolina. Ralph Brown is the baseball coach and assistant to Mr. Akin in football at BGA. Gerald Johnson is head coach at Central High School in Nashville, and Ralph Spangler is the head coach at Ashland City. And these are but a few. He says, "the biggest satisfaction in teaching is seeing some boy that you've helped straighten out, and then really go places."

This edited article was written by Dorinda Carlisle, and appeared in the Review-Appeal on July 25, 1957. James Boyd Akin died in 1983 at the age of 75. He was survived by his wife, Katherine, two daughters, and six grandchildren.

Mike Hudgins, Class of 1957

My daddy was about 10-years-old when he came to Franklin from Hohenwald. Captain Tom Henderson was one of Franklin's leading citizens, and he took my father under his wing. After he and Captain Tom's son, Tom Henderson Jr., became close friends, they both went to Battle Ground Academy in the 1920s. When Daddy was a student, there was an occasion when he was drinking and he got into a fight with the headmaster, Mr. Briggs. When he threw Mr. Briggs down a flight of stairs, Daddy got kicked out of school. Captain Tom wanted to keep his son and Daddy together, and he pulled Tom Jr. out of BGA. Then he footed the bill for them to go to Riverside Military Academy, where they both graduated.

I had dyslexia, and I was held back when I was in second grade. When I was in the fifth grade, my grades were so bad that my teacher, Mrs. Lee, went to my mother and daddy. She said, "Mike has already failed the second grade. Unless I can get his grades up, he's going to fail this grade, too. I want Mike to come live with me for the balance of the school year." That was from January through the end of May. I'd stay with Mrs. Lee from Monday through Thursday night. I made it through the fifth grade, but my grades were always on the bottom.

On Saturdays, back when I was growing up, I would ride my bicycle down to the Franklin Theater. I'd watch Roy Rogers movies, or whatever was showing. When I came back outside, the sun would be so bright I could hardly see, but my bicycle would always be there. If I was walking back home, I'd act like I was a tough customer. I'd just seen Roy Rogers beat up 10 cowboys, and I didn't want anybody messing with me. But by the time I got to the Corner Drugstore, I'd be normal again.

My daddy could drink a lot of whiskey. He was a US attorney for the Middle Tennessee district, and after a still was raided, he would get his law enforcement friends to give him a few kegs of confiscated moonshine. He always had a supply of whiskey. By the time I got to BGA, I raised worms in our basement. I sold them during fishing season. I would go down to feed my worms, and there would usually be new whiskey kegs down there.

On Halloween, everybody would go downtown and soap up the store windows. But we all knew all the police, and they all knew us. Officer Harris Irwin would say, "Hey Mike, it's 10 o'clock, you better go home." So I'd go home because Harris Irwin told me to. They'd treat us with respect, and we treated them with respect. Nobody got into too much trouble.

Even though my dad hadn't asked me if I wanted to go to BGA, I was glad I was going. We lived on Adams Street, very close to the campus, and I knew the school pretty well. I was already 14-years-old when I started eighth grade in September of 1952. I had already played football at Franklin Junior High, and I went out for BGA's freshman team. Mr. Smithson was our coach. It would take me a while to grow into a good football player.

Around the time I was starting BGA, Mr. Akin called me up. He said, "Mike, there's a boy that lives in Nolensville, and I'm going over to talk to him. Would you ride there with me?" So I went to Nolensville with Mr. Akin. I didn't talk to the boy. I just sat there and listened to the conversation. It was, "Son, where are you going to go to school?" and stuff like that. It meant a lot that a man like Mr. Akin thought enough of crazy Mike Hudgins to take me over to see this prospective student. He was my hero after that.

I was enthralled with the teachers at BGA, and with how orderly the school was. You were expected to do the right thing, and follow the rules, I liked to find out what a rule was, and then stretch it so far that nobody could recognize it. The next year, when I was about to start ninth grade, there was a faculty meeting about who they didn't want at BGA anymore. My name was brought up, but at least one of the teachers stood up for me.

When I was a freshman, the weather was bad and one day we practiced in the gym. Mr. Redick was coaching us, and he lined us up. He said, "Boys, you can always tell a good player from a bad one. Take Hudgins here. He's not that good, so we're going to take this other player and put him right here." We hadn't played any games yet, and he didn't know whether I was good or not. I just knew I wanted to play football, and I was waiting for the opportunity to prove him wrong.

I ended up being pretty good, and time had a lot to do with it. After I graduated from the eighth grade, I had started working on farms during the summer. I went to work for a guy named George

White, who lived out on Highway 431. I would show up at 5:30 in the morning. After I opened the gate and got all the cows together, we'd milk the cows. Then we did things like fix fences, paint the barn, or do whatever needed doing, and we'd milk again that night. I'd get home around dark. And I'd be out there the next morning at five-thirty.

And in between the seasons, some of us worked out with weights five days a week. Guys like Jim Burton, Flem Smith, Mickey Crowell, Britt Knox, and Box Hawkins would go from the classroom to the gym and change clothes, and then go to the weight room to work out. About dark I'd take a shower and go home. I'd have dinner and study, and then I'd get up the next morning, go to school, and do the same thing again.

I don't recall a day when I took a break from going to gym. I always envisioned myself becoming a good football player. I used to squat and jump up as high as I could – over and over and over and over. I developed very strong legs. I was an offensive guard, and during my years at BGA, I don't remember the guy playing in front of me on defense ever making a tackle.

I ended up being a little over six-feet tall, and I weighed 190 pounds. I wasn't all that big, but I was fast and there was something about hitting that I loved. Mr. Akin knew I had a propensity to jump offsides. I'd try to get across the line of scrimmage a little too quick. When I was a sophomore, we were playing a game, and the other team was on our two yard line. Even though I didn't usually play defense, Mr. Akin sent me in. He knew I might go offsides, but I guess he figured I might be able stop them from scoring. Being dyslexic, I've always done my own thinking. I didn't always listen or follow directions, but I'd try to find a different way to follow the same directions. I'd just get there a different way. That time I guessed right on the snap count. I tore across the line like a mad man and ran over the guy across from me, and we stopped them.

Mr. Akin and I had an agreement. I had to bring him my books at the end of class every day. He would count them. "One, two, three, four. Okay Honey, you can go on." I couldn't study at home without my books, and if I didn't show them to Mr. Akin so he could count them, I didn't get to play football.

When I was a junior we went to football camp. I'd been working out all summer, and my legs were as strong as iron. We had a scrimmage while we were at camp, and this guy from the other team clipped me and broke my leg right above the knee. When I had my leg broken, and I was put in an ambulance, Moises Behar, who was the manager of the football team, rode to the hospital with me. I ended up in a cast that went from my ankle all the way up to my chest. I was out of school for half a year.

When I was able to play, my tackling style was close and murderous. But my friend Pedro Paz was a great open field tackler. There were times when we kicked off, and Pedro would hit the runner head on. He'd pick the guy up, drive him back, and just drop him. That's the way we were supposed to tackle, but nobody could do it but Pedro.

Jim Burton was one of our best players. He was really tough and he was all muscle. Jim weighed about 225, and sometimes he would just step on my back and keep going. It's easy to remember things like the running ability of Jim Burton, or the quarterback skills of Mickey Crowell, and the way Mr. Akin coached. His leadership style was pretty basic. He expected his players to do their best. I knew that my job as left-guard was to make sure the guy in front of me didn't tackle our runner. Ralph Brown was the assistant coach, and he had a different approach. He would mix it up with the boys a lot more than Mr. Akin. They just had different management styles.

Mr. Akin had so much dignity. One Monday we had gathered in his classroom, ready to go down and practice. He said, "Let me see a show of hands of boys who are up on Saturday nights after 10 o'clock." Another guy and I raised our hands. "See me after practice, boys." After practice he told us to start running laps around the football field. We ran and ran and ran, and it got dark. We thought Mr. Akin might've forgotten us. We finally couldn't run anymore, and we started walking. Once we rested up, we started running again. It was dark, and Mr. Akin finally showed up. He said, "That's it, boys, go home." If he hadn't said we could stop, we might still be running. We respected him that much.

One day, Mr. Akin was in the backfield watching us practice. We were down near the goal post, close to the administration building. I think Charlie Shanlever was running to catch a ball, and he ran into Mr. Akin. Mr. Akin's ankle was broken, but he didn't yell and scream. He just sat on the ground and said, "Boys, call the ambulance." He went to the hospital and took it in stride.

Mr. Akin left pep talks to his players. He had a calm presence, and that allowed us to concentrate on what we were supposed to do. Before my last game, during the 1957 Butter Bowl, Mr. Akin said, "Boys, this is a big opportunity for us. We should go out and win this game." We didn't win it, but we went out and got a 7-7 tie.

I remember one day when we were in study hall. Mr. Redick was teaching in the classroom to the left of the stage, and DeBow Casey was keeping study hall. DeBow said something funny and we all laughed, and Mr. Redick came bounding out of that classroom. He said, "Who said that?" DeBow said, "I did," but he wasn't being defiant. Mr. Redick said, "Come here." DeBow walked over to the end of the stage, and started to come down the steps. But Mr. Redick grabbed him. He had one hand on the back of DeBow's neck, and his other hand on his belt. Then Mr. Redick took about three steps and threw DeBow through the door and into the classroom, Mr. Redick stormed out of the room, and we didn't know what to do. We didn't move. Mr. Akin finally came walking up the stairs, and he started looking around. That broke the bully spell. I don't think Mr. Redick wanted to be a bully, but sometimes he could be a bully.

My daddy loved to fight. He didn't fight because he was angry, he just liked to fight. I didn't like fighting, but I would stand up for what I thought was right. One day at BGA it was snowing, and one of the teachers had one of the students down on the ground and he was rubbing his face in the snow. At first I thought the teacher was just having fun with one of the students. I thought he might've just gotten a little carried away. But another guy was standing next to me, and he didn't see it that way. He said, "Do you like what you're seeing?" When I told him I didn't, he said, "You want to break it up?" So we walked over and I grabbed the teacher by the ankles, and dragged him away through the snow. I could've gotten into trouble, but I didn't.

It was Mr. Smithson's way or the highway. I was in one of his math classes one day, and this guy said, "Mr. Smithson…" Then Mr. Smithson said, "Two demerits." The guy said, "What?" and Mr. Smithson said, "Four demerits." Then he said, "What did I do, Mr. Smithson?" Mr. Smithson said, "Six demerits." But when his students got to college, they just breezed through their math classes. I respected Mr. Smithson, but I can't say I liked him.

Carl Smithson, 1955 (Mike Hudgins in center background)

One night Pedro Paz and I were talking, and one of us said, "Hey, there's a black guy who lives on the other side of the gymnasium, and he has a goat. Let's go get the goat and put it in Mr. Smithson's classroom tonight." Somebody had done something pretty close to that before. One day that same goat was turned loose in study hall, and it had run all over the place.

It was a big white billy goat, and we let him loose in Mr. Smithson's classroom, which was in Room One – the room closest to the dorm on the ground floor. Mr. Smithson had all these cardboard parabolas displayed, and when we came to school the next morning, the goat was standing there. It had eaten every one of those little parabolas, and there were little green balls all over the floor. Mr. Smithson went ballistic. He looked like he was going to have a heart attack. After he accused some other guys of bringing the goat, I went up to Mr. Smithson. "You're blaming all these other boys, but they didn't do it. Pedro and I did it. We went and got the goat, and we put him in your room." But he didn't believe me, and I went to Mr. Redick. I said, "Pedro and I put that goat in his room. Mr. Smithson just doesn't believe us, so I'm telling you that we did it." He just said, "Don't worry about it, son." And that was that. No demerits.

I wasn't good in math, and there were a lot of Saturday mornings after football games when I had to come back to his class and spend a few hours doing math problems. I was stiff, tired, and worn out, but I would be standing up at the chalkboard doing problems. And I never got any better at math.

I liked Ralph Naylor. He had a good sense of humor. He didn't take himself too seriously. He was keeping study hall one day, and we started singing, "For he's a jolly good fellow." Mr. Naylor jumped up, and said, "Boys, if I thought you meant it, I'd let you keep on singing it."

When he was keeping study hall, we'd get a cannonball and put it up in the back-right corner of the room. We'd prop it up with a pencil to keep it from rolling, and then we'd tie a string around the pencil. The string would be let out until it reached all the way to the front of the study hall. When somebody pulled the string, the cannonball would start to roll. When it started rolling, it went pretty slow at first. Then it would hit all those chair legs all the way down to the front of the study hall. We did that several different times, but everybody liked Mr. Naylor.

The Gilco

For dances, bands from Nashville would come and play in the gymnasium. There might've been a little rock 'n roll, but it was basically old-fashioned orchestra music. Patti Page-type, 1950s music. I was in love with Nelda Casey when I was at BGA, but I didn't have a car, and I wasn't much of a lady's man. Pedro Paz was really colorful. Pedro could speak perfect English, unless we were at one of our BGA dances. He would wear a white suit, and his hair would be all pulled back. He looked pretty good. He always had good-looking dates, and he danced with the pretty girls. We'd tap him on the shoulder so we could dance with the girl, and all of a sudden Pedro acted like he couldn't speak English. "No. No speak English." He'd pull that little trick all the time.

Unless there was a high school game or a dance, there wasn't much social life in Franklin. There wasn't much else to do except go home and go to bed. But when BGA had a game, or after a movie, we all hung out at the Gilco. The Gilco was just a typical drive-in with tables and booths, and there was a counter with a few stools. There was a kitchen back of the counter, and we'd have hamburgers and fries, and cold drinks or milkshakes, and the jukebox was usually playing.

The tug-of-war was something we anticipated all year long. We would take the rope from BGA, with the Greers on one end, and the Platos on the other end. We'd walk down Main Street, and when we got to where Franklin Road crossed the Harpeth River, the rope would be dropped off the bridge. I was a Plato, and we went down to one side of the river, and the Greers went down to the other side. Mr. Akin was in charge of the Platos. He would say, "Boys, this is what I want you to do. I want Mike Hudgins and Percy Fly to be in front of the line." Then he would tell us not to just start pulling, but to get a rhythm going, and to keep pulling in rhythm. Then he would stand there and about every three or four seconds, he'd yell, "Pull, pull."

Because I missed so much school when I broke my leg as a junior, I didn't graduate with the rest of my class in May, 1957. I went back to BGA for the fall semester. I got to play another year of football while I finished up my classwork. We had a good season, and I made the All-Midstate team. I got a scholarship offer to play football at Vanderbilt, and I also got a scholarship offer to play baseball at Florida State.

Baseball wasn't a game I was in love with, but I did have a particular skill to play the game. I liked football more than baseball, but I had never gotten over getting clipped and having my leg broken. I was always looking for somebody to hit me from behind. I couldn't live with that. I just couldn't do it. So when I graduated from BGA in January of 1958, I went to Florida State. But when I went down there to take my entrance exams, I had trouble. The instructor said, "Read these instructions and then start." But the instructions were so complicated, that I was still trying to read them when everybody else was on the second or third page. Over the years, I learned that there are some things I can't do, and to stay away from them. There are other things I can do real well, and I specialize on those.

I flunked out of Florida State. I was totally undisciplined. I shouldn't have gone from a school with 200 students to a school that had 15,000. If I'd stayed at BGA until the end of the year and played another season of baseball, maybe I would've been ready to go to Florida State. But I flunked out, and came back and finished at MTSU. I should have probably gone to UT and played football, but I still would've been looking for some guy running up to clip me. If it hadn't been for that, I honestly think I could have been an All-American at UT. I've made a lot of bad decisions along the way, but I eventually had a very successful career in the insurance business.

BGA was everything to me. There was so much commitment by the teachers. We never had any inkling that they were teaching to make money. I had differences with some of the teachers, but I felt like they were there for us, and we knew that BGA was a special place. I never told Mr. Akin what he meant to me. I was just too caught up in myself to think about going to thank him. But after he died, I decided to look up as many teachers as I could. I wanted to look men like Mr. Bragg and Coach Brown and Coach Mayes in the eye and thank them for what they gave me at Battle Ground Academy.

The information in this narrative came from an interview that took place on February 22, 2013.

Britt Knox, Class of 1957

I was the youngest of four children. My brother, Jack, who had gone to the Citadel on a football scholarship, was nine years older than I was. My brother, Joe, who had an academic scholarship to Princeton, was six years older, and my sister, Phoebe, who was two-and-a-half years older, went to Vanderbilt and was a world-class opera singer. I was the least likely to succeed in my family. I just didn't have any direction. But when I put my mind to something, I could have a lot of determination.

In 1952, my dad and I were in a real bad automobile accident. I was in eighth grade, and we were on our way to watch Jack play against Furman in Greenville, South Carolina. We stopped in Chattanooga for gas, and the last thing I remember is getting into a sleeping bag in the back seat. That probably ended up saving my life. We were on a two-lane road in Georgia. It was after midnight, and there was almost no traffic. Daddy had a tendency to really move on, and I think he was probably going 100 miles an hour in our old Hudson. A truck had stopped in the road just over the top of a hill. Another car was coming, and in the collision, the motor was driven back on the side where I would've been sitting. I got slammed up against the back of the front seat, and Daddy was just chopped to pieces. It happened near Thompson, Georgia, early in the morning of October 17th, 1952.

When they got me out of the car, somebody said, "The little boy is dead." I had a blood clot on my brain, and my wrist was broken. I was in a coma for a while, and the doctors thought that I would have trouble with my head injury. They said I might not be able to do much of anything, but Daddy didn't accept that. Later on, and for years afterwards, there were times when my eyes would be out of focus. But if I said I didn't feel good, Daddy would say, "You're babying yourself." He was the son of an oil man. He'd grown up in Texas and he was kind of a cowboy, so I learned not to talk about how I felt.

My dad had wanted to serve in World War Two, but he couldn't. He'd fallen off of his horse when he was a little boy, and there was a metal plate in his arm. That arm was a little bit smaller than the other one, and he was very self-conscious about it. My father was a tough, tough, disciplinarian. He loved me, but sometimes he was unreasonable. I was not real close to him. It took me years to get rid of the resentment I felt. He was a tough guy, but man, could he draw. He did very well in the cartoon business, but he had a drinking problem.

Because of his drinking, he ended up having to start over, and he went back out to Texas and worked on a ranch. That's how he met Bob Corley, who ended up marrying Harry Guffee's sister-in-law. I met Dr. Guffee and his family when I was about five. They were very kind and giving, and it was like having a second family.

My sister Phoebe was dating Flem Smith, who went to BGA. Flem would talk about the school, and one day late in the summer of 1953, Mr. J.B. Akin came to my house. I was back from my paper route, and I had taken my bicycle apart in the front yard. He walked up and said, "Well, I can see that you're a mechanic and a paper boy. Let's take a ride to Franklin." I'd spent a lot of time in Franklin visiting the Guffee family. Mr. Akin drove me to BGA, and took me around the school. When we went down to the gym, he showed me the jerseys for the freshman football team. They were gold with white numbers, and I really wanted to wear one of those jerseys. Then I asked him how much it would cost to come to BGA. He said that if I rode the bus, brought my lunch, and bought used books, it would cost about $25 a month.

Then I told him I'd have to get out of school early enough to keep carrying my afternoon paper route. He said okay, and we made a deal. After that I went home and told my parents I was going to BGA. My parents didn't send me to BGA. I made the decision to go there myself. I did it because I was running away from the situation I was in after the wreck. I could hardly shoot a basketball, and I was pretty down. I went to BGA because I was having such a hard time.

I remember when we had our first assembly. It was in 1953 – Coach Ralph Brown's first year. I also remember going to an evening program. The parents came to the cafeteria, and the students were all wearing ties. The atmosphere was the way I imagined schools were in Great Britain.

When I went to BGA I weighed 96 pounds. I was a little guy, but I was on the freshman football team. Mr. Redick was my first coach at BGA, but the season only lasted for about two or three games because so many guys got hurt. And Mr. Redick taught me Civics that first year. He was a toughie. His nickname was Bull. When I was a freshman, we had big desks in the study hall where two people would sit. Mr. Redick was teaching a class down front, and Bob Napier and I were sitting at the same desk. I had a stocking cap pulled down on my head, and I was trying to make Bob laugh. All of a sudden, Mr. Redick came up and smacked me. When I went home, I told my father that Mr. Redick had hit me. He just said, "Good, I think I'll call him and ask him do it again." He never asked me why I got hit. That's pretty much the way it was.

Another time, I was sitting with Howard Smithson. I looked out the window and saw Mr. Redick walking from the administrative building over to the mess hall. I just leaned out the window and bellowed, "Mooo." Man, when he turned around, there was fire in his eyes. A lot of guys had problems with Mr. Redick. He didn't like certain people, but I got along with him okay.

Bob Napier

And some boys didn't care for Mr. Smithson. He was kind of a an unpredictable guy, but I really liked him. He lived in Nashville, and he would ride the bus to BGA. Because I initially rode the bus, too, I got to spend some time with him. One way or another, he kind of learned about my story. I felt like Mr. Smithson really liked me, but that didn't keep him from giving me demerits, or throwing me out of the class and all that.

After the first semester, I wasn't doing very well and I told Daddy that I wanted to leave. I said, "I can't carry my paper route with all this homework." Daddy said, "I'll tell you one thing. If you quit, you're not gonna play basketball or football or anything else. But you're gonna keep carrying that paper route. And I said, "Then you can pay for BGA, and I'll give up the paper route."

Over the summer, Mr. Redick suggested to Mr. Akin that I should get a chance to be on the varsity, and I got a letter inviting me to football camp. I hadn't been sure that I wanted to stay there, but something changed when I got that letter. I started thinking about the guys at BGA, and that's when I decided to go back.

I took Physics and Chemistry and Bible from Mr. Akin. He was just a phenomenal teacher. He didn't have a lot of personality, but he knew how to teach. He was a real anchor. Mr. Coverdale was a business guy. He was always counting pennies. Mr. Daly Thompson was a great teacher. He was a nice old man, but I was a little afraid of him. Mr. Bragg taught me first year Spanish. He was so straight and proper. He was pretty strict, and we didn't screw around in his class. He was a by-the-book guy. I didn't have any idea about the combat he experienced on Iwo Jima and Okinawa.

There was a teacher named Abe Hatcher who taught Latin and several other courses. He was a real nerd. He'd come into his classroom and the chairs would be all over the place, and one would always be missing. The students just wanted to see how he would react. Once there was a trash can turned upside down on his desk. There was a possum underneath the can, and it growled at him.

BRITT KNOX, CLASS OF 1957

Pedro Paz

I had a big year in football when I was a junior. Pedro Paz was the hardest hitter we had. He was tough. Pound for pound, he was the best football player we had. Pedro could've played for anybody in the country. He was just that good. But in the second game of my senior year, I got a clipped going down on a punt and hurt my knee. I kept trying to come back and play, but I hurt the same knee about four more times before the end of the season. I hadn't really started playing basketball again until my junior year. I'd dressed for a few varsity games as a junior, but Mr. Akin thought I fouled too much, and I didn't play a whole lot. When basketball came around again, I was still hurting and I finally quit. I ended up wishing Mr. Akin had tried to talk it over with me, but he just seemed a little irritated. All he said was, "Okay." So when it came to sports, my senior year was discouraging. I hadn't gotten to play much, and when I did play, I usually got hurt.

During my senior year at BGA, I was wrestling with Bob Napier and I jarred my head. All of a sudden my eyes went out of focus, and I got numb all over. That would happen to me sometimes. It was because of the wreck. But I was afraid it might keep me from playing football, so I didn't talk about it. When I went to see a neurosurgeon, he told me that I couldn't play football anymore.

I wasn't a boarding student, but my parents were going out of town, and I stayed at BGA for a couple of weeks with Hervin Romney, Larry Stumb, and some other guys. One day I was upstairs, and when Hervin came through the door, I hit him in the face with a big wad of wet toilet paper. Boy, did he get mad. Well, that started it. Next thing you know, water from a hose was coming through the window. One of the teachers, Mr. Guiton, lived in the other part of the house, and water was coming through. We got a whole lot of demerits for that, but it was really funny.

When it came to the Greers and Plato, I was a Greer. We had basketball games and track meets and, of course, the tug-of-war. It was like something from the movies. We'd march with the rope on our shoulders all the way down Columbia Pike into Franklin, and then over to the bridge on Franklin Road. Then we took the rope and dropped it over the side. I think we flipped a coin to see what side of the river we'd be on. The Nashville side was better than the Franklin side. I remember getting pulled into the river, so we must've lost the coin flip.

I came to BGA around the time rock 'n roll was coming on the scene. Songs like *The Great Pretender* by the Platters, and all those Elvis Presley songs still take me back. And romance was a big part of my life in high school. Lillian Campbell was my sweetheart. The first time I saw Lillian was at a dance in the old gym when I was a junior. I was kind of bashful, but I remember saying something about it being my birthday. Then I said, "Sweet Sixteen and never been kissed." And she said, "Well, I ain't taking care of that." I was really smitten over Lillian. She was just so smart and pretty, and she was a really, really good person. We dated for the rest of the time I was at BGA.

BGA was a major turning point in my life. It gave me a different direction. I thought the only reason to go to college was to play football. I didn't really want to go to college, but it was kind of expected. I decided that I'd go to the Citadel, and that I'd pay my own way. Between the money I'd made from being a paperboy, and what I received from being injured in the wreck, I had $1500. That was enough to cover my first year's tuition, my uniform, my books, and my room and board.

When I got to the Citadel, I thought I might become a trainer and get a scholarship. My plan was to go for one year, and see if there was something I could work out. So I became an apprentice trainer. At that time, I probably weighed about 170 pounds. But I ate with the football team and got to know the players, and I was still growing. I got up to about 190 pounds, and I was really in good shape.

When I went home for the summer, I made another appointment with the neurosurgeon. He examined me, and he said the results really looked good. Then I asked him if I could play football. He looked at me and said, "If a man wants to jump off the Empire State Building badly enough, I guess I'd tell him to do it." All I heard was that he didn't say no. So I decided to walk on at the Citadel in my sophomore year.

Before I left, I was at home, sitting at the table. Daddy and my brother Joe were arguing. When Daddy was walking out of the room, I said something that upset him. He had a terrible temper, and he hit me. I grabbed him and picked him up. He was a big guy, but I was 19 and I was strong, and I threw him on the floor. He was really angry and cussing. I just said, "I'm sorry."

I made the team at Citadel and I got a scholarship, and I was playing a lot until I got hurt. But after I came back from being injured, it didn't take me long to realize that I wouldn't be playing much anymore. I finally told Coach Teague, "I don't think y'all have any place for me here. I'm leaving," I thought I could go to Alaska and get some work helping to survey the Alcan Highway. I packed my bags and hitchhiked to Washington DC, but the congressman who I thought could help me get to Alaska was out of town. So I got on the bus, and went home to Nashville.

When I told my father what I'd done, he was angry. He said, "You've got to go back to the Citadel, and you've got to go back right now." When I told him that the coaches weren't going to let me play, he said, "Hell, if I was a coach, I wouldn't let you play either. But that doesn't have anything to do with it. Go back and give it a try. If you don't make it, then become the best cadet they have. But you've got to go. Not for me. Not for your mother. But for yourself." And I went back.

The coach let me back on the team, but I hardly ever got to play. It was a struggle. But in 1960, when I was a senior, we went down and played an unbeaten team, Tennessee Tech, in the Tangerine Bowl. We were way ahead, and people in the stands started chanting, "We want Knox. We Want Knox." I went in and made three or four tackles in a row. And on the last play of the game, I sacked the quarterback for about an eight yard loss. We won 27-0.

Everybody got on the bus, and we were all cheering. The line coach, Coach Ratteree, came back and sat down next to me. He put his arm around my neck and said, "Britt, I know this has been tough.

You've got more guts than anybody I know. And I'll promise you something. You're going to benefit from this." Then he just got up and walked off. And that was it. That was the end of my football career.

I still felt like I should've played more than I did. I really just had one year of football at BGA before I got to college. I was very fortunate to have played on the best team the Citadel ever had, but I still wonder what would've happened if I hadn't gotten hurt so much.

I graduated from the Citadel in 1961. I had a degree in Civil Engineering, and I got a job working on the Flaming Gorge Dam in Utah. But I had been in ROTC at the Citadel, and when the Berlin Crisis flared up, I got called to active duty. I was assigned to Fort Knox, Kentucky, for two years. I was a basic training company commander. I got out of the service and worked as a mining engineer, but I had reserve requirement and before long I got called up to active duty again. I was assigned to the 101st Airborne Division.

I went to jump school at Fort Campbell, Kentucky, and the first jump I made at Fort Campbell was out of a helicopter. The pilot was a guy I had known at Fort Knox. I said something like, "How can I get to be a helicopter pilot?" He thought I should just put in for it. When I did, the Pentagon told me to come up for an interview. I talked to them around November, but I didn't say anything about my head injury. They said there was a rotary wing class starting in February at Fort Rucker, Alabama, and that's what I signed up for. Flight school was not easy. The cockpit was designed for smaller pilots, but I adjusted.

I got through it okay, and shipped out to Viet Nam. Most of the time I sort of felt invincible, but I went down six different times. I was wounded when we were supporting a Korean unit. A Korean major, who was our interpreter, had his hand on my shoulder. I had just turned to my left to tell him something, and a round came right through my altitude indicator. My co-pilot, who was flying the chopper, was hit in the face and killed. The aircraft turned on its side, but I was able to straighten it back up and we made an emergency landing.

I didn't realize I'd been hit until I looked down and saw blood on my arm. I bled a lot, but my wound didn't seem to be that bad. I was playing solitaire and trying to be cool, and all of a sudden I was having a hard time playing my cards. I was close to going into shock, but I was just waiting to get another helicopter replacement. That was just sort of the way things were over there.

The first time I went down was in December, 1966. I had only been in Viet Nam for about three weeks. I was flying with a old warrant officer who had been a special forces guy. He was a good pilot, but we were flying the oldest aircraft in the unit. We were out doing a resupply, and we got an emergency call for a special forces evacuation. When we saw where we had to land, he kept saying, "We can't do it."

We had to land the aircraft right on the edge of a big cliff. If we came in straight, our blades would've hit the side of the mountain. So we had to do a pedal turn, and when we started hovering, the aircraft shook like crazy. Guys would climb in as soon as we touched down, and then we'd take off. We did that twice, but the third time we came in to land, the crew chief was guiding us in, and we hit a tree. The blades were damaged, and once they get out of sync, they start throwing parts. The pilot was able to ease the chopper out and let it fall, and just about the time we got to ground, he pulled in the power.

The helicopter started bucking and jumping, but he set it down on the road, and we all were able to walk away.

Six months later, I was taking off from a beach in a high wind. I'd been going in and out of there all day, and we lost an engine. My anti-torque was gone, and the helicopter started spinning around. It was a terrifying situation. The aircraft hit the ground hard and rolled over, but somehow nobody got hurt. We flew seven days a week, and most of the time we just went out on routine missions. But in September, three months after we crashed on the beach, the copter I was flying had a hydraulics failure. We had to make an emergency landing on an island controlled by the Viet Cong. We got out of there okay, and a month later, we went down after getting hit in the cockpit.

I went home on leave, but I extended my tour. By the time I came back, everything was different. The war was different. It was really getting bad. We had moved north to Bien Hoa. We had lost two or three crews, along with several aircraft. I was a platoon leader. I was in charge of 12 aircraft and 50 officers and enlisted men. There was a rocket attack on January 28, 1968, and two or three more aircraft were lost.

The gunships took off, and I was getting ready to line everybody up. We were drawing fire from everywhere, and from the city of Bien Hoa. One of the gunships got hit, and I heard the call, "Sidewinder One going in." So in case we could do anything, I lifted my chopper up and flew to the crash. The fire was so bad we couldn't see anything. The gunship was carrying 48 rockets and lots of ammunition. It was burning, but my crew chief and door gunner jumped out and rescued three guys before the gunship exploded. When it blew up, one of its rockets hit my main rotor. It just rolled our helicopter, and I got banged around a lot. Then I was just sitting there. I was in the twilight zone. I didn't have any pain, or any fear. I thought I was dead. There was no way I should've still been alive.

My unit had been shot up so badly, and we had lost so many men, that we had to stand down. I told my commanding officer that I was finished. I wanted to be transferred to a battalion position, because they didn't fly as much. I was waiting for my orders to come through. None of my guys were flying. We were just relaxing and playing football, and after a while, I changed my mind. My orders came, and I looked at my guys and decided to just stay where I was. When the guy that was going to take my place showed up, I took him up on a little rinky dink resupply mission. While we were out flying, we got an emergency call.

A unit from the 199th Light Infantry had been out for two weeks on a search and destroy mission. They were closing in on their night position. They were going to be evacuated the next day, but they had been surrounded by a regiment of North Vietnamese Army. The NVA were hardcore soldiers.

So we went around low. It was getting more intense, and the guy on the radio was really getting shook. Two or three of his guys got killed while I was talking to him. It was close to dark, and we had to line up to drop napalm. They would talk to us on the radio, and when we were in the right spot, we'd just kick it out the open door.

Then we came in and hovered about 200 feet above the trees. My crew chief and door gunners were using a rope to lower supplies as far down through the jungle as they could. They had straps on, and they were almost hanging upside down. I was flying an old bird, and we were taking a lot of fire. I knew we were taking hits, but I had to maintain 6000 rpm. Anything less than that, and we would've gone down.

We could smell the damage. I remember saying, "Guys, we weren't even supposed to be on this mission. You don't have to stay." But those kids kept doing it. They were tough. Really tough. They were my heroes. But my company commander was monitoring us on the radio. He knew we were taking hits, and he finally ordered me to return to base.

After we got back, an NCO from maintenance showed up and asked who had been flying the aircraft he was working on. Then he threw some rounds that had hit the chopper out on the floor. He said, "Somebody was looking after you. You had one of these rounds in your blade grip." The blade grip is what lubricates the blades, and it was a miracle that the aircraft made it back to base.

I didn't do anything while I was in Viet Nam that any other helicopter pilot wouldn't have done. It was just a way of life. I don't know any of them that didn't go down several times. That was just how it was. I stayed in the military for twenty-one years, and when I got out, I went to work for the Corps of Engineers.

One of my duties with the Corps of Engineers was to go down to Peru and open up an office. Peru was an adventure. I spent a lot of time in Iquitos, which was on the headwaters of the Amazon. It could only be reached by river or by air. We were trying to intercept the flow of drugs coming up from South America. Most of my work was in jungle towns. My team built all kinds of facilities, including runways. And because so much drug traffic came down the river, we even built a floating command post. It looked like a big barge. There were also planes that would detect unidentified aircraft. If the planes didn't respond when they were contacted, they would be shot down.

I worked in South America for six and a half years as a resident engineer. While I was down there, and especially while I was in Colombia, I was very restricted. I had to have an armed guard with me because of the terrorism. I couldn't walk on the streets. I started drinking every day, and when I came home, I *kept* drinking every day. All together, I drank for 53 years.

I'd read that it was normal for people who'd had head trauma to drink, so I kept blaming my drinking on what had happened to me in the wreck. But when I finally went up to Washington DC to get examined, they put something in my veins so they could look at my brain. They gave me all sorts of tests, and they diagnosed me with post-traumatic stress disorder. But I just shrugged it off. I didn't pay much attention to PTSD until I ended up in rehab. That's when I finally started facing things. Then I got involved in Alcoholics Anonymous, and my life changed.

Going through AA was a real experience for me. There were so many things that I hadn't been dealing with correctly. It's a wonderful program. Very spiritual. It got into me more than any church I've ever been to. It made me more of a believer than I ever was before. It wasn't that I hadn't believed, it's just that up until then, I'd tried to avoid it.

BGA turned me in a direction that changed my whole life. If I hadn't gone to BGA, I'm not sure that I would've gone to college. I would never have had the opportunities I got If I hadn't gone to BGA. That's where I learned how to study. When I was a senior, I was the last guy in class to turn in my final Math exam. I stood there while Mr. Smithson looked over my test. He finally said, "I think you made it, Britt, but do me a favor. When you get to college, just don't study engineering." But because I'd learned how to study, I made better grades at the Citadel than I had at BGA. And along with Math, thanks to Mr. Akin I did well in Physics and Chemistry. I couldn't have possibly ended up getting my degree in Civil Engineering without the background BGA gave me.

When my BGA classmate Buck Ramsey died, Mike Hudgins and I both went to the funeral. Mike was riding with me to see Buck's ashes being spread. We were talking, and he said, "We need to get together and have lunch sometime." So we did, and the next time we asked Pedro Paz to join us. And from there it just kept growing and growing. Sometimes upwards of 20 of us will get together. We'll talk about our lives, and the time we spent at BGA. It's become very special. I feel blessed that I went to BGA.

This interview took place on November 16, 2012. Britt Knox died in Woodbury, Tennessee, in 2024. He was survived by his wife, Faye, four children, six grandchildren, and four great-grandchildren.

Buddy Benedict, Class of 1960

Some of my friends went to high school at MBA, but the whole nuance of MBA back then wasn't something I thought I should be involved in. If I'd had my choice, I would've probably gone to Hillsboro. But my father said, "You'll never make it in class with girls around. You're going to BGA." That was about the end of the conversation. So I came to school at BGA because my father said that's where I was going. BGA was sort of a bubble, but it wasn't a bubble in the way that MBA was.

From fifth grade through eighth grade, I'd gone to Camp Hy-Lake. Several members of the BGA faculty worked there during the summer. They needed summer jobs. Since Jonas Coverdale, who was the head of BGA, owned Camp Hy-Lake, that wasn't a problem. That's where I got to know Jonas Coverdale and the headmaster, Paul Redick. They'd come to BGA from Castle Heights, which was a military school, and at camp they were called Major Coverdale and Major Redick. I also got to know Ralph Brown, Cannon Mayes, David Wood, and Jimmy French, who all taught at BGA at one time or another.

Hy-Lake drew guys from across the Southeast. Sometimes campers went on to become boarding students at BGA. Even though I knew a few of the men on the faculty, when I started BGA in ninth grade, I didn't know many of the boys.

A lot of things started unfolding for me when I got to BGA. I was learning to be an athlete, and my coaches helped me develop a sense of discipline. Luckily, everything went through Major Coverdale. He had his feet squarely on the ground, and he was a people person. He was like the Buddha. He called you by name, and treated you like you were his equal. There was nothing arrogant or egotistical about him. He was a plain ole guy who knew how to deal with boys. He was a mentor to everybody at BGA. How he dealt with people made an impression on me for the rest of my life. But Major Coverdale was getting on up in age when I got there.

Major Redick took over before my senior year, and Paul Redick was not Jonas Coverdale. He had an entirely different personality. He was very much of a disciplinarian. He didn't let you get by with much of anything. He was a strong leader, especially among the athletes. I'll have to say that Paul Redick favored athletes over the average student. If you were an athlete at BGA back in those days, you were looked at a little differently than everybody else. I graduated over 50 years ago, and looking back, I think that wounded a lot of people who weren't athletes. If they tried to be athletes, they usually got laughed off the team for one reason or another. We weren't bullies overtly, but we knew how to kid guys who didn't play sports. And sometimes we did it unmercifully.

The potential that you had as an athlete was something the school really wanted to develop. BGA had students that never would have been able to go there without financial help. Tom Fiveash's father had passed away when he was young, and he lived with his mother. He didn't come from my socioeconomic background, but he was a heck of an athlete. A lot of great athletes came out of BGA. There were less than 300 students when the school won that State Championship in 1960. During those years, it seemed like the chemistry of BGA was beginning to unfold. All those guys were coming to Franklin from different places, and the school had coaches who knew how to get the most out of their players.

We didn't have a lot of students, but we had Ralph Brown. He knew how to get us to play ten feet off the ground. You didn't know you could do it, but he knew you *could* do it. And he had a way of getting you to do it. All of us were just plain ole guys that Ralph Brown took and said, "Hmm, I might have something here." When I was a senior – the year before BGA won the State Championship – we were in the 1959 Butter Bowl. I like to kid the guys in the class behind me. I tell them, "Hey, we're the ones who got you all so high up in the rankings. All you had to do was just walk it in." But BGA was able to win that championship because it had people like Ralph Brown that could motivate you. And Paul Redick and John Bragg also motivated us to be something we didn't think we could be.

Coach Brown had a way of pitting us against each other competitively, and of pitting us against him. He would go to the practice field with you and race you – and generally beat you. But he had a method to his madness. Fifty years later, he still kids me about when he outran me in a 50-yard dash at football practice. I say, "Yeah, you were sitting over there in your shorts and t-shirt, and I'd just finished two hours of practice in full uniform. Sure, you outran me." You talk to him now, and he can tell you about every play, every player, and every whistle.

He was the freshman football coach when I was a freshman. I got a notion of who he was back in those days. He was a motivator. Then Mr. Akin retired as head coach, and Coach Brown took over the varsity. But Ralph had this touch about him. He could see something in you that you didn't see yourself.

Ralph Brown was one kind of genius, but J.B. Akin had a whole other kind of genius about him. First of all, he was our chemistry teacher. He was a laid back kind of a guy, but he could see what you needed to do to be successful in his class, and he'd make sure you got there. Not in an overbearing way, but he could just pick it out. Mr. Akin was my first varsity basketball coach. I played for him when I was a sophomore. I proved some things to myself during that year that I didn't know I could do, and Mr. Akin was responsible for it. But he never wanted any credit. He'd just say, "I told you so," and he'd go on about his business. But he wasn't a rip-snort, go get 'em kind of guy. He was kind of quiet, but he knew how to deal with boys.

Then he turned the basketball team over to Jimmy French. Frenchie wasn't much older than we were. Coach French was one of the most avid competitors I've ever met. Of course, being little and getting as far as he got in athletics, he had to be. He was really competitive, and he taught us how be competitive. We knew how badly he wanted to win. He had a passion for what he was doing. We made it to the state tournament in 1960. Jimmy was a natural leader. He just knew how to do it. Everybody respected him because we'd seen him play at Vanderbilt. A little guy who was five foot seven dribbling between everybody's legs.

Coach Jimmy French

You didn't want to get on the bad side of Paul Redick. You didn't want to cross him. If you did, he'd never forget it. You wanted to make sure you had your ducks in a row with Mr. Redick, and I had a lot of friends that didn't have their ducks in a row. Because they had tried to challenge Mr. Redick, they spent Saturdays with demerits in Saturday School. My first cousin, George Paine, really knew how to get under Mr. Redick's skin. He really enjoyed doing it. All sorts of things went on at BGA. You never knew what was going to happen next, and that kind of made BGA special.

The competition between the Greers and Platos was a big part of the school. I was a Greer. We used to beat the Platos in everything until whoever was in charge decided to even things up. The Brown brothers were all super athletes. John Brown was a Greer, and his twin brother, Allen, was a Plato. So to even it up, they put John over with the Platos. Man, that killed us, especially when we played each other in flag football. The faculty really encouraged that rivalry. Most of the time I was there, we had the tug-of-war on the Harpeth River, right beside the bridge on Franklin Road. It was a pretty intense.

I probably respected Daly Thompson as much as any other teacher. I learned a lot more Latin from him than I ever thought I could learn. He was very kind to me, and as a result I was a good Latin student. But if you got him riled up, you had better take a backseat. He had the patience of Job, but if he got enough of you, that was it. That put the fear of God in you. When he got to that point, you better get out of the way 'cause he's going to get you. But some guys were really asking for it.

A lot of things were done in study hall to irritate the monitor. Somebody was always rolling pencils down the floor of the study hall, or intentionally being in the wrong seat. Just to be playful. The one that got irritated the most, but who had the longest fuse, was Daly Thompson. We had a guy named Pete Minton, who did things that kept us on the edges of our seats. Mr. Thompson would finally get enough of it, and he'd look down from that stage at the front of the study hall. "Now, Mr. Minton, I don't know how we're going to get along without you, but we're going to try. Now, get out of here." Toby King was another one of his nemeses. And there were times when he'd get ahold of Soapy Roberts. But for the most part, nobody ever pushed him that far, because they saw what had happened to the few that did.

My senior year, we played in the state tournament at Vanderbilt, but we got beat in the first game. I remember running up and down that Memorial Gymnasium floor. It was the biggest basketball floor I'd ever seen. I got out of breath just from looking at it. When Jimmy French got out of coaching, that deprived a lot of kids from getting something really special from getting what he would've given them.

John Bragg was my English teacher. His face had an unusual side profile, and we used to call him *Chin*. I'm not sure he appreciated that much, but he was a gifted English teacher. I have a vivid memory of Canterbury Tales. I can still recite part of the prologue to the Canterbury Tales. It was something we all learned to recite.

We called Ralph Naylor, *Goober*. He was the butt of a lot of jokes. He was married to Mr. Briggs' daughter. He was kind of the laughingstock, which was probably unwarranted. He was a good teacher, but he'd get run over in study hall. He was no Daly Thompson. He'd lose control of the students pretty fast, and that made him somebody you would make light of.

Mr. Smithson was one of the most feared teachers at BGA. And he was probably the best teacher I had when I was there. He really knew how to teach math. Sometimes you hated him, but he didn't care whether you hated him or not. You were going to learn algebra or calculus. He was called *Goat*, and that upset him to the nth degree. He was nice to me, but I think it was because he favored athletes quite a bit.

The Silvertones (Buddy Benedict on drums)

I played in a band when I was at BGA. I was the drummer. Russell Farnsworth played the guitar, Barry Poston played the tenor sax, John Brown played the piano, and Mac Gayden also played the guitar. At first Mac couldn't play three notes on that dang guitar. We had Silvertone amplifiers. We got shirts that matched the color of the amplifiers, and we became the Silvertones. We played at BGA some, and also at a birthday party or two. Mac Gayden ended up making music his career. We'd play Rock and Roll – *Johnny Be Good* by Chuck Berry, and that sort of stuff.

Later on I was in a band at Vanderbilt with some other guys from BGA. I still played drums, and Jimmy Hunt, who was a year ahead of me at BGA, played guitar. Rod Daniel was in my class and he played the bass, and Howard Harlin, another one of my classmates, also played with us. Dianne Lackey, who went to Peabody, was our girl singer. She would sing songs like *Easier Said Than Done* and *He's So Fine*. She was a big hit, and I ended up marrying her.

BGA shaped us irrevocably. Sometimes we thought it was done a little too strictly, but back when he told me I was going to BGA, my father had known exactly what he was doing. And the faculty at BGA knew exactly what *they* were doing. Things were different then. We didn't have to contend with things like drugs. We just had to worry about getting caught with a cigarette someplace where we weren't supposed to be smoking. There were ditches you could run into, but BGA kept us between those ditches. They kept the reins on us. We knew what we could do and what we couldn't do. While we were there, we learned a lot about what was right and wrong. Some of who I became goes back to those teachers at BGA. I doubt if I would've been the same person if I'd gone to Hillsboro.

After I graduated from Vanderbilt, I went into the business world. My route was all laid out for me. My family said, "These are your choices. This is what you need to do." My father's reputation was one of my greatest assets, and when I was 37, I was about to become president of my company. But I couldn't do it. I went to my partners and said, "I've got to step away from this." I wasn't going to ride the elevator up to the 25th floor of the First American Center anymore.

My wife and I really had to shave back our lifestyle. We left all the clubs where you spend money to spend more money. The kids left private school. My father couldn't understand why I'd leave that golden brick road, and go to Vanderbilt Divinity School. But if you're the senior pastor in a church, you're the head teacher. I had learned a good bit about how to lead people when I was at BGA. Being involved in student government helped me with that, and it has gone with me everywhere.

Instead of just shutting it off, I guess BGA gave me the attitude, or the ability, to consider doing something like that. I think my experience at BGA helped me understand that there might be other things for me to try. It gave me the attitude to open myself up to other possibilities. Along with my family, BGA had a lot to do with giving me the courage to leave the business world and become a preacher.

I was on the BGA board for eight or ten years – back when John Bragg was the headmaster. He'd had ambitions to run the school for some time, and the stars finally lined up for him. There were some real trying times financially. We were competing with Brentwood Academy, and all those schools in Nashville that had been started to avoid integration. They were popping up everywhere. BGA was 15 or 20 miles away, and we were kind of left in the lurch. That's when we decided to open the school up to girls. It was the right decision, but it wasn't very popular. Had we not done that, BGA might not be here now.

John Bragg and Charlie Warfield, who was the chairman of the board, led us through all that. There was a power structure on the BGA board, and there was a group of business people that kind of ran Franklin. Men like Howard Johnston, the Harlins, and Stewart Campbell wanted the school to stay the way it was. Mr. Bragg had to manage those people. He had to deal with the dynamics of people who were determined to hold their ground. When we said we're going to have to do this for the school to survive, there was a feeling that no, that's the easy way out. You can do this other thing instead.

But we were finally able to convince everybody that if we didn't increase the student body, within four or five years the result would be disastrous. We had to change the facilities. We had to make bathrooms for girls, and do all the other things that had to be done to become coed. It was hard.

The faculty went along with it, but a lot of the parents did not. John Bragg was accused of being too political, and cowering to the powers that be on the board. But they didn't appreciate his gifts. He saw the bigger picture. He could see that if we didn't admit girls, we wouldn't have a school. So in addition to being a gifted English teacher, he made a great contribution to BGA while he was headmaster.

The information in this narrative came from an interview that took place on April 12, 2013.

Larry Brown, Class of 1961

I was the second youngest of six brothers. Our mother wanted to get us out of the house when summer came along, and I was six or seven years old when we went to Camp Hy-Lake. The camp was owned by Major Jonas Coverdale. He left Castle Heights Military Academy to become the head of BGA. My oldest brother, Bill, went to MBA, but my parents liked Major Coverdale and they sent the rest of us to BGA. They wanted us to be wherever Major Coverdale was.

And there might have been another reason we didn't go to MBA. In 1952, my second-oldest brother, Tommy, was in the eighth grade at MBA. My next brothers, John and Allen, are twins. John was the better athlete, and John Sloan, the chairman of the board at MBA, offered a scholarship to John, but not to Allen. After that, my parents put Tommy in BGA, and that's where the rest of us went.

Until I was 10 or 11 years old, we lived on a 90-acre farm on Dickerson Road in East Nashville. We had horses and cows and chickens and pigs, and we were very fortunate to grow up where we did.

After we moved across the county to Franklin Road, I went to Robertson Academy. There were some good athletes in my class. I got to know guys like Tuck Woodring and Johnny Webber, and they both ended up going with me to BGA. But more kids went to BGA from Hy-Lake than from any individual grammar school.

I knew Mr. Redick in a different way than most students at BGA. His son, Bill, and I were friends, and I spent the night at the Redick's all the time. I enjoyed being around Mr. Redick. He always had a story to tell, and he was a really good storyteller. Major Coverdale could have a really great sense of humor, but he could also be stern. He could change in a second, and I was kind of afraid of him. At BGA he was usually in his office or doing something off campus, but I got to know him a lot better at Hy-Lake.

By the time I got to BGA in ninth grade, I had been on the campus so much that I felt like a student before I ever went. I'd already heard Tommy, John, and Allen talk about the teachers. One of the main ones was Mr. Smithson. There were times when he talked so much in class that he'd get some spit on his lower lip. Once it was there, it would be there the whole time he was lecturing. He'd throw chalk and erasers at us, but he was a great teacher. When I took college math, it was so easy it was boring. I was really well-prepared for college. Mr. Smithson was also the B-Team football coach, but he wasn't all that interested in sports. He mostly coached for fun.

Coach Brown (Gag Photo)

We called Mr. Naylor, *Goober*. He seemed to be listening to a different drummer, but he was a pretty good teacher. He was in charge of our yearbook, the *Cannonball*. I worked on the yearbook, and I was one of the people responsible for having a picture showing Coach Brown in a pair of panties. We cut some pictures out of a Playboy, and put them on a photograph of him coaching. We tried to kind of hide it in a collage of other pictures, but Mr. Naylor found it. Everybody who was involved got 25 demerits.

I had Mr. Thompson for two years in Latin. We would play pranks on him in study hall. There was a bell up there on the desk. When a teacher rang it, everybody was supposed to be quiet. So we'd hide the bell from Mr. Thompson. He might be falling asleep, and somebody would go up and get that bell. Then he'd wake up and say, "Who stole my bell?" He had a real deep voice. He was a good man.

Mr. Akin taught Bible and Science in a room on the first floor. We were in the downstairs corner room, but a new lab was built while we were there. He was a good science teacher, and he really knew the Bible. He was the head coach when I was a sophomore, and he let me dress out with the varsity for one game. I got in for one play, but except for that, I was on the B-team, I liked Mr. Akin a lot.

My relationship with Coach Ralph Brown started at Hy-Lake. He got to know a lot of his athletes at camp. He loved sports, and he was quite a motivator. He had a baseball team up at Camp Hy-Lake. We'd get on the camp bus and he'd take us around to play different rural teams in baseball. When I was a junior, Coach Brown came in and took over the varsity from Mr. Akin, and we had pre-season practices at Hy-Lake. We'd be up there for a week or two, and we had a couple of practices a day.

In the morning we'd sit up there on the hill looking down at the field. We were supposed to be down there waiting for him in the morning. We could hear him open the screen door of his cabin, and the sound of his cleats. Then he'd blow his whistle, "Take it around boys!" And we had to start jogging around the field, After a couple of days, the straps of our shoulders pads were like sandpaper. Everybody would be raw. We also did a lot of sprints. It was hot, it was awful, and nothing got washed. But it was good, rough training. That was part of what made us so good. We were in great shape. Coach Brown had the philosophy that we might be behind when the fourth quarter came around, but we'd have a chance.

One of the things Coach Brown had us do in football camp was play Bull in the Ring. Bobby Morel was just a freshman, but he loved hitting people. He'd start hollering, "Let's play Bull in the Ring, Coach! Let's play bull in the ring!" Trying to hit Morel was a joke, but Coach Brown wanted us to be physical. At first, Charlie Fowler wasn't the rough-and-tough guy that he ended up being. Most of us were pretty much do-or-die kind of guys, but Charlie had sort of a happy-go-lucky attitude. His stamina wasn't good, and I remember him passing out during one of the pre-season practices. It was kind of scary.

We lost our first three games of the 1959 season. They were good, close games, but we ended up on the losing end all three times. But after that we went on a winning streak, and we played Manchester in the Butter Bowl in Pulaski. Coach Brown had studied their team. They had a good running back, and he had me tackle that guy on every play, whether he had the ball or not. That's the kind of strategy he would come up with. He'd pick out somebody and say, "This is how we're going to beat this guy." But after I let a guy run right by me and score a touchdown, Coach Brown told me to quit doing that.

I liked track more than I liked baseball, so when spring came around, I ran track. Tom Fiveash was a year ahead of me. Tom was a moose, but he could pole vault. I thought it looked like fun, and I decided I'd pole vault, too. At that point in time, they weren't fiber glass poles. BGA had two metal poles, and since Tuck Woodring liked pole vaulting, his father had bought one of them. Coach Mayes was the track coach, but Tuck, Hal Herd, and I mostly learned to do it by trial and error. We'd just run down, stick in the pole, and take off. It was just plain old fun. When I was a junior, I jumped 11'6" in the state track meet. That was good enough to win the state championship, but it didn't seem like that big a deal at the time.

That track meet was around the same time that we had the Greer-Plato the tug-of-war. It was at the Kinnard's pond, and I was up in the front. But the rope broke three different times. We finally just charged into the water and went after each other. We were laughing and having fun, but I ended up facedown in the mud and the water. I couldn't holler for help or anything. I thought I was going to suffocate, and it was a couple of minutes before I could get up.

At the end of summer we went back up to Hy-Lake for my last football camp. I thought our football team would be pretty good, but I wasn't sure how good. We had some good athletes, but we still needed a good coach to pull everybody together.

Charlie Trabue was a natural athlete and a very competitive guy. He matured earlier than the rest of us, and that gave him a head start. He was big, and he was a good, hard runner. He was also good in baseball, and good in basketball. Charlie was just an all-around athlete. He could've played at Alabama.

1960 Tug-of-War (Mud Brawl)

Paul Guffee was also a good athlete, but when we were younger, he was just a skinny guy. He and I were about the same size when we were freshman, but he grew a lot after that. By the time I got to be a senior, Paul had beefed up a little bit, but he still wasn't real big. Guys like Gary Anderson, Burt Phillips, and Tuck Woodring were not great athletes, but they would die for you. They were tough, and that's what made our team the way it was.

Duke Shackleford was a year younger than I was, but he would beat me in anything I played against him. Horse shoes, ping pong – you name it. He was just a very gifted athlete. Duke played baseball and I ran track, and one day he was walking past the track on his way to the baseball field. Somebody said, "Hey Duke, I bet I can beat you in a 440." They raced, and Duke beat the other guy without a problem.

Whitey Morrison was a great punter, and a very good receiver. Even if one of Duke's passes was off target, Whitey would catch it. Alvin Ford was also in the class behind me. He was another good, natural athlete, and so was Sid Tompkins. I was a cornerback and Bobby Morel was the defensive end on the same side. I was right behind him on every play. Bobby was a maniac on the field. He was really good.

Coach Brown was a great motivator. When I was a senior, we played down at MUS. Early in the game he pulled me off the field. He said, "Go over there and sit down. You don't even want to play." That was all he had to do. He knew how to get you fired up. That makes for a good team. He could get us raring to do anything. We did something we called *The Growler*. We'd be playing some team, and when they came up to the line, we'd start growling at them. We'd do that at some point in just about every game. And it would work. The other guys usually looked scared.

I remember a lot about the game we played at Columbia that year. They had a real good team, and their best player was a guy named Regen Peebles. It was kind of early in the season, and we had been winning. But they had been winning, too, and they were beating us in the third quarter. We'd been tackling Peebles for the whole game, and being in shape was crucial. It was a knock-down, drag-out game, and as the second half went on, they got tired and we didn't. We ended up winning by twenty points, but when the game was over, I was worn out.

My father never really got to watch my football games. He was too busy. He was up on top of the press box, filming the games. He filmed every game we played. On Saturday he'd take them to a guy that lived near us, and he would develop the films. On Sunday we'd take the films to BGA and watch them.

We won all of our regular season games, and we played Isaac Litton High School at Vanderbilt on Thanksgiving Day in 1960. I definitely remember running out on the field before the Clinic Bowl. I remember how perfect the grass looked. We hadn't ever seen grass like that. And the stadium was full of people. It was very exciting. As far as being nervous before a big game, most athletes would probably say the same thing. You're real nervous before the game, but after the first play, you're back in the middle of it. My attitude was let's do our best, and see how it works out.

Coach Brown was a strategist. There was a certain play that he had been setting up since the start of the game. Duke would fake a handoff to me or Charlie Trabue, and then he would hold the ball down where the defense couldn't tell he had it. Whitey Morrison or the split-end, would have gone in like he was going to block the safety, and then he'd take off. Duke threw it right on the money, and it went for a touchdown. We'd been running it all year, and it worked again in the Clinic Bowl. That season meant a lot to me. The guys on our team all bonded from going unbeaten and being state champions.

The only reason I got a college scholarship was because of Coach Brown. During Christmas Vacation, he was with his family over in North Carolina, and he took some game films with him. He went to see a couple of coaches, and he got me a scholarship at North Carolina State. That was a pretty big deal, because my parents didn't have the money for me to go to a school like Vanderbilt.

I started in my last two years at North Carolina State. When I was a junior we were co-champions of the ACC, and we were conference champions when I was a senior. When I was a freshman at BGA, Jim Burton had run over me one day in practice. When I was in college, I got run over by Brian Piccolo when we played Wake Forest, and by Ken Willard when we played North Carolina. They both ended up being stars in the NFL.

With five brothers, I grew up not being around girls, and I would've liked to go to high school with girls. Even though Judy Kinnard was my steady girlfriend for a while, I think going to an all-boys school held me back some. But I was very fortunate to have gone to BGA, and to have such deep relationships with the guys and the teachers who were there.

When somebody dies young, things change. My brother, Tommy, had died in 1963, and then Paul Guffee died in 1968. Looking back, I think Paul reflected the character of the team more than anybody else. To lose a friend that young was devastating. Right after it happened, I'd be happy when I was asleep. I'd be dreaming, but then I'd wake up.

The information in this narrative came from an interview that took place on June 14, 2013.

John Coleman, Class of 1961

I grew up in Franklin, so I knew about BGA my entire life. I was always a huge fan of the school. When I was going to Franklin Junior High School, I would bum rides on BGA's team bus to go to football games at places like Pulaski and Columbia. If there was room, whoever was driving would usually let me ride to the game.

When I was in eighth grade at Franklin Junior High, at the beginning of football season, the coaches decided that instead of having one captain for the whole year, we'd have game captains. Paul Guffee was easily the most outstanding person in our grammar school class. He was our halfback, and although he was on the small side, he was always a hitter. He wasn't big enough to do much damage, but he would hit with everything he had. He had a great sense of humor, and he cracked a lot of jokes.

Paul was very unimpressed with himself, but he was our most respected player. He was the captain for our first game.

At practice the following week, Paul stood up and said, "John is going to be our next captain." I was a starter, but I wasn't very good. People were kind of looking around and thinking, "Is that really a good idea?" And Paul said, "This guy works harder than any of us. At the end of practice, when everybody's dog-tired, he always wins the sprint drills. He hits as hard as he can in practice, and he is going to be our next captain." No one argued. I was blown away. Then, *of course*, we went out and got our butts kicked in that game. We had a terrible football team. We were so bad that our coach, L.I. Mills, wouldn't allow a team picture to be taken at the end of the year.

My dad had started out as a farmer, and then he worked in the produce business in Franklin. He had a little fruit and vegetable stand, but he never made much money. My mother was the secretary for the Williamson County Health Department. That was pretty much all the income we had. When I was in the eighth grade, my mother was diagnosed with cancer. Dr. Harry Guffee knew my mother's situation, and the Guffees invited me to live with them for the six weeks when my mother went into the hospital. Paul Guffee and I had been going to school together since first grade.

I had a paper route. I delivered papers on my bicycle, and the first night I was there, I asked Paul if I could borrow an alarm clock. He said, "I'll just take you in the jeep." We were only 14 at the time, but he already had a car. The next morning he took me to get the papers, and I got it done a lot faster than I could've done it on my bike. Then we went home, took our showers, and went to school. He might've taken me one other time, but that was it. The rest of the time I ran my route on my bike. Getting up that early every day just wasn't the way Paul grew up.

That was about when Dr. Guffee asked me where I planned to go to high school. I told him I didn't know. He said, "Well, you've got three choices. One is Franklin High. And there's also a Methodist school over in Hartsville that takes Methodist students of limited means. The other choice is BGA. Where would you like to go?" My family wasn't well-off, but I said, "I'd like to go to BGA." Then he just said, "Well, you're gonna go. I'll take care of it." He arranged a scholarship for me through the Franklin Rotary Club.

In the spring of my eighth grade year, Franklin Junior High had a track team. Hal Herd was our high jumper, Paul Guffee threw the discus, and Tom Hudgins was our shot putter. I was a distance runner. Coach Cannon Mayes, who was a teacher at BGA, had heard about us. He knew we were coming there to school, and he invited us over to BGA. He wanted to time us or measure us in our particular event. But BGA didn't have a permanent track. There was just a makeshift, lopsided little track on the practice field next to Mr. Redick's house. It was marked out with rows of stakes, and twine connected the stakes. That was the only track the school had.

There were some older guys from BGA who ran on that little dirt course. Guys like John Colton and Asa Jewel were running close to five minute miles, which was pretty good for back in those days. So we all showed up, and I ran a 6:03 mile. I was really disappointed. I'd expected to run it in five minutes. I thought I was a lot better than I was, but that was the start of my track career at BGA.

I played freshman football that fall. Ralph Brown was my coach, and he did a great job. I was a defensive end. I didn't get to play a whole lot, but it was the appropriate amount for my skill level. After freshman football, I went out for freshman basketball, but I got cut by Coach Brown right off. I thought I should've made the team, but it turned out pretty well for me. A couple of days later, Coach Cannon Mayes came up and said, "John, last spring you ran a mile around the dirt track. You looked pretty good. You're going out for track, right?" When I said I was planning to, he said, "Well, you can start training anytime you want to."

I had a paper route, and I was always riding a bike and running all over town. I might've been the only person who carried papers on a bicycle. Almost everybody else had motor scooters and motorcycles. Most guys had paper routes just so they could buy gas or make payments on their motorcycles. I used what I made to pay for school lunches and buy my clothes.

For several years, after working all day at the Health Department, my mother would go over to the Dan German Hospital and cook dinner. She would leave the hospital around seven. At the time we lived over on Murfreesboro Road, about a mile-and-a-half from Dan German. I didn't want her to walk home by herself, so I would run to the hospital to meet her, and then walk her home. So I was already running a lot, and after Coach Mayes mentioned training, I started running with a purpose in mind. I decided that I'd run from here to there, and I realized that I liked running. And I also realized that I had some ability. Running was on my mind from then on.

I ran track that spring, and I ended up being the only freshman who lettered. The following fall, Coach Mayes asked me and a couple of other guys to find out if there was enough interest for BGA to start a cross-country team. There was enough, and the cross-country team started in fall of 1958, when I was a sophomore.

Coach Mayes got permission from the Kinnard family to use the grounds at Willow Plunge as our home course. The races would start back by the eating area, and some of the terrain was God-awful.

It was a really difficult surface to run on. Very thick grass, and sometimes there would be mud that was up to your ankles. It was the same for everybody, but it was to our advantage because we were used to it. We had meets against Clarksville, Nashville East, and also the military academies – CMA, Castle Heights, and Sewanee Military Academy. Those were the main schools we ran against. And we traveled with the football team when they played at SMA. The meet was run at half-time, and we got through before the start of the second half. It was great to have a crowd watching us finish.

BGA was a little harder than the Franklin Junior High had been, but it wasn't much different from what I expected. There were some great educators. Coach J.B. Akin was an iconic teacher. He was fair to everybody. Treated everybody the same. He expected you to work hard, and if you didn't, he would let you know about it. And he would also praise you.

One summer, I worked at BGA. I did stuff like fix the dorm rooms. If furniture needed to be moved around or fixed, or if the football field needed to be mowed, I'd be doing those kinds of things. And a lot of times Coach Akin would be working right next to me. There were times when we'd be sweating together all day. He was a worker. After we got through working, he would go take care of school business. He was a great man and a great teacher. I had him for Bible as a freshman, and later on I had him for chemistry and physics.

He had coached football, basketball, and baseball for years, but I never heard one negative thing about him as a coach. It wasn't long before he stepped down from coaching, but he kept serving as athletic director. I ended up buying my first car from him. He said, "John, this car hasn't been driven very much. My daughter drove it back and forth to Duke a few times, and that's all it's been driven." It was a blue 1950 Ford, and he sold it to me for 50 bucks.

Mr. Bragg was a really great English teacher. His nickname was *Chin*, and I had him for Senior

English. He was very exacting. Back then there was a term for when you were being treated unfairly when it came to grades. We called it being *cobbed*. Mr. Bragg was exacting, but he was fair.

Don Hasty was a dorm student from Shelbyville. He would take friends home with him on the weekends, and one night we were driving between Shelbyville and Lewisburg. We saw a billboard on the side of the road, and there was a big corn cob extending from the top of the sign. We managed to saw it off from the rest of the billboard, and after we got it in Don's car, we drove it all the way to BGA. It was so big, that part of it was hanging out the window. We got Mr. Stutts, who was the equipment man for the school, to help us get the corn cob all the way up through the window and into Mr. Bragg's classroom. When he came in Monday morning, it was waiting for him. Don and I were in his first class. He said, "Who did this?" We kept quiet.

Daly Thompson was the best. By the time I had him, he was pretty advanced in years, but he was totally with it. He was a great Latin teacher. If somebody acted up, he would be all over it. He'd say, "Hmm, I see you back there, boy! Straighten up!" His nickname was *Monkey*. Everyone loved him. I think I remember him swatting Padge Beasley a couple of times. I also had Mr. Thompson for second year Bible.

Mr. Naylor was quite a card. I had him for English and French. He was like the absent-minded professor. Sometimes he'd open the window up to let in some air, but he usually kept his windows down. Well, one day he forgot that the window was down, and he went over and spat all over the window. Then he looked at us and shrugged. It was like, doesn't everybody make a mistake every now and then? He was very quick to kick people out of class too, and sometimes it was the wrong person. He'd say, "I saw you back there. Get out of here." And the culprit would still be sitting there.

Mr. Smithson was a really good man. He was as good as any teacher at BGA. He knew math up one side and down the other. He had an amazing knowledge of the subject. He expected you to work hard and to do the best you could. He knew who had the ability and who didn't. He would pick on the good students that weren't doing their best, just as much as poor students who were doing the same thing.

I was never a big fan of Mr. Redick. I thought he played favorites. It seemed like the guys who had gone to Hy-Lake were his pets. And if you didn't come from a pretty good family, he would treat you differently than students who were not as high on the social pecking order. I had been his son's classmate for years and years, but he didn't treat me that way. But when I was a senior, I had him for American History and he was totally fair to me in class. Mrs. Redick was a wonderful person. Absolutely delightful. I knew her from about the time I was in third grade. And we all noticed how beautiful Coach Brown's wife, Helen, was. She was not only attractive physically, but she was a wonderful person. She treated everyone the same way.

The track had been built around the football field by the Spring of 1960. It came about because of Cannon Mayes. He raised the money and supervised the construction process himself. Once it was built, he would be out there raking to keep it level and to get rid of weeds. But it wasn't a 440 yard track. It was closer to 410 yards. We had to go around something like five times to make a mile. And Coach Mayes spent a lot of time measuring off the distances for the various running events.

Coach Mayes was a real straight shooter. He always had a plan. He had a plan for the sprinters. He had a plan for the distance runners. He learned how to coach discus throwers and pole vaulters and high jumpers and hurdlers. When we were juniors, Paul Guffee was state champion in the discus, and Larry Brown was state champion in the pole vault. But we had other guys who weren't very good athletes, and Coach Mayes made them into pretty dadgum good track men.

Even though track is a very individual sport, Coach Mayes made sure we knew we were a team. When I was running the mile, the hurdlers would be on the sidelines cheering me on.

Cannon Mayes

When guys were competing in field events, we were all there pulling for them. I had him for Greek Mythology and Sophomore English, and he was a very good teacher. He didn't mess around in class. If somebody was out of line, they were out of there – with demerits.

Coach Mayes taught me a lot. He would coach me on my stride, and he even wanted me to hold my fingers a certain way when I ran. He thought that holding the ends of my middle and ring fingers against each of my thumbs would relax me while I ran. He would say, "John, with your hands going back and forth, and your fingers all over the place, you're wasting a lot of energy." There was a lot of strategy behind his coaching. For distance runners, he usually wanted us to maintain the same pace. He would say, "That's a lot better than going out too fast or too slow. If you run just a 72-second pace, you'll have the best results." But I was typically a fast finisher. I beat a lot of people in the last few yards.

I was a senior in the Fall of 1960. The other seniors on the cross country team were Mike Shinkle and Don Hasty, and we also had Dickie Gillespie, and a kid from Kentucky named Kirk Kirkpatrick. Nicky Rasmussen was a very good runner. He was an orphan who had been picked up by some GIs at the end of WWII. He had been brought to America from Europe and adopted by a Vanderbilt professor named Rasmussen. Coach Mayes took our team to the first state cross-country meet at Memphis State. We finished something like fifth in the state, but I led the whole way and I was able to finish first. I was excited to be the Tennessee Cross-County Champion.

Cross Country 1960 (Coleman front row, left, beside Rasmussen)

Although I was probably the only scholarship student in the class, I wasn't treated any differently by the other students. I studied pretty hard. I probably averaged doing three to four hours of homework a night. Doing well at BGA took a lot of work, but on the weekends there was time to have fun. I had some really good friends. I would go places like the Gilco, the Corner Drugstore, or the Franklin Theater with Whitehall Morrison, Bert Phillips, Jack Francis, or Larry Brown. Larry had a car, and around the time we got to be juniors, we started double-dating.

In those days the girls pretty much came and went. I don't remember taking the same girl twice to any BGA function. We'd go to dances or to parties at somebody's house, and the music might be Chuck Berry or Little Richard or Johnny Mathis. We had a whole lot of fun. Paul Guffee's girlfriend was Barbara Beaman. She was BGA's head cheerleader and Homecoming Queen when we were seniors. Back then, dating wasn't usually exclusive. Almost all of us, including Paul, dated other people. Gary Anderson was the only one who had the same girlfriend all the way through high school.

The success of the football team was a big part of my senior year. We had a huge sense of pride that our little school of 250-something boys had the best team in the entire state. The school we beat in the Clinic Bowl, Isaac Litton, had something like 2,000 students. I stopped playing football when I was a sophomore. Even though I was a much better runner than a football player, when I was senior and saw how good our team was going to be, I couldn't help thinking, God, it would be nice to be a part of that football team.

When I got my scholarship to Vanderbilt, I didn't say anything about it. But somebody must've told Mr. Redick. He came up to me and said, "I heard you got a scholarship to Vanderbilt! Why didn't you tell me?" I said, "I didn't know you needed to know, Mr. Redick. I'm sorry. I got a scholarship to Vanderbilt. Now you know."

Paul Guffee and I, along with a third of the guys in our class, ended up going to Vanderbilt. We didn't lose touch, but we weren't as close as we had been. We joined different fraternities, took different classes, and made new friends.

Paul and I were both in Pre-Med. We had classes together, but a lot of the classes were big, and I wouldn't see him that much. We weren't in the same dorm. We joined different fraternities, and we made different friends. Paul and I were still friends, but we weren't as close as we'd been.

When we were juniors, Paul didn't pass the second semester of Organic Chemistry. It had nothing to do with him not being smart enough. He could've gone to summer school, made a C, and moved on. But he told me that he wasn't going to go to summer school. Then he said he wasn't going to Med School either. That really shocked me, but later on, I thought I understood. Dr. Guffee wanted Paul to be a doctor, and that's why Paul was in Pre-Med. I'm not sure that he didn't fail Organic Chemistry on purpose. That was around when I heard that he'd gotten involved in a theater group. He wanted to be an actor. I thought, "Well he has different interests. Good for him."

So when he was a senior, Paul got into a theater group and started acting. He graduated on time, and then he went into the Air National Guard. He also started learning how to make movies. After he finished serving in the Guard, he moved to New York. I was in Medical School, and one day I got a phone call from my mother. She was crying. She said, "Did you hear about Paul? He was found dead in New York at his apartment." At first people thought he had been murdered. But before long the prevailing opinion was that he had committed suicide. That's what I heard pretty soon after he died, and that's what I've understood ever since.

We had been friends from first grade through college. We had kind of drifted apart, but there was never a time when we didn't have each other's back. We had always been friends and respected each other. He always wanted to know how I was doing. "How's school. How are things at home? How's everything else?" He was my friend.

BGA had a huge bearing on the way my life has turned out. Since I was in the fifth grade, my goal had been to go to Vanderbilt. Going to BGA kept me on that path. I wasn't class valedictorian, but BGA prepared me for Vanderbilt. At BGA I learned to be thorough. At BGA I learned how to be honorable. In my medical practice, I can't remember doing anything that I'm ashamed of. Things don't always turn out perfectly, but I've never lied to a patient about why an outcome was the way it was. Even if I've been up all night and have 20 other patients to see, I always see every one of my patients.

I wish a lot of things could've stayed the same, but nothing ever does. I wish I could go up into that study hall and watch Mr. Thompson dealing with some student who was misbehaving, and relive so many of the other things that happened back then. I don't think anybody who went to BGA in my era could've asked for a better education, or for a better preparation for life. I don't believe there was a better school that I could have gone to. About five years ago I asked Mr. Bragg, "Do you remember that corn cob?" He remembered it. "Well, now that you can't hurt me, I'm going to tell you who did it."

The information in this narrative came from an interview that took place on December 3, 2013. Dr. John Coleman died in California in 2025 at the age of 82. He was survived his wife of 49 years, Angela Martinez Coleman, their two children, and one grandchild.

Charles Trabue, Class of 1961

I was signed up to go to MBA. That's where I wanted to go. I had a letter from Coach Tommy Owen, the great MBA coach, saying how glad he was that I was coming there to school. The letter was framed, and it was hanging on my bedroom wall. One evening in December, Parmer played a basketball game against Burton in the old MBA gym. I played for Parmer, and after the game, I went down to the locker room to change. All of a sudden, my father and Coach Ralph Brown were down there. My father said, "Just go with Coach Brown."

Coach Brown was a good recruiter. He had driven the BGA bus onto the MBA campus, and parked right in front of the gym. He was taking me up to Fort Campbell to see a BGA freshman basketball game. So I rode on the team bus with guys like Buddy Benedict, Tom Fiveash, Bill Cherry, Terry Geshke, and Mouse Sinclair – among others. It was a really, really, fun trip.

I already had a connection with BGA through Camp Hy-Lake. I had been a camper there for three or four years before that. A lot of BGA guys went to Hy-Lake. I was 10 years old when I first went. I had been kind of anxious when I first showed up at Hy-Lake. I went into the cabin I was assigned to, and when I looked up in the rafters, there was Bill Redick talking like Donald Duck. We ended up being classmates at BGA, and guys like Buddy Benedict, and John and Allen Brown, were campers who were already going to BGA. I'd already gotten to know Major Redick and Major Coverdale. They were called majors from when they taught at Castle Heights, which was a military school, but by then they were at BGA.

I had never considered going to BGA, but all of a sudden that's where I was going. Back then I just was doing what I was told. Like a good son. But it worked out. My class at BGA had a collection of really exceptional athletes. It was a perfect storm of athletes.

I'd been at Parmer for eight years, and going to BGA was a lot different. I had to be driven a couple of miles to where I could catch the bus, and from there it took a long time to get to school. I had one teacher for the whole year at Parmer, but at BGA I had a different teacher for each subject. But the biggest difference didn't really dawn on me until I was older. Parmer was a pretty homogeneous group of kids. Everybody lived in Belle Meade, or in the surrounding area. At BGA there were guys that came to school after doing their farm chores. They were wearing overalls and work boots. They probably had to get financial aid to be there. It was an interesting mix.

Charles Trabue and Paul Guffee, freshman year

During all my years at Hy-Lake, I'd been hearing about Paul Guffee – mostly from Bill Redick. I'd heard what a great guy Paul was, but I'd never met him. But one day, right before we started at BGA, he came up to Hy-Lake with his father. I remember the first time I ever saw him. They pulled up on the hill, and we were out there on the athletic field. He was walking toward us with this big grin on his face, and somebody introduced me to him. He'd heard about me, too, and I remember us sizing each other up.

Because I was bigger, I was kind of a big deal in the freshman class. Paul Guffee was still a little shrimp. Our freshman year, Paul was a good five or six inches shorter than I was, and he was skinny. I had an advantage, but I wouldn't say I was the king of the roost. I was big, but my asthma was pretty bad. My allergies would get on me in the fall, and I missed the first week of school. When I finally got to class, I was a week behind everybody else.

The thing that I feared the most when I was a freshman was that we would have to scrimmage the varsity. We had a great varsity football team in 1957. Jim Burton was 6'1" and 225, and he had sprinter speed. And there were guys like Mickey Crowell and Bill Cherry and Tom Fiveash and Mike Hudgins. They were awesome. I lived in fear of having to scrimmage against Jim Burton, but we never had to.

I guess everybody felt like they had a special relationship with Ralph Brown. He was that kind of guy. He was my mentor for four years. In a lot of ways, he is still my mentor. He was my freshman football and basketball coach. He was also the varsity baseball coach, and even though I was a freshman, he put me on the varsity baseball team. The first year or two I was at BGA, we played baseball on the football field. Home plate was close to the dining hall – near the southeast corner of the football field.

One day we were playing Clarksville. We had a one run lead, and they had the bases loaded in the ninth inning. I was just a freshman, and Coach Brown had me at third base. It would've been easy for him to take me out and put in somebody who was more seasoned, but he left me in. He showed me he had confidence in me. The Clarksville batter hit a ground ball a little bit to my left. I should've probably let our shortstop, Terry Geshke, field it, but I cut it off. I knocked it down and bobbled it, and then I got up and threw a strike to Buddy Benedict. I got the runner by about a half a step. Coach Brown was fired up, and he praised me for staying with it. That did so much for my confidence.

Coach Brown built the new baseball field across the road. He pretty much did it himself. I remember seeing him out there with a sled, smoothing the ground. And he got a tractor and cut the grass himself.

For my first two years, Mr. Akin was the head football coach. Since he had been through so many games by then, I guess every game was just another game. He never showed much emotion. Mr. Akin was a great man, but it was probably time for him to step down. And it was time for Coach Brown to take over. If Coach Brown had been the head coach of that 1957 team, I kind of believe that BGA would've played in the Clinic Bowl and been state champions. They were that good. One of my best friends, George McGugin, was in that same class at MBA. He's told me that if he had gone to BGA, he might not have made that team.

Paul Guffee and I became good friends, but we didn't get to where we were inseparable until our senior year. If I had a best friend at BGA before that, it was Bill Redick. I spent as much time at the Redick house as I did at my own house. The Redick's house was on campus, right next to the school. It was easy to just go over there after practice and spend the night. But later on, if I wasn't at the Redick's, I was at the Guffee's.

I was BGA's quarterback when I was a sophomore, and I wanted to keep being the quarterback.

Coach Brown was trying to make Paul into an end, so the summer before our junior year, I worked out with Paul at Willow Plunge. We would go out there with our shirts off to impress the girls. I would throw passes to Paul, but he couldn't catch with his hands. I had a pretty good arm, and when we were done, he'd have little x's all over his chest – imprints of where the end of the ball had hit him. Paul didn't become a good athlete until sometime in our junior year. He was just too little, he wasn't very fast, and he was a little awkward.

Bill Redick, Freshman Year

My tenure as quarterback ended when Duke Shackleford got to BGA, but I was still kind of an alpha dog. The summer before our senior year, Paul and I were up in Redick's room. We would wrestle around, and I'd always been able to handle Paul easily. But all of a sudden, he just flipped me over. Like with a flip of his finger, I thought. "This game has now changed." He'd grown and filled in. Up until then, he hadn't been big enough to do much in football. Then he was just... there. He went from not being a starter as a junior, to being All-State as a senior. And he became a good wrestler, and a great shot-putter. He could do a lot of things. Paul was larger than life. He was big and strong and almost always smiling. He was magnetic.

Bill Redick was funny, but he was also intense and serious. Bill and I spent a lot of time talking during our years at BGA. Talking about issues that mattered. We thought we were being grown-up. The Redicks were like my surrogate parents. They were both so welcoming. I always felt as much at home in their house as I did in my own house.

I remember one thing Bill did that seems like it happened yesterday. Mr. Smithson taught Senior Math, and he and Bill butted heads all the time. But because Bill was the headmaster's son, Mr. Smithson had to exercise a little caution. Mr. Smithson would try to egg Bill on, and Bill would do the same thing. One time, Bill had gotten hold of a fountain pen that had disappearing ink. He instigated some kind of argument with Mr. Smithson, and Mr. Smithson was arguing back. Mr. Smithson was sitting in his desk, and Bill was standing over him. Bill was holding his pen, and he spurted ink all over Mr. Smithson's face and down his white shirt. Mr. Smithson blew up. He grabbed Bill by the wrist, and dragged him out of the classroom and down to the headmaster's office. But by the time he got down there, the ink was gone. It didn't take Mr. Smithson long to see the humor in what Bill had done.

If you were up at the chalkboard trying to solve a problem, and if Mr. Smithson didn't like what you were doing, he'd throw chalk or erasers at you. He really kept you on your toes. He taught a difficult subject to people who might not have been gifted in that area. I think we all came out the better for it. I wasn't sure I'd pass the final exam. But when I got to Vanderbilt and took the placement test in Math, I was in the 98th percentile in the incoming class. He was hard and he required a lot of work, but he was fair. I had Mr. Naylor and Mr. Bragg and J.B. Akin, and they were good teachers, but Mr. Smithson was probably the best teacher I had at BGA.

I really liked Mr. Naylor. He taught us grammar and sentence structure, and that stayed with me for a long time. Mrs. Redick taught typing. We had these old fashioned typewriters, and the keys you struck came up and hit the ribbon. She would have speed drills. She would say, "On your mark, get set..." We'd all be poised over the typewriters, and then she'd say, "You may begin." We were all trying to win, and there were times when some of us would start off by hitting two keys at once. That would make them stick together, and we couldn't start typing until we got them unstuck. By then the other guys would have a big head start.

Mr. Akin taught Physics and Chemistry, and even though I wasn't good at them, they were interesting courses. And Mr. Bragg taught Senior English. We did a lot of reading, and they weren't books that I would have ever picked. Not easy reading. It was Thomas Hardy and Dostoevsky, and those types of books. But they served me well. I was an English major at Vanderbilt. I took a lot of literature courses, and I'd already read some of the books.

Mrs. Paul Redick

Paul Guffee, Senior Year

I took Latin under Mr. Thompson. If somebody got out of line he'd say, "Don't make me come to you." One time Mr. Thompson was sitting up at the head of study hall, and somebody rolled a cannonball down from the back. It crashed into the base of the stage. I remember Mr. Thompson looking up and sort of watching it roll down and hit the stage. I don't think he got up or did anything.

High school wasn't completely about sports. During parts of my junior and senior years, my high school girlfriend was Susan Brindley. After a football game, we'd usually go to somebody's house. We'd get something to eat and listen to music. Paul Guffee was dating Barbara Beaman. She was the most beautiful girl around back then, and Paul was the most handsome guy. They belonged together.

Susan and I double-dated with them a lot. If there wasn't a game, we'd see a movie or go to somebody's house. There'd be some refreshments upstairs, and a basement with the lights off. A record player might be playing Johnny Mathis, and guys would be trying to cop a feel in the dark. Where I was concerned, there was never any alcohol involved, but I remember Paul and Bill talking about how they'd gotten into some alcohol over at the Guffees when they were sophomores or juniors. They both felt pretty bad afterward, both conscience wise and hangover wise. But most of us who were involved in sports didn't drink or smoke.

Susan and I were together until the end of my senior year. She had an older sister who went to Vanderbilt. Her sister fixed Susan up with a Vanderbilt guy, and once she got a taste of the college scene, she wasn't much interested in dating somebody at BGA. We ended up going to the BGA final dance, but by then the handwriting was on the wall. She broke my young heart. And a song came out that year called "Runaround Sue."

Charles Trabue and Susan Brindley

We had some stars on our 1960 football team. With a couple of exceptions, our starters were good enough to have eventually played what's now called Division I football. But the thing that made us a really good team was Duke Shackleford. He would be a star quarterback today, even as big and strong as fast as people are now. He had a great arm, and his ability to throw kept defenses honest. And he could run. We also had Alvin Ford and Johnny Jewell, who both played some at Auburn. Larry Brown played at NC State. Charlie Fowler ended up playing in the NFL. Whitey Morrison could have punted for anybody. He got them really high. Bill Redick and Joe Torrence played at Center. We also had Gary Anderson. There wasn't anybody tougher than Gary. If there was a fight, he wanted to get in it. He was fearless.

And then there was Bobby Morel. When you were on the field with Morel, you had to hit him or you were going to get demolished. Bobby was a hitting machine. He was really compact, and when we played bull in the ring or something like that, he was going to come at you. It wasn't malicious. That's just what he did. Sid Tompkins, Bert Phillips, and Tuck Woodring were all good high school players. Paul and I played linebacker. Coach Brown had defenses that freed us up to make a lot of tackles. And what we didn't do, Bobby Morel and the others took care of. We were just a well-coached, talented team.

Even though he didn't play much, Bob Dunkerley made me a better player. Coach Brown had him work me over every day. Bob was pretty big, and when we had dummy drills, he would attack me. He was at defensive end, and I was supposed to block him. If I didn't want to get hurt, I had to hit him. Without Bob, I might not have played college football.

Sometimes during two-a-day practices – between practices – we'd go to the Gilco and get a milkshake, or we'd go hang out at Paul's house. There was a big playroom with a pool table and a refrigerator, and plenty of snacks and drinks. Dr. Guffee was our team doctor. He was a great guy, but he was kind of gruff and a little distant. It never seemed like he gave you his attention. His mind seemed to be somewhere else. You had to be hurt pretty bad before he'd admit that you were hurt. He talked so low that you could barely understand what he was saying. It would be something like, "He's not hurt too bad. He can go back in."

We thought we were going to be good. We'd scrimmaged some strong teams and handled them pretty easily. But our first game my senior year was against Carthage. They had beaten us pretty easily the year before, and they were good. Right before the game, five or six of us were standing at the end of the field on the little slope down by the gym. We all had pre-game butterflies. I'd kind of get into my own space for games. Unless we were playing a bad team, I was pretty wired up.

Mr. Redick and Coach Brown walked up, and Mr. Redick said, "Guys, you've put in a lot of hard work, and I'm really proud of you. Whatever happens, win or lose, you're going to be fine." He walked off and Coach Brown was kind of laughing. He said, "What Mr. Redick told you is all well and good, but you can forget about losing. We ain't losing to this crowd." That broke the tension.

Carthage was probably our toughest game that year. We won by eight points. At the end of the game, they were down on our goal line about to score. We dug in pretty hard, and they didn't get in the endzone. The next week we played Murfreesboro at BGA. They had a good team, and we hadn't beaten them in eons. We won, but it was as hard a rain as I've ever been in.

A few weeks later we played at Columbia. They had Hal Wantland and Regen Peebles, and they were all really good players. I remember Regen Peebles just ran over me. He put his cleat marks on my chest and on my face. He was the only player ever, in high school or college, who ever did that. He was as good as anybody. We were kind of sucking wind against them, but in the second half they just quit. We ended up beating them pretty bad.

From there we played tough teams like Tullahoma and Franklin County, and we also had some easy games. When we played Mount Pleasant, we punted on first down just to keep from running up the score.

When we were about to play Franklin County, their coach thought that stopping me was the key to beating us. Later on Coach Brown told me what their coach told his players. "Trabue is a Belle Meade guy, and if you keep hitting him, he'll break." I was pretty competitive, and I had a good game. I gained 100 yards and scored four touchdowns. We beat them 28-6, and we got the Clinic Bowl bid right after the game. There was a lot of joy in the locker room.

We wanted to show everybody that we could compete with the big boys, and that we could also sell tickets. There was a question about whether a school as small as BGA could do it. We set a record for the most tickets ever sold, and the game against Isaac Litton turned out to be a sellout.

Isaac Litton had a lot of great players. We kept reading about guys like Billy Tomlinson and Richard Cutrer and Jack Patterson. And they had a middle linebacker who was tough as nails. I remember sitting in the end zone before the game. Watching the stands fill up. We had done our calisthenics, and we were in the north end in-zone. Litton had a huge band. They were playing the Litton fight song, and we all just watched their team run out onto the field in their fancy uniforms. Coach Brown's assistant, Spencer Holt, looked over at us and said, "Boys, just remember one thing, you can't make chicken salad out of chicken shit."

Paul and I were co-captains, but we could only send one person out for the coin flip, so Paul went. I remember watching him from the sidelines, and being as nervous as I could be. I was probably more nervous than in any college game I ever played. The butterflies were all over me until the opening kick-off. Then they just vanished. Then it was game on. The ball came to me, and I had a pretty good return.

On the very first play of the game, Coach Brown had a couple of our guys sandwich Litton's middle linebacker. It knocked their guy for a loop, and the same thing happened two or three plays in a row. For the rest of the game his head was on a swivel. He wasn't very effective after that. That was Coach Brown. He said we had to do something to stop that guy, and we did it. Once it started, I didn't think the outcome was ever in doubt. We won 13-0, and we were named state champions.

A few months later, Paul and I went on a recruiting trip with Coach Brown to Georgia Tech. Bobby Dodd was the coach, and he wined and dined us. He told us he really wanted us to come play at Tech. That was on a weekend, and the signing day was the following Wednesday. He said if we were interested, he would come to Nashville for the signing and take us and our families out to dinner. We both said we wanted to come to Georgia Tech.

Well, I went back home and told my parents that I was going to play for Tech. But Wednesday came and went with no word from Coach Dodd. I learned later that my father called and basically told Coach Dodd, "Don't come up here." I never heard anything, and I finally just said, "Well okay, I guess

I'm going to Vanderbilt." When I finally learned what my father had done, I was upset. But then I decided there was no point in worrying about it.

In 1962, when Paul and I were sophomores at Vanderbilt, Ralph Brown left BGA and became Vanderbilt's freshman coach. The next year he came very close to being named the head coach, but Jack Green was hired instead. He was a good man, but he didn't have any imagination. His idea was to put all his best players on defense, and try to keep the other team from scoring. Then maybe we might get some points here and there. In my two years under Coach Green, we only won four games.

I think Coach Brown would've been a great college coach. He would've assembled a really strong staff. He knew assistant coaches on college teams from all across the South. They came to BGA to scout his players, and he had a lot of relationships. Vanderbilt would've been a lot better off, but in the long run, it might've been better for Coach Brown that he wasn't picked. He took a different path, and he's had a great life.

Paul was not very motivated when we were playing at Vanderbilt. During our sophomore year, right in the middle of spring practice, he disappeared. Earlier that spring he had bought a little Harley Sprint motorcycle. He rode it around for a week or so, and all of a sudden he was gone. I called around and called around, and finally found him in Houston. He was with his brother, Harry, who had gone to Rice. Paul had gotten on that motorcycle with nothing, and just ridden to Houston. He wanted to quit football. One thing I really regret is that I helped talk him into coming back to Vanderbilt. I believe that Paul might be alive today if he had broken free.

Paul didn't play much at Vanderbilt until he was a senior. He had kept growing, and by the time he was a senior, he was about 6'3" and weighed maybe 220. That wasn't big for a lineman, but he was as good an offensive guard as anybody. He showed what he could do against Steve Delong, who played for Tennessee. Delong was a first team All-American, and in 1964 he won the Outland Trophy as the best interior lineman in college football. When Paul and I were seniors, the last game of our careers was against Tennessee. Paul was nose-up on Delong. It was amazing how quick Paul got out on him and tied him up. He couldn't move. Delong had been averaging 15 tackles a game, but I think he only made two tackles that day. We won our final game 7-0.

I've thought about what would've happened if I'd gone to Georgia Tech instead of Vanderbilt. Who knows? But I wouldn't have met the woman I married. I wouldn't have the children I have. You can't spend your time looking back saying, "Man, if I'd only done that."

My father wanted me to be a lawyer. I didn't really have an idea about doing anything else, so I did that by default. I don't really regret it, but I didn't have much fun doing it. And I got out as quickly as I could. I think I might've been a good coach. I certainly had a good teacher in Ralph Brown. But if I'd done something different, I might've been sent to the jungles of Vietnam and never come back. Instead I went to law school and avoided the draft for a while. I eventually had to report, but my football injuries ended up keeping me out of service.

I'm glad I went to BGA. It was a small school that drew from a rural area. I wasn't the student I could've been in college, but BGA prepared me well enough to graduate from Vanderbilt in four years without failing any courses, and I managed to get through three years of law school. Paul graduated in four years, too, but he struggled. He tried to go into pre-med, but he couldn't make it through Organic Chemistry, and maybe some other courses.

Playing on a state championship football team was a moment of glory, but I don't think about it too much. It happened a long time ago. I've moved a long way from there. Every few months I have lunch with some of the guys from BGA. We still joke about Mr. Thompson, and talk about what a great man he was. It's fun to go back to all that, but it is bittersweet.

Bill Redick died a couple of years ago. He had done about as much as a person could do, and then some. Bill was as hard-headed as his father. But even though his father was a staunch conservative, Bill was a flaming liberal. Bill pushed the edge of the envelope. For the last 10 or so years of his life, he was deeply involved in the Capital Case Resource Center. He was committed to ending the death penalty. He and his father went for some years without being able to talk to each other, but there was a reconciliation toward the end of Mr. Redick's life.

When Paul Guffee and I were at Vanderbilt, he and I pretty much did everything together. But he just kept doing things – and there were things I did with him – that he shouldn't have survived. At BGA and at Vanderbilt, he totaled four or five cars. When I say totaled, I mean absolutely totaled. But he walked away from every wreck he had without a scratch. Dr. Guffee had the means, and Paul always got a new car. He drove fast and he was reckless. And he was really lucky.

It might be three o'clock in the morning, but there were times when we would get on motorcycles and ride them down West End Avenue at 70 miles an hour. Paul would wear a cape that he got from the theater. It would be flying back behind him. No helmet. No caution. Just a big grin on his face. He always had this big grin. I can see him right now. It reminded me of what Tom Cruise said in the movie, *Risky Business*. "Sometimes you gotta say, WTF." That was Paul Guffee.

Not long after I got into law school, Paul moved to New York. Whenever he came back to Nashville we'd get together, but it was always just to carouse. I knew Paul as well as anybody did, but I don't think I knew him very well. It eventually dawned on me that Paul probably had a death wish.

Paul has been dead since 1968. So many of my memories of BGA are tied to him. I miss Bill Redick, but I don't miss him like I miss Paul Guffee. Maybe it's because he had such an unfinished life. I still have dreams about Paul.

The information in this narrative came from an interview that took place on March 14, 2014.

Cora Miller Spencer

Cora Miller was born near Spring Hill, in Maury County, on the day after Christmas in 1913. At the time, her father, Albert Miller, was employed by the railroad as a laborer. Although Albert was illiterate, Cora's mother, Lula, could both read and write. Before she married at the age of 16, she was Lula Brown, and it appears that the Brown family had been living in northern Maury County for many years. They may have been associated with the family of Major Campbell Brown, a wealthy Confederate veteran whose property bordered Spring Hill. Albert Miller's family was also from Maury County. His father, Green Miller, had been born around 1835, and his mother, Caroline Baugus, was born around 1842. Both likely spent the first 20 years of their lives in slavery.

Cora's father, Albert, was born around 1875, and when he was old enough to do farm work, he began helping support the family. He married in 1894, and in 1900, when Albert was working as a farmer a few miles northeast of Columbia, the couple had a daughter. His wife died two or three years later, and he married Lula around 1905. By 1910, Albert and Lula had moved to the western part of Maury County, and he was working for the railroad. Cora was born, and by the time she was six, her family was living in Franklin. Albert was still a railroad worker, and Lula brought in extra money by doing laundry. At some point during the 1920s, he began working at a foundry, and along with raising her four children, Lula continued to take in laundry.

In 1930, with the Depression deepening, the Miller family was living on Granbury Street in Franklin, just around the corner from Battle Ground Academy. They were part of an integrated community known as Beasley Town. The neighborhood consisted of a number of modest rental houses that had been built and owned by W.J. Beasley, the owner of an adjacent sawmill. After attending elementary school through eighth grade, Cora worked for a few years, and in 1933, when she was around 19, she became a cook at BGA.

BGA Picnic, circa 1938 (Cora Miller, cook on left)

In 1935, her father died of cancer at their house on Granbury Street, but the family endured. A few years later, Cora met Walter Spencer at a dance in Spring Hill. When they married in 1943, the wedding was officiated by her neighbor, Elder Henry Brown, who had been working at BGA for over twenty years. By 1950, Cora's household included her mother, Lula, and two daughters, Rose and Willie. Her mother, Lula, died later that year, a few months after Jonas Coverdale became the head of Battle Ground Academy.

Cora had been the head cook at BGA since George Briggs was headmaster. The close relationship she had enjoyed with Briggs, and later with Glenn Eddington, would continue with Coverdale. He owned Camp Hy-Lake, which was around 100 miles to the east on the Caney Fork River, and Cora began to work there every summer. Then, after cooking for the campers for two months, Cora cooked for the BGA football players when they came to practice there at the end of the summer.

Cora's son, John, was born in the 1950s. After many years of paying rent, his mother may have already been trying to find a way to own a home. In 1958, she located a nearby structure that had become available on Ninth Avenue. But she understood that if she tried to buy it outright, the price would probably be raised on account of her race. When she went to Jonas Coverdale for advice, it was decided that he would buy the house on her behalf. In order to pay him back, a small amount would be deducted from each of her paychecks.

The Spencer family left Granbury Street and moved into their new home, but Cora would only live there for four years. In the early spring of 1962, she came down with pneumonia and died two weeks later. Her obituary listed her survivors and gave details regarding the funeral. It also mentioned her, "White friends, Mr. And Mrs. J.S. Coverdale, Mrs. George I. Briggs, the BGA faculty, and the student body." She was laid to rest near her parents in Mount Zion Cemetery, just southeast of Spring Hill, close to where her family may have lived for generations.

When Cora died, all but $109 of her loan to Jonas Coverdale had been repaid. In addition to preparing food for three decades of boys, she was a beloved and highly respected member of the BGA community. The school, then being led by Paul Redick, honored her a few months after her death. Her family accepted an ornate silver tray, and her eldest daughter, Rose, received scholarship support from BGA to help pay her college tuition at Tennessee A&I in Nashville. By the time Walter Spencer, her widowed husband, died in 1996, Cora's youngest daughter, Willie Spencer Dickerson, had become a noted local educator. Cora Miller Spencer did not go to high school, but her daughter, Willie, after graduating from college, embarked on a career that has spanned over 50 years, including a long tenure as principal of Franklin High School.

This article was researched and written by the editor in 2025.

Billy Adair, Class of 1965

I lived in Franklin, and I'd wanted to go to BGA from the time I was in second or third grade. I just assumed that's what I was going to do. I lived across Columbia Pike, and it only took me about five minutes to walk to school. I decided to play freshman football, so my life as a BGA student began in August, 1961. That's when I first met Coach Oxley. It was rougher than I thought it would be. Ninth grade football was a lot different from playing in junior high school. Bert Brown usually practiced with the varsity, but if the coaches got mad at him, they'd send him down to play with us. It wasn't great running into Bert.

Most of the kids I'd gone to school with before I came to BGA were from families that were fairly well off, but we also had some very poor kids. There was none of that at BGA. And the dumbest kid at BGA would've been average or above average at Franklin High School. The bright kids in Franklin and BGA were about equal. There were 10 or 11 of us who came from Franklin Junior High to

BGA. My best friends were Mike Pearson and Glenn Crowell, and there was also Stefan Smith, Allen Tanksley, Jimmy Short, Jimmy Sewell, Ronny Grimes, Jodie Bowman, and Chug Morton.

That helped because I was going from being with guys I'd been with for eight years, to being with a lot of guys I didn't know. It took a little getting used to. My freshman year, I was talking to one of the Nashville students about seeing something in the paper the day before. He said, "You guys get the paper here?" I thought he was kidding at first, but he was serious. Another guy said he didn't know we had television in Franklin.

The first day of class, I went home after school, and Mike Pearson was with me. I remember saying, "This place is *not* going to be fun." He said, "I think you're right." I said, "I'm not going to get a demerit while I'm there. I'm going to spend as little time at school as I have to." And I never got one demerit. I was a goodie-two-shoes. My freshman year was rough, but it was a cakewalk compared to my sophomore year. What happened was that I had Goat Smithson and Bo Stewart for teachers. Having them at the same time put me in a world of hurt. They both acted like their class as the only class you had. Why not give you five hours of homework a night?

Mr. Smithson taught Algebra II and Advanced Math. Even though he wasn't my teacher when I was a freshman, I'd gone to him once for help in math. I'd been trying to understand radicals, and he said, "Well, go to the board and work it!" So I went to the board and started in on it, and I heard this shriek. "What are you doing?" And he came up and said, "You've committed a cardinal sin of radicals." The next thing I knew, he had me in a headlock, and I was getting my head rammed into the blackboard. Three times. Not gently.

Then he said, "I'm going to show you how to fix this, and you will never make this error again." He was right. I never made that error again. When the study period was over, he said, "Now, know this. There will be two sections of Algebra II next year. There's no way you're not going to be in my class." Then he pointed at the two desks closest to his desk. "The people that sit in these desks have the privilege of incurring my wrath when I'm too lazy to get up and smack the perpetrator. This one will be your desk."

Well, the rest of the year came and went, summer came and went, and then it was first day of tenth grade. Algebra II. I looked at that desk, and I thought no way in hell am I going to sit there. This is not happening. So I went to the far corner, near the back. He walked in and said, "Hello class, how are you? But wait. *Something's wrong*." I was hiding behind a clipboard. Then he said, "I know what it is. Adair, Get up here." So I went up there, and he smacked me. He was as good as his word. For the rest of the year, if something upset him,

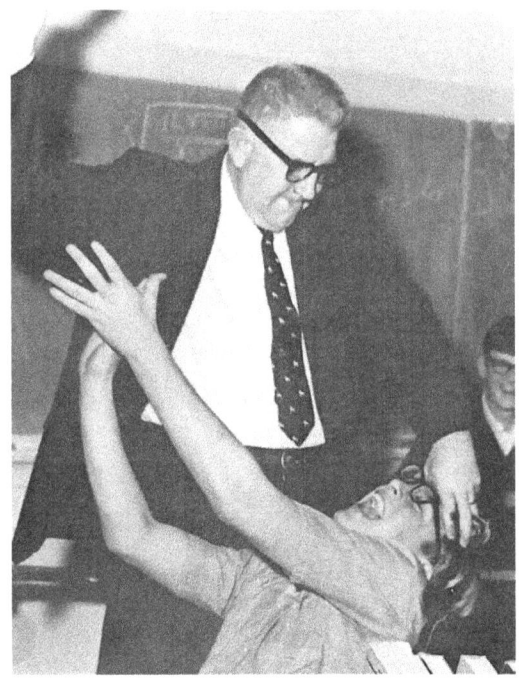

Mr. Smithson (Gag Photo)

Mike Pearson or I got smacked. It's not like I acted up. I was just handy. But I liked Mr. Smithson. The thing I figured out was that if he didn't like you, he wouldn't bother with you.

Sometimes he'd slap you on the back – pretty hard. Sometimes he'd pop you on top of your head. Then if somebody wasn't paying attention, he would hit the guy with a piece of chalk between the eyes. I never saw him miss, and I never saw him hit anybody in the eye. And if he was at the board and somebody wasn't paying attention, he would take the eraser and dust it on their head till it was clean. Other times he'd pull the hair on the side of your head – he called that picking cotton. And he did all kinds of other stuff.

Daly Thompson

There were a lot of impersonations of Daly Thompson, who taught Latin. *"Son, I'm gonna have to come to you."* That meant you were close to being in a world of hurt. If he came to you, you didn't want to know about it. Mr. Thompson was a big guy. By the time he was at BGA, he'd retired from being the Williamson County School Superintendent. But even though he was over 70, he was very powerful. He was a very nice man, but you didn't want to upset him.

I think I was a freshman, and Mr. Thompson was keeping study hall. A younger kid was talking, and Mr. Thompson had told him to be quiet. But the kid looked straight at him and kept talking. Mr. Thompson looked down at him and said, "Son, I'm going to ask you again to be quiet. Then I'm going to have to come to you." The kid looked at him and didn't stop talking. The rest of the study hall knew that if he told you to hush, you needed to hush.

Mr. Thompson left study hall and went downstairs, then he came up the back steps. He ended up standing behind this kid, watching him jabber. He stood there for a good minute. The kid never saw him. The next thing I knew, Mr. Thompson had him by the back of the neck. Then he lifted him up out of his desk, and backhanded him across the face. After that he set the kid down and said, "Son, I'm really sorry I had to do that, but you wouldn't listen. I said I was going to come to you." The kid was sitting there bawling. I mean, he got hit pretty hard.

I remember being in Latin class. We'd be reading out loud, and Mr. Thompson would be staring out the window. You'd be reading along and Mr. Thompson would say, "Son, I believe that was actually when Caesar crossed the mountains into Gaul." He had the book memorized.

Ralph Naylor was another one of my teachers. He was a different sort of guy, but I liked him *a lot*. He really helped me back when I was a freshman. I had him for English during the first semester, but there was a teacher named Bob Knight, who was teaching junior English. He couldn't keep his class in order, so he and Mr. Naylor switched classes. They put Mr. Naylor with the juniors, and we got Mr. Knight, who we called *Bub Nut*.

Everything was fine until one day when I was watching a tennis match. I was telling somebody about something *Bub Nut* had done in class, and I said, "I don't know about this guy. I don't think he's real bright, and blah blah blah blah." Well, Knight was standing right behind me the whole time. That semester was mostly writing, and until then I'd been making good grades, But after that my grades plummeted. In one month I went from making A's to making C's.

So I went to Mr. Naylor. I said, "Can I talk to you about something?" I gave him one of the papers I'd written. He said, "You got a C on this?" I said, "Actually I got a C-." He said, "Well, that's an A paper." When I showed him two of my tests, he said, "Those are much better than these grades." When I told him what happened, Mr. Naylor said, "I'll take care of this." And before I knew it, my grade was an A again.

Mr. Naylor was the butt of jokes from time to time. One involved an imaginary bomb. Mr. Naylor was kind of like the Absent Minded Professor, but he was a good-hearted absent minded professor. The guy sitting next to you would pretend to hand you imaginary bomb, and you had to take it and give it to the next person. I was sitting on the front row, and Bert Brown handed me the imaginary bomb. I tried to give it to Glenn Crowell, but Glenn wouldn't take it. I said, *"C'mon man,"* and Mr. Naylor looked at me. He said, "Adair, put that damn thing on the floor, and I don't want to see it go off!" So I had to get up and put it on the floor. People would set him up like that all the time.

His room was on the second floor, and every day after lunch he'd come in, push open the window, spit, and then pull the window shut. So one day somebody had an idea. Whoever it was opened the window before Mr. Naylor showed up. And sure enough, he walked up, closed the window, and spit on it. He just looked at the spit on the window, and then he went to his desk and sat down.

Ralph Naylor

Mr. Redick, the headmaster, was a strict disciplinarian, and Dan Fleming was the son of Sam Fleming, who was a BGA board member and one of the school's main benefactors. Dan was a horrible behavior problem. He had probably broken every rule that could've been broken three different times. So Mr. Redick called him to the office. He was going to paddle him, but when Dan assured him he was not, they got into a fight. I mean, an actual fist fight. Redick won pretty handily. He supposedly punched Dan two or three times in the face. Sam Fleming was apparently fine with it. I heard he'd given Mr. Redick license to do it.

Mr. J.B. Akin did more to run BGA – and especially to hold it together – than anybody. But it was all behind the scenes. He just quietly went around getting things done. He didn't look for any credit. I really liked Mr. Akin. I had him in Chemistry. I'd known him since I was a kid. He'd been a pretty successful coach before I came along.

Bo Stewart was another one of my teachers. It was his first year at BGA, and he taught Sophomore English. Mr. Stewart didn't like it if you argued about a test grade, but my friend Glenn Crowell took issue over a score he'd gotten. So he kept arguing, and Mr. Stewart finally said, "Mr. Crowell, leave the room with five demerits." When Glenn kept talking, Mr. Stewart said, "Mr. Crowell, leave the room with 10 demerits." By the time he got out the door, the demerits were up to 20. I said, "Glenn, shut up or you're going to be here for the rest of your life."

Boardman Stewart

Mr. Stewart made us do a lot of extra reading. We had to read David Copperfield, and that was on top of the other assignments he gave us. That was a lot of reading. The amount of homework we had was stunning. I wasn't the dumbest person there, and I would get home in the afternoon and study until dinner, and then study until I went to bed, and get up about five and study until I got to school. And I'd *hope* I had it all done. It was really that bad. Between Mr. Smithson and Mr. Stewart, it was an *amazing* amount of work.

I remember when Allen Tanksley and some other guys rolled Bo Stewart's yard. He thought it was funny. They were on the honor roll, but Don Patterson was out for blood. Mr. Stewart was completely fine with it. He said, "As long as they clean it all up, who cares?" But Patterson wanted them to be kicked out of school. Mr. Stewart had to talk him out of pushing for that.

Mr. Patterson was pretty hardcore, and one story involved one of my classmates who was a boarding student at the time. I think this was at the end of our sophomore year, and it was less than a week before the end of school. The teachers would come through and check the rooms, and Mr. Patterson came in and found a half pint of gin that my friend hadn't hidden well enough. I remember it was announced at assembly. "150 demerits, alcohol in the room." They had him doing yardwork, cutting the grass on the football field, and painting rooms. He was basically an unpaid janitor, or an unpaid yardman. They told him if that ever happened again, he'd be gone. I don't think they let him out until the end of June.

I liked Mr. Bragg, but he was a pretty hard teacher. There was a lot of outside reading, and a lot of memorization like *The Canterbury Tales*. It's funny, I thought about that just this morning, so I guess it must have stuck with me in some fashion.

Bill Bradshaw was my tennis coach, and I played for him for two or three years. He was a different sort of guy. He never would hit balls with us. He would just come out and we'd practice. He would just occasionally say something like, "Man, that's terrible footwork." But that was about it. There was no demonstration, but I basically liked the guy. I had him for every history and government class he taught. But his political views were a little odd, and some of the ways he expressed them were also a little odd. The first class I took with him was Ancient History, in my sophomore year.

Billy Adair and Glenn Crowell (walking on left)

The first big test we had, he said, "Adair, stand up and tell us about the honor code here and how it applies." So I answered it the best I could. But I thought, *what was that about?* When I handed in the test, I said, "Mr. Bradshaw, did you think something was going on?" He said, "No, I knew there wasn't. That's why I asked you." The next year I was in Modern History, and he did the same thing to Bert Brown. Everybody in the class looked at you like you had answers written on your arm or something. It was a trip.

I didn't take Biology until my junior year. I was in class with Coach Jimmy Gentry when President Kennedy was assassinated. I was sitting beside Frank Blackwell, who was my lab partner. I guess somebody came in and told us that he'd been shot, but it hadn't been confirmed that he was killed at that point. I remember Coach Gentry looking pretty horrified. He said, "Let's all pray right now." It wasn't 20 minutes later that somebody came through and said he was dead.

I ate lunch at BGA until my senior year, but I finally talked my parents into letting me eat off campus. Back then, the food at lunch was pretty horrible, and I had a car. It didn't take much convincing to get three or four guys to jump in my car and eat off campus – whether they were supposed to leave or not. We had an hour or so before we had to be back at school. It was easy to get around in Franklin in those days. We could go just about anywhere in a few minutes. And there were plenty of places to eat. We would go into town to Dodson's, or to one of the drugstores that had a soda fountain. And the Gilco was only a couple of minutes away from BGA. It was right across from Willow Plunge. It had burgers, fries, and shakes, and there was also a jukebox.

I'd gotten into music in the summer between my seventh and eighth grade years. My dad owned a furniture store on the square. It was a big, big, building. So the local radio station, WAGG, came to him and said, "You have room enough for people to come in and have an audience. Why don't we do a show from here? We can get local rock bands and maybe country bands, and let them play live." So they talked my old man into it.

I remember the first day. This band called The Valients came in, and they had two good guitar players. From the minute they started playing, I thought, I want to do *that*. My mom was musical, and although my dad wasn't, he liked music. So I said, "I want a guitar. Maybe for Christmas or whatever, and I want *this* kind of guitar." But the one I wanted was fairly expensive. It was a Gibson Les Paul Junior, and it cost $136. I also needed an amp, which was more money. My mother said something like, "OK, we'll get that for you, but if you don't learn how to play, I'll kill you." And she didn't smile when she said it.

It was Christmas of my 8th grade year when I actually got the guitar. I didn't take lessons, but I got some chord books, and when the Valients played at my old man's store, I'd watch how they did certain things. It was a lot of trial and error, and mostly error. You know, make mistakes and then try to figure out what you did wrong. My parents got a little concerned because they couldn't get the guitar out of my hands. And it kind of went on from there.

When I got to BGA, I'd been playing for about eight months. Well, I kept on practicing through my freshman year and the next summer, and then I started a band. I got Allen Tanksley and Bubby Beasley and another couple of guys, and we were really into it. We didn't have a name at first, but during my sophomore year we finally had our first gig.

We called ourselves the Telstars. We had a party at Bubby's house. We'd been playing for about 45 minutes, and I was having the time of my life. I was thinking, this is so cool. And a guy came up and said, "What are you guys making tonight?" When I told him, he said, "Well I've got a deal for you. I'll double it if you stop playing." We were pretty awful. Later on we added a couple of saxophone players, but neither one could play much.

I kept playing guitar and practicing, but I eventually wanted to learn how to play the bass. After I started to figure it out, I started getting calls to sub for other bands. I'd borrow a bass and play with the Fairlanes when they needed a sub. I really liked playing bass, and before long, I'd pretty much quit playing guitar.

The next band I was in was the Silhouettes. That was in the late spring of my junior year. A guy named Howard Hudgins had subbed with us one night, and he liked the way I played. He said, "I'm going to start a band, and I'll call you." I thought, *yeah, sure*. But a couple of months later, he called me. Along with Howard, we had Jack Jackson, Bill Davidson, and another guitar player named Paul Jenson, who was very, very good. It was a different world, as far as how much better that band was.

When I was playing with the Silhouettes, we had some gigs at Fort Campbell. I was 16 and I remember walking up to the bartender and saying, "Sir, I don't want to lie to you, I'm nowhere near 21, but can I buy a drink in here?" He said, "Kid, if you can see over this bar, I'll sell you anything you want." I said, "Well, I'd like something that tastes good, but isn't very potent." He made me a Singapore Sling. I had three of those, and I was blitzed by the end of the night. But I was in better shape than a couple of other guys in the band, and I had to drive all the way home on Clarksville Highway. But I didn't really drink all that much back then.

I played with the Silhouettes for about a year and a half. I liked them, but I wasn't as close with those guys. The next year I was to going to college, and I decided that I'd just quit playing. That lasted for about a week, and then I started sitting in with The Charades. They had Allen Tanksley and Jerry Smith and Drew Nixon, and a couple of other guys who weren't very good.

I sat in with the Charades a time or two, and Allen said, "We're getting rid of our guitar player. Do you want to come with us?" I told him I did, but then I changed my mind. By then I'd started my own band, the Exotics. We had Glenn Crowell and Bert Brown, and before long we also had Loy Hardcastle and Jeff Cook, who was the only one who hadn't gone to BGA. I think our first rehearsal was around the first week of February in 1965. Before long I started to really like what was going on with the Exotics.

The Exotics (Jeff Cook, Loy Hardcastle, Billy Adair)

During my senior year at BGA, we'd make about $150 bucks a gig, which was pretty good money for back then. That year I made about $5,000 playing with the Exotics, which was *astronomical* in 1965 dollars. In the summer, we might play three or four nights a week. We played all over the place. There were high school sorority and fraternity parties that people would have in their driveways. One night we played at Jerry Carter's house on Woodmont Boulevard, and 1500 people were there. It was *crazy*, but nobody caused problems.

And we played *a lot* at Willow Plunge during the summers. It was a good place to hang out, and it was beautiful. Gorgeously maintained. And the people that ran it were really nice. Later on in the afternoon I'd go there and hang out on my days off. If there wasn't a dance, it would stay open till around dark. It was just a good, fun place.

And while we were playing, we watched the girls dance. As small a town as Franklin was, I think we had the most beautiful girls in the world. I had friends who came to town and they'd say, "What is up with this place?" There was Diane Wagner and Sally Snow and Betty Fowlkes – all of the Fowlkes sisters were gorgeous. And Bridget Custer and Damon Akin and Teresa Taylor. And in Nashville everybody went gaga over Nancy Welch. But I didn't date too many girls from Nashville. Everything was fine in Franklin.

When it came to girls, there were advantages to playing in a band. But it didn't always give me a leg up. Sometimes I had a leg down. Everybody else learned how to dance, but I never got to because I was always up there playing. And you had to have a certain type of girlfriend. She had to be very patient. She knew there was a good chance that on Friday or Saturday night you were going to be playing. So her choice was to either stay at home, or go, and if she went, she did a lot of sitting.

Right after our senior year, a couple or three weeks after graduation, the Exotics had a long gig down in Daytona Beach. But one night the tail end of a hurricane was coming through, and we couldn't play because the gig was outside. So some of us went to a club to hear The Allman Joys, back before they changed their name to the Allman Brothers. And they came to see us a time or two. They said they liked the way we played. Duane Allman and I got to be friends, and while we were down in Daytona, he taught me to play *Satisfaction*. When we came back, the Exotics were the only band in town that could play stuff like that. We were like, "Yeah, check this out." A couple of years later, Glenn and I sat down and made a list of everything we could play. It ended up being over 300 songs.

I'd gotten along with Mr. Redick just fine in school. He'd always been nice to me, but a few months after we graduated, we had a problem. The Exotics were invited to play at a school dance at BGA. A teacher named Tony Cobb was in charge of social functions at the school. He hired us, and he said they also wanted the Spidells. They were an all-black vocal group that we sometimes backed up. I said, "Tony, are you sure this is a good idea?" It was the mid-60s, and I knew how a few members of the faculty felt about race. But the Spidells were hired, and they came to BGA and put on their show. They were *really* good. Then I saw Mr. Redick come up beside the stage, and his face was beet red.

The Spidells weren't doing anything wrong. They were just doing their usual dance routine. But Mr. Redick looked at Billy Lockridge, who was their leader. He said, "Young man, you will not do that kind of suggestive dancing here. You will cease and desist right now." The whole place just went dead silent. Billy looked at me and said, "What do I do?" I said, "Man, I am embarrassed. And I'm sorry."

The Spidells

Tony Cobb was pretty mad. He went up to Redick, which I thought took some guts on his part. He said, "This was to be my event. Why don't you let me run it as I see fit?" I would see Mr. Redick after that, and it was all fine and good. But I thought, *Come on*. A few guys came and went, but the Exotics stayed together until we were out of college. We went through Hendrix and Clapton and all that, and then along came *Blood, Sweat, and Tears* and *Chicago*. I liked that a lot. That was about the time I decided that I really liked big band music. I wound up playing in the jazz band at Vanderbilt, and everything kept going. I got an invitation to join a group called, *Sweet Thunder*. The rest of the band were all studio players, and they were at least a level a better than I was. And they also invited Glenn to sing.

By then I was doing a little studio work, and after a year or so, I was doing a lot. It was fun. Most of the session work was for people who were convinced they were going to be the next big thing. But I also played for groups like *Alabama*, and I did a lot of work on TV shows – people from George Straight, Ronny Millsap, Janie Fricke, and Rodney Crowell to Carl Perkins, *The Drifters*, *The Coasters*, Chubby Checker, and Jerry Lee Lewis.

A few years after I graduated, I stopped by BGA for a visit. I went to see Mr. Smithson, and he was teaching an Algebra II class. They were working on quadratic equations. He had some kids at the board, and one kid was screwing up *badly*. But instead of ramming the kid's head into the blackboard, Mr. Smithson came over to me. He said, "*You* go work the equation and give us rules." I'm thinking, my God, I haven't done any math since I left BGA. But I went to the board, and everything came out right. So I sat down, and he went on with the class. About 10 minutes later, he came back to where I was. He was standing at my desk.

He said, "You do know what would've happened if you'd screwed that up, don't you? You would've died right here." I just said, "I know." Fear works very well. Some years ago, I think it was in the early 80s, I was on a bike, and I rode back to where Willow Plunge had been. There were huge trees growing up through what was left of the pools. They had just come straight up through the concrete. I hated to see it that way. I'm very glad I went to BGA. It sure made college easy. I mean, it really did. It was a complete snap. Overall, I had a really good time. It was a great experience, and I'd do it all over again.

The information in this narrative came from an interview that took place in 2012, and was supplemented by additional conversations between Billy and the editor. Billy Adair died in Nashville in 2014, at the age of 66. He was survived by his wife, the internationally-noted jazz pianist, Beegie Adair.

Kenneth Phelps, Class of 1965

I came to BGA because the high school in my hometown, Lewisburg, had burned down. I didn't want to go to school in a Quonset hut, and since my best friend, Bob Thompson, was going to BGA, I told my mother and father that I was going to BGA, too. So I took the exam and got in, and during my first year, I roomed with Bob.

I'm not sure what I expected, but I liked BGA. I liked the atmosphere. There was something going on all the time. I was on the bottom floor of the Old Dorm, along with most of the other freshman boarders. BGA had a totally different environment from Lewisburg. Everybody in Lewisburg knew everybody else. If your grandparents hadn't been born there, you were a foreigner. And everybody went to church.

One of the first people I got to know at BGA was George Elder. He came into my room and asked if we had any food. We didn't, and he left. When everybody was moving in, I noticed a guy who turned out to be one of my classmates. A servant was unpacking all of his stuff and putting it away for him. Before long, I watched him cut off the sleeves of a tailored shirt. He wanted a short-sleeve shirt. He was obviously a little different from everybody else.

The guys at BGA weren't like my classmates at Lewisburg. The BGA students were all fairly affluent, but there were a lot of poor kids at Lewisburg. A good many of the kids back home were just trying to get through school. And the academics were like night and day. There was a lot of copying off each other's homework and copying off each other's tests in Lewisburg. That didn't go on too much at BGA. But my grammar school teachers had been good, and the discipline was strict. If you got a whipping at school, you were going to get whipped again when you got home.

There were a lot of guys like me – boys from small towns – at BGA. Intellectual pursuits were more important than they'd been in Lewisburg, and I was drawn to that. I'd always been a big reader. I was also drawn to athletics, and that first year, I made the basketball team. I was tall enough, but I wasn't very coordinated. The basketball conditioning program started right off the bat. I liked getting in shape, and I got to know some of the other guys in the program.

The only time I ever got homesick was when I was when my grandfather died. I was a freshman. I went back for his funeral, and I spent the weekend at home. My grandfather was a wonderful man, but I hadn't really grieved or gotten upset. It wasn't until I got back to school on Sunday that I started facing everything. I just wasn't thinking right. One of the guys went and told a teacher that something was wrong with me. The school eventually called my parents, and they drove up from Lewisburg and got me. That was the first time that I hadn't wanted to be at BGA. I spent the night at home, but I was back in time for basketball practice the next day.

Our headmaster, Mr. Redick, and I ended up having our differences. One of his nicknames was *Bonehead*, which was very appropriate. He came across as something between a used car salesman and an itinerant evangelical preacher. He was very, very confident, and he had a big ego.

One of the first teachers who got my attention was Daly Thompson. He taught me Latin when I was a freshman. I'd never had a teacher who was that old. And there was a formality about him. The feeling he conveyed was that it was his responsibility to teach you. When I think about Mr. Thompson, the first thing that comes to mind is one day when we were in Latin class talking about World War Two. He had this deep, slow way of talking, and he was telling us about how Cordell Hull was negotiating with a Japanese emissary for a peaceful settlement of the differences between Japan and United States. They were in the middle of their discussion, and an aide came in and told Secretary Hull that the Japanese had bombed Pearl Harbor. Then Hull looked at the leader of the Japanese contingent, and just said, 'You yellow-bellied son of a bitch!'

The next year I had a young guy named Boardman Stewart for sophomore English. He really made an impression. He reminded me of Sherlock Holmes. Being in his class, made me feel like I was in a British boarding school. We stood and recited passages, and most of the grammar I ever learned probably came from the books he had us read. He was knowledgeable and entertaining, and he projected a lot of confidence.

When I was a freshman, it had been decided that I needed remedial work in reading and spelling.

I was a terrible speller. I was sent to Mrs. O.C. Hatcher. She worked with students who needed help, and later on she taught me speed reading. I ended up being able to read 1000 words a minute. I used speed reading when I read *The Robe*, which was one of the books Mr. Stewart assigned, and I ended up making an A on the test.

Bill Brown taught Algebra II when I was a sophomore. In spite of being the new head football coach, he was very soft spoken and humble, and very honest. He didn't seem to have taught much before he came to BGA. I could tell that he was only two or three pages ahead of where the class was in our textbook. But he was working hard, and getting advice when he needed it. If he didn't know how to work a problem, he would ask one of the students to come up to the board and do it. That impressed me. A lot of teachers had too much ego to do something like that, and it got in the way of their teaching.

Mr. Naylor taught junior English. He was a nice man, but just about everybody gave him grief. I don't know how he got through it. We'd pretend that we had an imaginary bomb that was about to explode. We'd pass it up and down each row, and Mr. Naylor finally said something like, "Get that bomb out of here!" We would also step over an imaginary wire when we came through the door for class. He made us stop doing that, too.

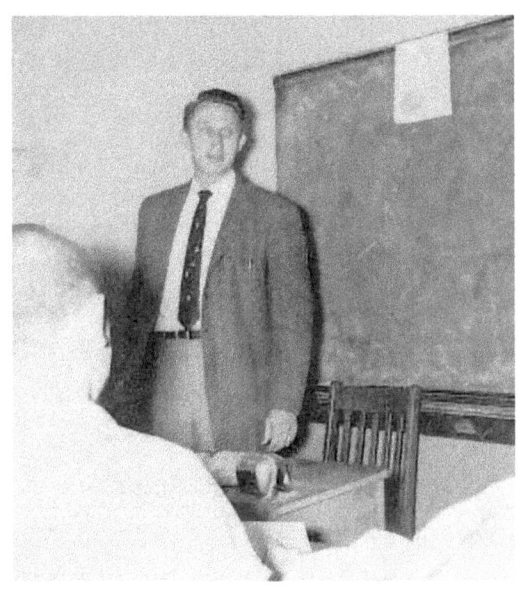

Ralph Naylor

Another memorable teacher was Mr. Smithson. I had him for Math when I was a senior. I sat in the back of the room where he couldn't hit me or throw books at me, or do any of the other things he did. I thought he was very entertaining, and he did a good job of teaching us. He gave a ton of homework, and how much he gave us largely depended on what kind of mood he was in. I had always liked math, and I did well in his class. I was obsessed with doing well in school, and no matter how much math homework I had, I did the problems two different times so I could double-check my answers.

Another teacher was John Oxley. He and I had a connection. Both my mother and father had gone to Lambuth College, where Mr. Oxley's father had taught biology. Mr. Oxley lived on campus and ate with the boarding students. I sat at his table at dinner, and we got to know each other pretty well. Some of us would take turns feeding and holding his baby so Mrs. Oxley could eat.

Mr. Oxley had gone to college at Southwestern in Memphis, where I ended up going. He taught the course I took at BGA using his college textbook, and using the notes he'd made when he was a student. It was a difficult course. I remember one time when I studied and studied. I had learned how to derive all of the formulas, but at the last minute, he decided to give us an open book test, which really ticked me off. I decided not to open my book, and I made a hundred on the exam. I took freshman physics in college. If you weren't a Physics major, you were supposedly dead meat. It was a tough course, but

I did really well – at least until we got past the part I'd had at BGA. Things went a little downhill after that.

John Oxley

Mr. Campbell was a retired teacher from Nashville. He taught U.S. history. Before we took our final exam, he gave us all the questions, so we all did real well. But when I went to college and took American History, I knew absolutely nothing that I hadn't learned before I started BGA. Mr. Akin taught Chemistry. He was calm and confident, and very knowledgeable. He worked well with his students, and I was extremely well-prepared for college chemistry. When I was a senior, Coach Jimmy Gentry created a course called Human Physiology. Sutton O'Neill and I actually dissected a pig, which was usually college level stuff. I enjoyed that very much. It gave me more confidence, and I felt like I was learning what I needed to learn.

I didn't like Mr. Bradshaw, the tennis coach. He taught Government and History, and he represented a lot of things I hated. He was arrogant, and he was also abusive and partial. In the summer he taught tennis at a country club. At school, during tennis season, he spent most of his time with the guys he taught at the country club. He worked with them, and that was about it. I was on the team for four years, but I wasn't very good and I can only remember one thing he ever helped me with. I liked my classmate, Steven Plonka. He was different. He was very smart, particularly in math. He had thick glasses, and he was short and pudgy. Every year, he tried out for the tennis team, which I thought took a lot of guts and courage. He kept getting cut, but he finally made it when he was a senior, and he ended up lettering.

The Cuban Missile Crisis took place when I was in 10th Grade. Some of us were scared. BGA was a politically conservative place, and some guys thought the communists were going to blow America off the face of the Earth. A lot of us just thought that everything would be all over. The next year, when President Kennedy was assassinated, I was walking between the dorms. Somebody raised his window and said, "Kennedy has been shot. The next thing I heard was that he was dead. Even if they disagreed with his political beliefs, almost everybody thought that Kennedy was a good man. Most of us had read *Profiles in Courage*, and we knew he had been a war hero. When our classmate John Jackson died the next spring, it affected everybody. Back then we thought we were all going to live forever. John sat at my table at lunch. He was a nice guy. When he died, it hit everybody. Nobody talked about it, but everybody felt it.

I worked hard when I got to BGA, but I was in the middle of the class when it came to academics. In my sophomore year, I got up into the upper quarter, and when I was a junior, I made it into the top ten. When you were a boarding student, if you made good enough grades, then you got to go home over the weekend. At three o'clock on Friday, your parents would pick you up. Or when you were senior, if you had a car, you'd be able to drive home. You just had to be back in time for study hall, which was at seven o'clock on Sunday night. I kept working, and I ended up being class salutatorian.

One teacher who made a big impression on me was a young guy named Danny Allen. He came to BGA when I was a senior. He lived in the dorm, and I started talking to him. He finally invited me to come down to his room, and we talked about all kinds of different things for maybe four or five hours. It might have been the first time that I really engaged in a truly open, emotional, and intellectual discussion with another person. That kind of opened a door for me. I realized that there were people around I could talk to. I didn't have to be invisible. There were people I could be open with.

When I was a freshman, BGA hosted an event where the boarding students would meet girls from Franklin. The Franklin girls were in one room, and we'd be in another room. Then we'd line up and get paired off, and the boys in the back would be hoping there wouldn't be enough girls. Whoever they put you with was your date. You were supposed to talk to her, and all the rest of it. My first year I got paired off with a girl who was nice and sweet, but her mother had made her come. She was clearly not excited about being there – or at least not being there with me. Even though she was well-endowed, she was not very attractive, but I went ahead and did my duty until it was finally over.

The next year came around, and the same event happened again. I wanted to change my luck, and I got in a different part of the line. But when I got to the front, I ended up with the same girl. I was real nerdy, and she was not very happy about how things had turned out for her. But we got through it. The teachers at BGA were happy, and her mother was happy.

We had a wonderful cook named Cora. She made great fried chicken and plenty of other very good dishes. Sometimes the upperclassmen tried to make the food sound unappetizing and gross. If the younger kids wouldn't eat it, there would be more for us. So we'd call the Kool Aid, *bug juice*, and hamburgers would be called *scabs*. At some point one of the cooks died, and we asked the kids, "Where do you think her body went?" When they said they didn't know, somebody would say, "Well, that's what we're eating it today. And she tastes pretty good."

Even though a teacher was living in the dorm, there would be occasional acts of violence. It could be a little like *Lord of the Flies*. They would pick out somebody who was going to get a red belly, which meant having your stomach slapped until it turned red. I stayed away from all that. As far as I was concerned, it was just cruel and heartless. Then one night they came after me. I picked up a broom handle, and if anybody came close, I was going to try to kill him. But largely through the efforts of a very athletic guy who ended up going to the Naval Academy, they finally got me. They didn't hurt me, but after it was all over, I went down to the guy's room. I wanted to kill him with my bare hands. He knew how mad I was, and he crawled on top of the radiator, and got in a fetal position. But I calmed down before I hurt him.

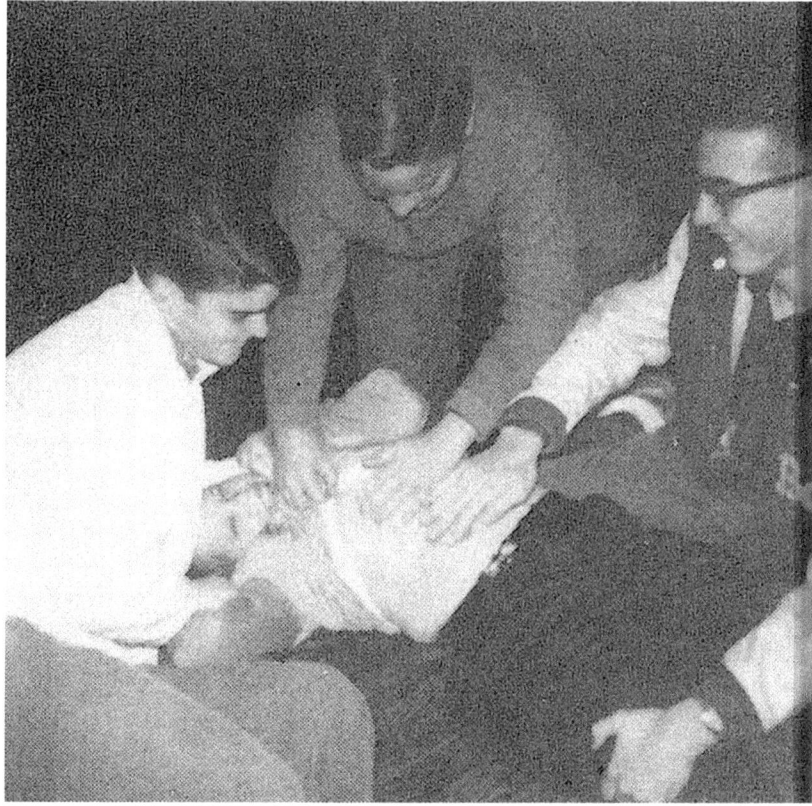

Red Belly

There was an older boarding student who had a hard time. He had a bad case of acne, and there were pockmarks all over his face. Guys would come by his room, and say things like, "Unclean. Unclean. Leper. Leper!'" And they would also give him red bellies. He was persecuted all the time. At some point someone told me, "There is nobody more cruel than a high school boarding student."

I don't know who instigated the Cripple Derby. I disapproved, but there were four guys who'd had polio, and they ended up competing in something that was supposed to resemble the Olympics. And around the same time there was also the Blubber Derby for guys who were overweight. They raced each other, and they might have done some other stuff. Just about everybody went out to watch them. Most of the guys who participated kind of laughed it off, but not everybody. That wasn't our finest moment.

I was the dorm proctor when I was a senior. The lights were supposed to be out at 11 o'clock. My job was to go down the hall and make sure everybody's lights were off. One night, I came across a guy I knew pretty well. He had been brutalized in some way, and he was disoriented. He was almost psychotic. After I took him into the bathroom where nobody could hear us, I tried to reassure him. It was a traumatic situation. Until then I hadn't realized that a person had the power to psychologically break somebody else by being cruel. In the end that experience made me more humane than I'd been before.

I was only in one tug-of-war. It was when I was a senior. Everybody got on buses and we went out west of town to the bridge over the Harpeth River. The rope was gigantic, and we got a pep talk about how the tug-of-war was a BGA tradition. I was a Plato. I remember that once we started pulling, everybody on both sides thought they were winning because the rope stretched. We won, and I remember two of the Greers holding on to the rope, and then dropping into the river, which was very muddy. Everybody was muddy from getting down in the mud, trying to get a foothold.

I was on the wrestling team my senior year. My coach was Jimmy Gentry, who was a fantastic guy. One day he came up after practice. He said, "Kenneth, I need to talk to you. You're going to have to sit out the match next Thursday." When I asked him why, he said, 'Well, the other school has a black wrestler in your weight class." The administration had found out about it, and they'd decided that they didn't want a BGA student wrestling a black person. I told Coach Gentry, "That's just not right." Coach Gentry said he agreed with me. When he asked me if I wanted to talk to Mr. Redick about it, I said I did.

So I went to see Mr. Redick. He did most of the talking. The main thing I said was that the situation was personal to me. I was a student at BGA. The other guy was a student, just like I was. We were two human beings. I told Mr. Redick that I couldn't go along with not wrestling somebody because he was black. What kept running through my mind was all of the things that BGA had taught me while I was there.

Jimmy Gentry

I had learned about character and fairness and honesty. I had learned about being open-minded and taking responsibility for my actions. Not wrestling in that match was going against all of those things. Mr. Redick might have even said something about taking it to the board, but I don't know whether he did that or not. Before I left, I just told him that if I wasn't allowed to wrestle, I was leaving school. I was supposed to think it over over the weekend, and then come back to him on Wednesday. When I walked out of his office, Mr. Redick was obviously displeased, but he couldn't do anything about it. I went and told Coach Gentry, and he thought that was the right decision.

At wrestling practice on Monday, I think I was wrestling Don Dickinson. He was out of my weight class, and I dislocated my shoulder. It popped right back into place, but it was really sore and tender. They took me to see Dr. Guffee, and he said I shouldn't wrestle, which was unusual. Dr. Guffee would usually let you keep participating as long as you could endure the pain. So I was free from my ethical responsibility. The team went ahead and wrestled on Thursday. Somebody could've wrestled in my place, but we ended up forfeiting that match.

When I was on the wrestling team, I was in the same weight class as David Kefauver. We'd go up against each other every day in practice. He worked out all the time, and he was a whole lot stronger than I was. I couldn't do much with him, but I never stopped coming at him. That is part of what I learned at BGA. You just don't give up. You give as much effort as you possibly can, and you keep going until you can't do it anymore. Trying was more important than winning and losing. In Lewisburg the general approach was, "I'm gonna give effort if it really matters." At BGA, doing the best you possibly could was a matter of honor.

I learned how to work at BGA. I also learned to respect the character of other people, and to appreciate characteristics like honor and kindness and concern for other people. I won the Roberts Watch at graduation. It turned out to be a real burden. I kept thinking about all the guys who were more deserving of the watch than I was.

The information in this narrative came from an interview that took place on October 15, 2015, and from additional conversations. Dr. Kenneth Phelps died in Lewisburg in 2022 at the age of 75. He was survived by his wife, Debbie, seven children, and eight grandchildren.

Steve Plonka, Class of 1965

I came to BGA from Huntsville, Alabama, but I was only two generations removed from Europe. Both of my father's parents were born in Poland. Dad was an electrical engineer in the Space Program. Along with having the brain to be an electrical engineer, he was a teacher. He taught a lot of Germans and other foreign students who had recently come to America. When I was in sixth grade, he took me to one of his classes. He was teaching base-eight mathematics. None of the adults were getting it, but it made perfect sense to me.

I went to parochial school through eighth grade. At the time, the schools in Huntsville weren't very good, and when I got out of elementary school, Dad told me we were going to look at a high school in Tennessee. I was totally clueless. So we came up and met Mr. Redick, who led us around. There was a break between classes, and I remember seeing all these students in the old administration building. It was the year BGA won the 1960 state championship, and there were a lot of football vibes in the atmosphere. It was a very welcoming environment. I took an aptitude test, and the next thing I knew, I was ready to start BGA as a freshman boarding student.

Rascoe Rhea, who was from Lawrenceburg, was my first roommate. I was coming from a very insolated Catholic background. Life in Huntsville had been going to school during the week and playing in the band, and then going to church on Sunday and being an altar boy. BGA was different, but it was also a very structured life. Athletics, supper, night study hall, and lights out. I'd never had to make up my bed before, not to mention having somebody else inspect it. It was an adjustment, but all that discipline was good for me in a lot of ways. I needed to get away from my mother, and have my horizons expanded. I don't remember ever being homesick.

I was about as wide as I was tall when I got to BGA. I pretty much had the same dimensions all around, and a couple of guys from Huntsville came up with a nickname for me. They called me "basketball." But somehow I got it into my mind that I was going to play football. English was my last class of the day, and I remember leaving for the first practice. I was with David Kefauver and Jim Smith. They kept quiet, but they looked at me like they wanted to say, "Are you sure you want to go out for football?" I lasted for about one practice. It wasn't going to work for a variety of reasons, including that I had a massive allergy to grass. It was not a pretty picture.

Coach Jimmy French taught Algebra One when I was a freshman. He was my favorite teacher of all time. When we were about a month into school, he said, "Steve Plonka, I want to see you after class." He wanted me to be the manager of the freshman basketball team. So all of a sudden, I got exposed to a bunch of athletes. That led me to do a lot of shooting. There wasn't much else to do while I was waiting to wash a bunch of jocks, and I ended up being a pretty good shot. I gradually became more athletic, and three years later I would be able to make the tennis team.

There were jokes about my weight from the boarders, but not from the day students. Early on, someone left a little box of Midol on my desk in my dorm room. I was fat, and since it looked like I had breasts, the implication was that I might need some Midol. And guys would pinch each other all the time. Just about everybody got pinched, but it was a different kind of pinch. They'd use the knuckle of their thumb and the top knuckle of their middle finger. I'd have bruises all over me, and especially on my chest. I never let my mother or father see me without my shirt when I went home. It was hard, but we all managed to survive.

During the second part of my freshman year, my roommate was Rick Beziat. He was a really good tennis player. He also played the guitar, and he loved Chet Atkins. I would just sit there and listen to him play. When I was a sophomore, I lived in the basement of the freshman dorm again. I was made a proctor at the beginning of the year, and I was paired with Robert McMillan, who was a junior. We lived down by the showers. He had a terrible case of acne and, of course, he was teased a lot. He paid a horrible price, but he was such a good guy. You see a whole different side of a person when you live with him.

After the first semester, I got moved upstairs. I roomed with Kenneth Phelps, who became a lifelong friend. Kenneth was extremely bright. He was capable in so many ways. He and Bob Thompson had both come to BGA from Lewisburg in the ninth grade. They roomed together the first year, and when I roomed with Kenneth, I started spending a lot of time with Bob.

One of the first teachers who stood out to me was Daly Thompson, who taught Latin. There was something about Mr. Thompson that commanded respect, but sometimes a kid would get out of line. When that happened, he'd take off his glasses. He'd say, "Son, don't make me have to come to you." Bo Stewart was my English teacher when I was a sophomore. One day he was explaining different points of view in literature. He stood up in his chair, and stepped onto the desk. Then he looked at all of us and spoke like he was the author, "I am omniscient." From then on, I never had any trouble remembering what omniscient meant.

Bob Thompson

Ralph Naylor was clearly a bright man, but he was very unusual. Between classes at BGA, the steps would be crammed with students. Some guys would be going upstairs, and some guys would be coming downstairs. One day, Mr. Naylor was coming down the stairs. He stopped to talk to somebody, and after a brief conversation he said, "When I ran into you, was I going up the stairs or down the stairs?" And whoever he was talking to said, "Well, Mr. Naylor, you were coming down the stairs." And he said, "Okay, good. Then I haven't had lunch yet."

Another time he was in the student center. Next to the drink machine and the snack machine, there was a storage closet. It was where all the drinks and snacks were kept. One day somebody saw that the key to the closet had been left in the door. Whoever it was turned the key and opened the door. Mr. Naylor was standing there in the dark. The kid said something like, "Mr. Naylor, are you okay?" He said, "I'm fine." Then the guy said, "But why are you in here?" Mr. Naylor just said, "Well, everybody's got to be somewhere." When I was a freshman at Vanderbilt, one of the assignments I had for English class was to write an essay about the most interesting person I'd ever known. I wrote about Ralph Naylor.

I had an aptitude for math, and I was pretty well-prepared when I got to Mr. Smithson's class. So I never felt Mr. Smithson's wrath. He never threw a piece of chalk at me, or hit me with his rose stem, or any of that stuff. He had a great influence on me. I loved that man. He was terrific. He was the coordinator for the state math contest. BGA would send students, and I went to the contest every year. If one of us placed first, he would get an automatic 100 on the final exam. If you came in second, you got a 95. If you came in third in the state, which was the best I ever did, you got a 90.

Sometimes we'd walk into Mr. Bragg's Senior English class, and he would have written something on the blackboard, or put up a picture. Your assignment would be to write a two-page theme about whatever the subject happened to be, and that really made me think. Studying the picture or analyzing the quote, and then having to figure out how to write about it, was an important part of my education. Coming up with ideas, expressing those ideas, and then writing them down was something I ended up doing a lot in my business career.

I was in Bill Bradshaw's government class when President Kennedy was killed. Bear Robertson stuck his head in and said that Kennedy had been shot. He said that they didn't know if he was going to live. Well, Mr. Bradshaw was no JFK fan, and he made some crack, but I don't remember what it was.

Bill Bradshaw

Mr. Bradshaw coached the tennis team. Even though I was on the team, I never had ten seconds of tennis instruction from him. But he did coach some of the other guys. There were eight of us on the team, and I was on the bottom part of the ladder. When I was a senior, we had the district tournament, and I had to play a guy named Bill Finger from Hillwood High School. He beat me like a drum. Later on I found out that Mr. Bradshaw told my teammates that I should have beaten the guy. He said I hadn't done enough to prepare. I should have gone up to him and said, "You never spent any time showing me how to be a better tennis player. All you did was drive the car when we went somewhere for a match." But I didn't have enough gumption to say anything.

There was a big room at the back of the Administration Building that served as the student center. There were two ratty ping pong tables, and one or two drink machines. There was also a store with a sliding partition. It was open for about 15 minutes after study hall was over. And across from the store was a little room with a few chairs and a little black and white TV. Lights out was at 10 o'clock, but on Saturday nights some of us would sneak out of the dorm. As soon as the teachers were out of the way, I'd go over with guys like Bill Abernathy, Jim Bassham, and Calvin Houghland and watch a TV show called *Night Train*. It featured black musicians, including local performers like Ironing Board Sam. We thought we were really getting away with something, and for some reason, we never got caught.

I was a model student back when I was a freshman, but I hadn't done too well as a junior, grade wise. Maybe that's when some of the teachers thought I changed. I guess it was kind of like, "Where's sweet, innocent little Steve? I was on the honor roll, but I couldn't make the privilege list. I deserved to be on it, but nothing was enough. Making good grades wasn't enough. Managing the basketball team for three years, and playing on the tennis team wasn't enough. And I never understood exactly what was wrong with my attitude. But God bless Mr. Smithson. He kept trying to get me on privilege list.

One way or another, I had gotten on Mr. Redick's bad side. I sat at his table in the dining hall when I was a senior. Maybe he was trying to rehabilitate me.

There were always stories about the food at BGA. Joe Shapard once found a piece of glass in the mashed potatoes, and somebody else found a fried spider in the bacon. When you're cooking that much for so many people, there will be times when things don't come out right. But every once in a while on Sunday, the cooks made homemade bread. It was the best bread *ever*. Butter and Jelly on that bread was like dessert. I remember that bread like I had it yesterday.

Mrs. Kennedy worked in the administration office. One morning when I was a senior, she pulled into the circle to drop off her son, John, who was in our class. It had been snowing, and I made a snowball. I lobbed it up in the air, and when it came down, it hit right where the windshield was already cracked. That made the crack bigger, and by the time the story got to Mr. Redick, it was like I had reared back and thrown an ice ball as hard as I could. So he told me to be in his office at three o'clock. I showed up and told him what happened, and how sorry I was, but he'd already decided what he was going to do. Nobody else was around, which was probably intentional.

Paul Redick

He just said, "Come over here and stand behind my desk. Now bend over and grab the edge of the desk." Then he reached over and got this big canoe paddle. I had already heard about the paddle, and about the technique Mr. Redick used. He would keep the paddle horizontal when he swung it. That way there wasn't any air resistance to slow it down. Then just before it made contact, he'd flip it so the flat side was what hit the boy's butt. He hit me so hard, that at first I couldn't breathe. I remember walking out of that building as fast as I could, and just going back to my room.

Jerry Porter was a year ahead of me, but we were friends. If I had a reputation of having a bad attitude, Jerry's reputation was worse. He got paddled when I was a junior. Mr. Redick hit him five times. Some of the guys had to help him up the stairs to his room. Jerry was a good guy, and he ended up going to the Naval Academy. The lesson I took away from the whole experience is don't get on the wrong side of whoever is in authority. Once you do, it's hard to get back. I learned how only one or two people can pull strings and make things hard for somebody else.

When you came up the stairs of the Senior Dorm, there was a long hallway to the left. There were seven rooms on each side, with two boys in each room. There was also a faculty apartment on the second floor, and Don Patterson lived there with his wife. We called Mr. Patterson *Bulldog*. At some point we noticed that there was a little hole in the wall above the water fountain. His apartment was on the other side of the wall, and we concluded that it was a peephole. So we drew this big eye around the peephole, and somebody wrote, "Bulldog Is Watching You."

Don Patterson

Mr. Patterson had a white Thunderbird, and he parked it right out beside the dorm. In the late spring of my senior year, I ran into some trouble. When I went outside after supper, I accidentally bumped up against the outside rear view mirror of his car. So I opened the door and got in. I did the best I could to adjust it, and then I got out and forgot about it. A few days later, he came up to me and said, "Well, I'll give you a choice. I can give you 25 hours, or you can wash my car." I wanted to know why he would give me 25 hours. He said, "I saw what you did to my car the other day. I saw you bump into the mirror." It turned out that somebody had been messing with his mirror a lot. I told him that except for the one time I tried to fix it, it wasn't me. But he didn't believe me. He said he'd get back to me, and a couple of days later, he asked me which option I was going to take. I said, "Well, I can't stop you from giving me the 25 hours, but I am *not* going to wash your car." I was feeling my oats. I was two weeks from graduation. What was he going to do? Keep me from graduating? After a couple of days, he said to just forget the whole thing.

I remember the rope for the Tug-of-War being delivered when I was a senior. They laid the rope out on the track. I knew it would be long, but I was surprised by how heavy it was. You could only pick up about two feet of it. I was a Greer, and we ended up going into the river. The rope stretched when everybody started pulling, and we thought we were winning. We must have relaxed a little, and the Platos apparently knew what was coming. As soon as they felt us ease up, they all really started pulling, and that sealed our fate.

When I went to Vanderbilt, Vietnam was just getting started, and Dad said I should go ahead and get into the ROTC. I was planning to go to medical school, and he thought that it would be better if I was already an officer when I entered the service as a doctor. So I took ROTC. I was a late bloomer when it came to physical development. It didn't really kick in until my sophomore year at Vanderbilt. After my junior year, I went to summer camp at Fort Bragg. It was infantry-oriented, and it really appealed to me. That's when I decided that I wanted to have a career in the military. When I went home from summer camp and told my parents, I thought my father would be proud, but he got mad. He thought that when I got to Fort Bragg, somebody had put stars in my eyes. I tried to explain it to him, but it didn't register.

After college graduation, I reported to Fort Benning and went through the basic course for infantry officers. Then I went to Ranger School. Back then, there were three phases to Ranger School. The first phase was all physical training. Hand-to-hand combat and the basics of patrolling. All of that was near Fort Benning at Camp Darby. The second part was the mountaineering phase, which took place in the mountains of North Georgia. It was all mountaineering skills and patrols. The final phase was in the swamps around Eglin Air Force Base in Florida.

There was value in not knowing what was coming. It was eight weeks and two days under stress. Meaning hunger and extreme fatigue. It was worse than anything I would experience later on. I found out that if I was tired enough, I could sleep standing up. There were training situations when I'd be taking orders from guys, and ten minutes later, they'd be taking orders from me. We were all college graduates, and if they wanted to, guys could make you look bad without making themselves look bad. You had to figure out the system pretty quickly.

We ended up with a 12-day extended patrol in the swamps. We were out for 12 days solid. We didn't eat very often. It was simulated combat conditions. Choppers couldn't get in because of the weather. No resupply. I knew I was hungry. I knew I needed to eat. But it just wasn't as hard for me as it was for a lot of other people. I learned that in large part, hunger is in our minds. A lot of the guys in Ranger School didn't pass the requisite percentage of patrols, but I was able to get through it. I came out with a level of self confidence I'd never had before. After Ranger School I was assigned to Fort Carson, Colorado. I met Marilyn Levering while I was stationed in Colorado, and we were married in the Catholic Chapel of Air Force Academy in 1971. Then I went to Viet Nam.

I had three jobs when I got to Viet Nam. I was the leader of a rifle platoon. Boots on the ground. The First Cavalry Division had started having elements stand down, and we took over part of their area of operation near Bien Hoa Air Base. We would go out on patrols, and there were miles and miles of bunker line. My second job was serving in a security battalion, which meant dealing with what were called sappers. They were enemy soldiers who were adept at getting through barbed wire without tripping alarms and flares. They'd bring in explosives and blow up whatever they could. I also had an administrative job.

I saw a lot of lives ruined in Vietnam. Some kids couldn't handle it. Their escape was drugs. I'd find them asleep in a foxhole. I'd wake them up and say, "Don't you realize what you're here for? Don't you realize what could happen?" They'd just tell me they couldn't deal with it. I never figured out how to motivate those type of soldiers. It was a tough, tough environment.

The worst fighting I saw was during the Easter Offensive in 1972. We weren't fighting the Viet Cong. We were fighting the North Vietnamese Army. They were well equipped, highly organized, and their supply lines were all in place. My unit didn't really belong to a battalion. We were an independent rifle company, so we had a little bit of autonomy. The NVA was supported by tanks and armored personnel carriers. We were falling like cards, and I prayed like crazy. It was ugly. I wrote a letter to my father. I told him I didn't think I'd be coming home, and to take care of Marilyn if I didn't make it back. But I'd been well trained. I got shot at, and I shot back. I never lost a soldier. I don't know how many we killed on the other side. They didn't leave their dead. You'd just find blood trails.

After Ranger School and four years as an infantry officer, the Army said they had more junior officers than they needed. I left the Army in the late summer of 1973. I was a biology major and a chemistry minor, and I'd grown up with the space program. There were a lot of connections between the space program and IBM, and I started my career there immediately after I left the Army.

I began my career in administration. I was good at math, but I didn't know anything about computers. Marilyn and I were living in Columbia, South Carolina, and I worked at IBM during the day, and got my MBA at night at University of South Carolina. My day job was doing things like ordering computers and collecting money. The business school curriculum included an IT course, and one of my assignments was to create a flow chart. It was easy to do, and I showed it to one of the IBM sales reps. He thought that what I did was great, and said I should think about being a systems engineer. I wasn't completely sure what systems engineers did, but I took the company's aptitude test, and did well enough to become a systems engineer. They moved me from Columbia to Augusta, Georgia, and after three or four years, I realized that I was helping make all the salesmen rich. So I got a position in sales, and from there I moved up through a series of senior executive positions.

Marilyn was with me all the way, but she was struggling with several diseases. She suffered with Lyme disease for over 30 years. She endured an enormous amount of pain, but she was the most incredible, sweet, and caring lady I've ever known. My classmate, Kenneth Phelps, had become a brilliant and caring physician, and was well known and highly respected in the medical community. He stayed in touch with me over the years, and he would always ask how Marilyn was doing. I would keep him up to date on her symptoms, and he'd ask a lot of follow-up questions.

Along with all the other problems Marilyn was dealing with, once the Lyme disease started, she started having seizures. She had them every day, and they could go on for hours. They made her pain much worse, and the pain would make her seizures worse. It was a horrible cycle. One day Kenneth called me up. He said, "Has she ever tried Baclofen?" She hadn't. Kenneth wrote the prescription. She took the first pill while she was having a seizure, and fifteen minutes later, the seizure was gone. And she didn't have any more seizures. For the rest of her life. She died in November, 2024.

If I were to give advice to people, I'd say they should make a list of those who had a positive impact on their life. Keep track of them, and don't miss a chance to tell them what they meant to you. At some point they'll be gone, and you'll wish you'd made that phone call. Before he died, I made sure that Kenneth Phelps knew how much he meant to Marilyn and to me.

It's interesting to think about where we start, and see where we end up. It's interesting to go back in your life and think about the forks in the road that you didn't recognize at the time. Coming to BGA was a big fork in the road for me. If I hadn't come to BGA, I wouldn't have gone to Vanderbilt. Without Vanderbilt, I probably wouldn't gone into the ROTC. If I hadn't gone into ROTC, I wouldn't have gone into the Army and to Ranger School, and I would never have gone to Fort Carson and met Marilyn in Colorado. I thank my Dad every day for having the wisdom to send me to Battle Ground Academy. BGA was an incredibly positive experience for me.

The information in this narrative came from an interview that took place on April 28, 2025.

Paul Clements, Class of 1965

Even though I grew up less than half a mile from Montgomery Bell Academy, I ended up going to BGA, which was 18 miles to the south. Two of my classmates at Woodmont School, Tom Henderson and John Tompkins, were also going to BGA, but the stage for traveling to Franklin had already been set. When I was in fifth grade, my father took me to a basketball game at BGA. All I remember is DeBow Casey making long, two-handed set shots. The next fall, my father brought me to see a football game. And the following spring, I came back and took the entrance exam in the study hall.

Several of my future classmates turned out to be highly intelligent, but considering a few of the guys who got in, the test could've been something of a sham. I think BGA was hurting for students, and as long as a boy was reasonably literate, he was admitted.

The summer before I started BGA, I spent two months at Camp Hy-Lake. There was a close connection between Hy-Lake and BGA. They were both out of the same mold. Jonas Coverdale, who had just retired as the president of BGA, owned Hy-Lake. Paul Redick, who was about to begin his first year as headmaster, was the assistant head of the camp. And a lot of BGA teachers worked there during the summer. Before Ralph Brown, David Wood, and Jimmy French became my seventh-grade teachers, they were my counselors at Hy-Lake. Jimmy French was my geography teacher, and on the first day of school, I said, "Do I call you Jimmy, or Coach French?" He said, "Coach French."

I was struck by how antiquated BGA was. It seemed like things hadn't changed all that much since 1911, when the academic building was built. The floors creaked, the stairs creaked, and everything smelled old. And there were old pictures on the walls. You'd go down the hall and see all these guys who had gone to BGA over the past 50 or 60 years. One of the teachers, Daly Thompson, had been in the BGA graduating class of 1910. He'd come back to teach in 1914, and then left to fight in World War I.

And there were things to see from long before Mr. Thompson came along. The Battle of Franklin had been fought on the site of the school, and it wasn't unusual for a mini ball or a piece of shrapnel to be dug up on the campus. It didn't seem like much time had passed since the battle was fought. BGA just seemed old.

Even some of the seniors looked old. They looked like grown men. I was eleven when I started seventh-grade, and there were several burly guys walking around who needed a shave. Tom Fiveash could've passed for 40. Along with Jimmy French for Geography, I had David Wood for English and Ralph Brown for Math. I'd never had a teacher like Coach Brown. He was dynamic and charismatic. And Ernest McCord taught us Word Wealth down in Room One. He was a kind man, and he'd have the class play a word game called "Hangman" a lot. It was basically a blackboard version of the show, *Wheel of Fortune*, which would come to television a couple of decades later.

A day or two after school started, we had our first sub-freshman football practice. It was in a little half-acre field across Academy Street, just beyond the gym. Our coach was Johnny Bennett, who had just started teaching at BGA.

When Coach Bennett lined us up at the first practice, I was across from this guy who was a lot shorter than I was. We were supposed to take turns tackling each other. I was thinking, "This guy is too short to be any good." But tackling him was like running into a tree stump. Then it was his turn to tackle me. We were in the southeast corner of the field, and there were bushes right behind us. Coach Bennett said *hut*, and the short kid drove me back into the bushes. I ended up with pieces of hedge coming out of the earholes of my helmet. It didn't hurt, but he had totally dominated me.

Then I got to tackle again, and I decided to get serious. I took off and stayed low, but it was like running into a stump again. When his turn came, I ended up even deeper in the bushes. And he kept putting me into the bushes until we finally went on to another drill. After practice, we took our uniforms off to get dressed. When he took off his shirt, I began to suspect that what happened to me could've had something to do with all the muscles he had. His name was Roger Jackson, and we ended up being close friends. Less than a decade after he crushed me at practice, I would be in his wedding.

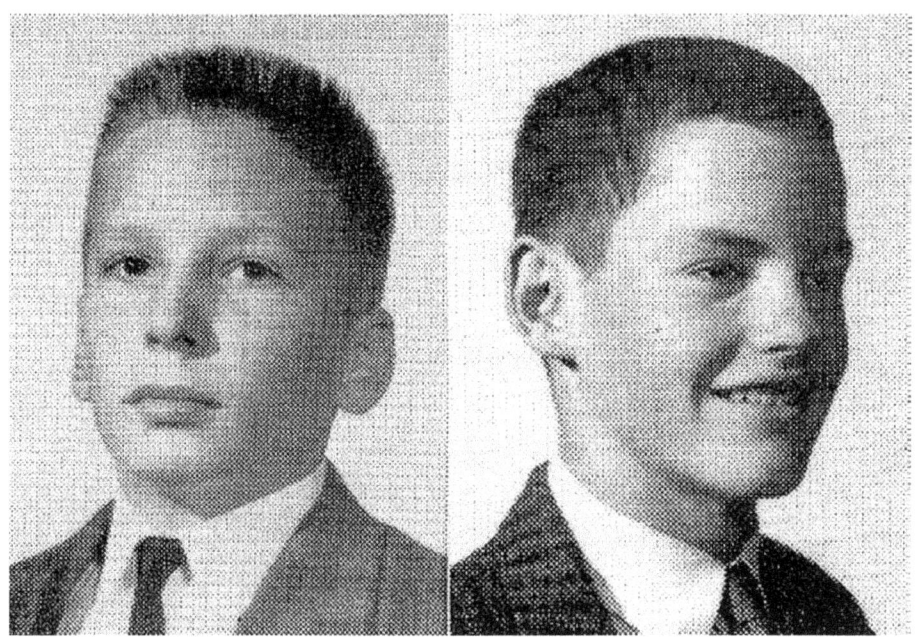

Roger Jackson and Bert Brown, 7th grade

Not too long after that, we were having another practice. The weather was lousy. Most of the eighth graders skipped practice, and Coach Bennett was furious. He took it out on everybody who showed up. We had head-on tackling for a lot of the practice. I got paired up with Bert Brown. For the entire drill. Bert not only weighed about 125 pounds, he was pretty familiar with puberty by then. I weighed ninety-something, and puberty was a long way off for me. Every time we'd hit helmets, I'd go black for a couple of seconds. I couldn't see anything, but I'd flail out with one of my arms. Over the course of multiple collisions, I think I tripped him up a couple of times. I didn't get in the next game, or in any other game that year. But the eighth graders who skipped practice all got to play. And, as usual, they lost.

Mr. Bennett also drove the BGA bus I took to school every morning. He drove the Hillsboro Road bus, and there was also a bus for the guys who came to school on Franklin Road. The buses had probably been used when they were bought, and they were pretty banged up. One of the more crucial defects involved the latches on the windows. There were times when somebody up front would have a moment of flatulence. Then there would be a growing chorus of groans, and row after row of bus riders would cover their noses with their shirts.

Somebody would usually stand up and try to hold his breath long enough to open a window. There were times when the guy would get the window down and put his head out into the fresh air, but other times it was like watching an execution. The guy would get weaker and weaker as he struggled with the latches, then his hands would slide down the glass like he was going into a sulphur-induced coma. And along with the occasional periods of near asphyxiation, people were always throwing broken pencils and anything else they could find at each other. The trip from Nashville to Franklin, including the routes along the side streets, took around 50 minutes, but it probably seemed a lot longer to Coach Bennett and his counterpart on Franklin Road.

I was devoted to BGA football. We'd have pep rallies in study hall on Fridays, and one of the cheers would start with, "Hope beat…" If we were playing Carthage, the chant would be, "Hope beat Carthage, Hope beat Carthage." Over and over and over, until just about everybody was fired up. The pep rally cheers were different from the cheers during the games. When we played a rural school, even though there were guys at BGA who lived on farms, one of the cheers would be, "Beat dumb farmers." The other team would have fans who lived out in the country. Some would be wearing their overalls, and there we were yelling, "Beat dumb farmers." It made me cringe a little, even back then.

Back in seventh and eighth grade, when there was a football game at BGA, instead of going home and having to come all the way back to school, I'd just stay in Franklin. Those Friday afternoons were idyllic. Other guys from my class stayed, too, and we'd play touch football, or find something else to do. Tom Henderson was always there. His grandparents lived not far from BGA on Lewisburg Pike. Tom's grandfather, Captain Tom Henderson, had gone to BGA around the turn of the century, and served in World War One. A couple of times, Tom and I had dinner with Captain Tom and Mrs. Henderson. They were both born in the 1880s, and they'd known all sorts of former slaves and Civil War veterans. They were from a different world.

Tom Henderson, 8th grade

Most of my classmates were as much in awe of the varsity football players as I was. We went to just about every game, but we spent more time on the sidelines playing Smear, also known as Smear the Queer, than we did watching the games. Somebody might have a little plastic ball, and whoever had the ball would try to stay on his feet for as long as he could. He'd run and dodge and fight people off, and when he got tackled, everybody usually jumped on top of him. Then somebody else would grab the ball and start running. BGA's 1959 team was pretty good, and we ended up going to Pulaski and watched them tie Manchester in the Butter Bowl.

That seventh-grade year moved on to basketball season, and David Wood, who had graduated from BGA only six years earlier, was the coach. I didn't make the team. Later on, Tom Henderson told me that when I was shooting layups, I kept going up off the wrong foot.

One of the most surprising things about BGA was how bad the food was at lunch. The breakfasts and dinners were supposed to be pretty good, but the lunches never got any better. We eventually understood that Mr. Akin was trying to save every penny he could. The milk was watered down. One day a week, we would have what were supposed to be hamburgers. But we called them scabs because of how thin they were. I ate a lot of white bread and peanut butter sandwiches, and the peanut butter usually had a pool of oil on top of it, which meant that we had to pour off as much of the oil as we could. After lunch we'd go out to the little grassy roundabout between the old dorm and the new dorm, and we'd played Smear.

For our class party that winter, we had what was billed as a "possum hunt." The site of our gathering was at a farm a few miles from Franklin on Lewisburg Pike. It was about where Sullivan Farms was eventually built, but back then it was way out in the country. It was cold, and the 30 guys in our class spent a couple of hours walking around in the woods and looking for possums in the dark. We made a lot of noise, and somehow we never saw even one possum. After our hunt, we ended up playing a big game of Smear out in front of an old mansion that looked like it was built before the Civil War. When 30 guys played Smear and everybody piled on whoever had the ball, it was a very bad idea to be on the bottom of the pile.

Rope Breaking, 1960

That spring we had the tug-of-war between the Greers and the Platos at Kinnard's Pond, which was near Willow Plunge. I was on the south side of the lake when the rope broke, and the Greers and Platos charged each other and met in the middle of the pond. It was only a foot or two feet deep, and guys were scrapping and wrestling and throwing mud. Later on somebody said that a car had been picked up and carried into the pond. They left it there with Mr. Smithson inside.

My eighth-grade year in football wasn't much better than my seventh-grade year had been. A new teacher named Bill Bradshaw was the coach, and I got to play right end for one offensive series during the entire year. We were playing MBA at BGA, and I caught a pass and managed to streak down the field for about three yards. And that was it. But the highlight of the year occurred one day at practice. My friend and nemesis, Tom Henderson, had torn up my math homework that day. I think I got a couple of demerits when I was trying to retaliate, and I was determined to get revenge.

We practiced on the baseball field. Tom was one of our best players, and he was returning punts. That's when I saw my opportunity. Somebody would kick the ball, and I was in line to go down and cover the punts. When my turn came, I took off early. Very much on purpose. I had Tom in my crosshairs, and I got to him just after the ball did. I put my helmet into the general area of his groin as hard as I could, and he went down. When he was getting up, he managed to mumble, "Good tackle," but it was a while before he was able to stand up straight.

When I was in eighth-grade, Cannon Mayes taught Mythology. His classroom was in the basement of the old dorm. Along with having us memorize the details of Greek and Roman deities, he would demonstrate how accurately he could throw a piece of chalk. Coach Mayes would wait until somebody was falling asleep, or not paying attention. He'd keep talking while he slowly reached back for the chalk. Then he'd fire it at whoever had attracted his attention. He was usually right on target.

I liked the headmaster, Mr. Redick. I had gotten to know him at Hy-Lake. When he was at camp, he was friendly and he smiled a lot. But it wasn't unusual for him to get mad and lose his temper when he was at school. Looking back, I suspect that he wasn't cut out to be a headmaster. He would've probably been much happier just coaching and teaching. But whether he was at camp or at school, he was a great storyteller.

Mr. Redick was very outspoken when it came to politics, and most of the teachers at BGA probably saw the world the same way he did. The 1960 presidential campaign between Richard Nixon and John F. Kennedy took place during my eighth grade year. Right before the election, we had an assembly, and Mr. Redick said something like, "Everybody who's for Nixon, stand up." Just about every student in study hall stood up. When he asked who was for Kennedy, only a handful of guys stood up. One of them was Winston Grizzard, whose nickname was "Weenie." He had a lot of guts. He participated in some of the civil rights demonstrations that took place in Nashville a few years later.

Ralph Brown and David Wood and Jimmy French were still my teachers when I was in eighth grade. Coach Brown and Mr. Wood taught math and English again, but Coach French taught history. I developed a love for the Civil War in that class. It was one of the best courses I ever took. Anywhere. On our tests we drew Civil War battlefields, including geographical details and where the various divisions were positioned. I was wired for history, and it meant a lot to be able to go to school where the Battle of Franklin was fought.

The BGA football team in my eighth grade year was awesome. Charlie Trabue, Duke Shackleford, Bobby Morel, the whole group – they were like demigods. They were unbeaten during the regular season, and accepted an invitation to play in the Clinic Bowl, which was the premier bowl in the state. Because BGA was such a small school, there was some question about whether we could sell many tickets, or draw enough fans to the game. Coach Brown got up at Assembly and said, "We're going to sell $10,000 worth of Clinic Bowl tickets." Everybody thought he was out of his mind. We ended up selling a lot more than that, and school spirit went through the roof. And we screamed ourselves hoarse at the Clinic Bowl, which we won, and which made BGA State Champions.

It didn't happen much, but one of the practical jokes that the upperclassmen would pull off was rolling a cannonball from the back of the study hall. The floor sloped down to the front, and there was no stopping a cannonball once it started rolling. The desks were bolted into the floor, and the cannonball would hit metal legs all the way to the stage. It was a little like a pinball machine.

Every now and then, something would happen and Mr. Redick would get incredibly angry. He'd jerk his glasses off and turn red. He'd look like he wanted to kill somebody. And, *of course*, that would egg some guys on. BGA was very authoritarian, and the big symbol of authority was the little silver bell on the table in study hall. When the teacher wanted everybody to be quiet, he would tap the top of the bell. The dinging was supposed to make whoever was talking be quiet. But there were times when somebody would take the clapper out of the bell. Mr. Redick saw that as a direct assault on authority.

And if somebody took the entire bell, he would get apoplectic. Bells kept disappearing, and one time he made the whole student body sit in study hall until somebody admitted to taking the bell. We all sat there for about an hour. A guy finally got up and confessed. It turned out that he hadn't even done it.

He just confessed so everybody else could leave. When I was in eighth grade, Geoff Winningham was president of the senior class and editor of the yearbook. His younger brother, David, came to BGA the next year, and was in my class. Several years later, David was cleaning out a closet, and he came across a box that had belonged to Geoff. When he opened it, the box was full of little silver study-hall bells.

When ninth grade came around, there were almost twice as many guys in my class as there had been the year before. The atmosphere of the school was completely different. There were all these strange guys fighting to establish themselves in the pecking order. It took a long time for everything to settle down.

I had Jimmy French again, but this time he was teaching first year Algebra. Coach Brown had gone from math to teaching Bible. When I was a freshman, my Latin teacher was Daly Thompson. Aside from how old he was, Mr. Thompson was noted for several things. One was the way he talked. He spoke with an unusually slow cadence. We'd be in Latin class, and he'd say, "Son, come up here and read for me please." He was very mild-mannered, but he wouldn't put up with disrespect or disobedience. He was in his 70s, but he could still supposedly do pull-ups and push-ups.

There was a kid in our class named John Mallernee. There were times when John could be a hellion. One day in study hall, he defied Mr. Thompson. Mr. Thompson came down off the stage, and got John by the back of his hair and pulled his head back on the desk behind him. Then he slapped him across the face a couple of times. Everybody in the study hall, including John, knew he had it coming. Mr. Thompson wasn't angry. He just walked back up to his seat on the stage, and went back to grading papers.

My sophomore English teacher was Boardman Stewart. He was probably 23 or 24, and he'd gone to college at Washington & Lee. He was very formal, and he was a stern task master. I wasn't doing that great until he had us read Shakespeare. For some reason it made sense to me. When my grades shot up, some of my friends said, "You've gotta be cheating," I said, "Off who? You guys are making 60s and 70s, and I'm making 80s and 90s."

In tenth grade I had been faced with the prospect of having Carl Smithson for Algebra II. He was a ferociously rigorous teacher. Three hours of homework a night, and you'd better do it all. Part of his method was hands on, meaning sometimes he would get physical with his students – in a painful but good natured way. But I was put in Bill Brown's class. He'd never taught algebra. He was a nice man, but between his lack of experience and my lack of interest in the subject, I didn't end up learning much algebra.

Boardman Stewart

When I was a sophomore, I had Bill Bradshaw for Ancient History. When it came to politics, he was a radical right-winger. He was a member of the White

Citizen's Council, which was to the right of the John Birch Society, and he was obsessed with communism. He preached that America was on the verge of being taken over by the communists, and that we might not make it to college before America fell. But Mr. Bradshaw was likeable, and he was a very good speaker. At some point he told us that he knew a man named Byron De La Beckwith. Many years later, De La Beckwith was convicted of killing the noted Civil Rights leader, Medgar Evers, in Mississippi in 1963. But I thought that if Mr. Bradshaw had seen a black person on the side of the road with a car broken down, that he would've stopped and tried to help. It was like he had a certain political story in his head, and he just couldn't let it go. But he was entertaining, and I ended up taking every one of his classes.

In October 1962, during my tenth-grade year, Mr. Redick stood up in Assembly and told us that a nuclear attack was possible. As soon as we were alerted, we were to immediately go outside and begin getting on the BGA buses. They would shuttle us to a nearby rock quarry out on Carter's Creek Pike. The Cuban Missile Crisis was unfolding, and the quarry contained a number of caves. It would be forty years before it was understood how very close we had come to seeing the world we had known come to an end.

Compared to what we would've endured in the wake of a nuclear attack, the pain we experienced was minimal. Along with the playful tortures of Mr. Smithson, we inflicted pain on each other. It probably had to do with BGA being an all-boys school, and because of all the testosterone there was. Some guys learned to pinch with the knuckles of their thumb and their middle finger, and it could draw blood. And some little fat kid walking around after lunch might get a red belly. He'd be thrown on the ground, and while somebody else held his feet and hands, another guy would pull up his shirt. Then he would get slapped on the stomach until his belly turned red. There was also what was called the smoking test. The victim would be held down, while somebody kept hitting him on the sternum with the knuckle of his middle finger until it hurt enough to stop. Along with all that, guys would routinely get slapped on the side the head from behind, or get tripped, or have the books they were carrying pushed out from behind and knocked on the floor.

Along with being the best basketball player at BGA, Tom Henderson was also a master organizer. Tom had been in the middle of our games of Smear when we were younger, and he was largely responsible for inventing the game we called Pile Drive. Pile Drive was pretty much like football, but the game had to be played in slow-motion. One team would have some big running back, and because the tacklers were moving in slow motion, the runner was hard to bring down. It would end up that the team on offense would be pushing their runner from behind, and the team on defense would be pushing him back. That would go on until one side finally collapsed, and there would be a huge pile.

Guys got hurt a lot, and Bill Brown, who was the varsity football coach by then, finally banned his players from playing Pile Drive. The rest of us kept playing. If we ate lunch fast enough, we'd have about 30 minutes for our clothes to get ripped, to be poked in the eye, or to have our ankles sprained. It was really fun. Tom was also the commissioner of two basketball events that took place on the outdoor court behind his house in Nashville. Varsity players were eventually prohibited from playing in either the Henderson Invitational League or the Henderson Invitational Tournament.

Roger Jackson, who crushed me in our first football practice back in seventh grade, had become one of my closest friends. He was on the wrestling team, and we took each other on all the time. There were times when I could almost stay with him, but years later it occurred to me that Roger might not have been trying as hard as I was. Mr. Redick apparently noticed, and he eventually came up to me in the hall. He said I should be on the wrestling team. I appreciated him taking an interest in me, but I didn't end up doing it.

I hadn't gotten any demerits back when I was in seventh or eighth grade, but when I was a sophomore, I got some bogus demerits from Mr. Oxley for standing up right as Assembly was starting. Some books had fallen off my desk, and I was picking them up. I thought, "Okay, if that's how things are going to be…" I still had braces at that time, and I started bringing extra packets of little orthodontic rubber bands to school. I'd shoot them against the blinds that were behind the teachers in study hall. They'd made a noise when they hit the blinds. The teacher would look around to see who did it, but I never got caught. Sometimes I got demerits when I hadn't done anything, but I never got demerits when I deserved them. It became sort of a game.

Demerits were given for all sorts of infractions. And because BGA was so restrictive, guys took a lot of pleasure in seeing what they could get away with. One thing they did was speak in code about forbidden subjects. Subjects like sex. It wasn't unusual to hear the question, "Have you ever picked any fruit?" As long as you only got one or two demerits in a week, you didn't have to serve any time. But every demerit after that meant an hour of detention. When all the other students went home after school on Friday afternoon, you had to stay in study hall. If you got five demerits in a week, that meant you had three hours to serve off. If you couldn't serve everything off on Friday, you had to come back to school on Saturday. And sometimes people got a whole lot more than five demerits.

Assemblies could be pretty memorable. When the civil rights movement was picking up steam, Mr. Redick stood up on the stage and said something like, "I can promise you this – a Negro student will *never* be admitted to Battle Ground Academy." It was a solemn decree. Around the start of my junior year, things at BGA were changing, at least for me. Some guys had seemed like adversaries when we were freshmen, but we had finally gotten to know each other. A feeling of closeness and acceptance was setting in.

That fall, Jimmy French had daily pre-conditioning sessions for basketball. We'd go out and do a lot of running. I really wanted to play. I practiced basketball all the time, and I'd gotten a lot better. We'd run 440s, and I tried to win every time. Coach French finally said, "You're a good runner. Why don't you go run Cross Country?" But I could've cared less about Cross Country. Then he said, "I'll tell you what, if you'll run Cross Country, I'll guarantee that you'll make the B-Team."

Not long after Cross Country was over, I was in Mr. Bradshaw's American Government class in Room One. It was around noon on Friday, November 22nd, 1963. The last period before lunch. I was sitting on the back row. Bear Robertson came to the door and interrupted the class. He said, "'Somebody shot the president." Mr. Bradshaw thought it was a joke. Guys were always messing with him, but he was good natured about it. He just said something like, "Oh, that would be a tragedy." When class let out, we all went to the student center, where there was a little TV room. The president *really had* been shot. A few guys saw it as a tragedy, but overall it was like a carnival. There was a widespread perception that Kennedy was an "unconscious agent of the Communist Party," and there was a sense of excitement about seeing a piece of history unfold.

On TV that night, there was nothing but assassination programming, and a few other guys and I went over to Tom Henderson's house. It was raining, but we just played basketball outside until it was pretty late.

There was another tragedy five months later. I was riding home on Hillsboro Road. Mike Everhart was driving, and Buddy Calvin was beside him in the front seat. We had just passed the intersection of Hillsboro Road and Old Hillsboro Road. I was doing homework in the back, and I heard a gasp. Mike pulled off the road, and he and Buddy opened their doors and ran back down the road. I had no idea what was going on.

John Jackson, Junior Year

John Jackson's station wagon was upside down in a flooded creek. Jim Smith was in the water, holding his arm. John was on the bank screaming, and blood was coming out of his ears. Steve Barnes and Jim Parish and Winky Cherry were wet and they were standing on the bank. I didn't want to go down there. Instead I started directing traffic so the ambulance could get through. John had a history of driving too fast. He had pulled out to pass a car, and when he whipped back into his lane, his station wagon hydroplaned right through the guard rail. That was before the time of seatbelts, and John was thrown out. He screamed for a little longer, and when he quit screaming, he began to turn blue. The ambulance finally came, and we followed it to Vanderbilt. We were saying, "He'll be alright," but by then he was already dead.

Pretty soon after that, a highway patrolman came to Assembly and showed a film called *Mechanized Death*. It showed actual traffic accidents. There was lots of blood and guts and screaming, and victims were shown dying on the scene. Two or three students fainted right there in study hall.

By the time senior year rolled around, it seemed like everybody in our class had become pretty good friends. That year I had Mr. Bragg for English, which meant memorizing parts of the Canterbury Tales. Mr. Bragg didn't talk about being on Iwo Jima, or how he'd helped clean Japanese soldiers out of caves. And I had waited until my senior year to take Biology under Jimmy Gentry. His descriptions of old time Franklin were really compelling, but he never said a word about being a liberator of Dachau. And I never heard about Mr. Smithson being in the Battle of the Bulge and winning a Bronze Star.

The 1964 Olympics took place in October. I had a few creative classmates, and somebody decided that along with contests between the Greers and Platos, there could be additional competitions. One was called the "The Cripple Derby." There were several guys in school who had been stricken with polio when they were children, and a couple of them might have helped plan the event. I don't remember that ridicule had anything to do with it, and most or all of the crippled guys participated. Around the same time, somebody came up with "The Blubber Derby" for the guys who were overweight. There were several participants, and they seemed to take the competitions seriously.

When we were seniors, Spencer Holt taught Physical Education. When he introduced soccer in P.E. class, we went ahead and played the game, but it was kind of a joke. After a while, Mr. Holt was crazy enough to put together a public exhibition. It took place at BGA – at halftime of one of the football games. Those of us who weren't on the team took the field, but we didn't play the game the way it was supposed to be played. Along with tripping whoever we could, we didn't try to evade defenders. When somebody started toward us, we'd just kick the ball at them as hard as we could. It was quite a while before soccer became a popular sport in the area.

Roger Jackson was not only as tough as nails, he was a good student. He was probably the most admired guy in our class, but he had zero interest in being popular. That he befriended me spoke volumes about how independent he was. Being a boarding student, he didn't usually watch television, but he loved the series, *Rawhide*. He said he liked *Rawhide* because of the way it presented courage and honor. That was pretty much the code that Roger followed.

One weekend, several boarding students – from Roger and George Elder all the way down to seventh graders – were walking back to BGA after watching a movie in Franklin. They were in separate groups, and they'd almost gotten back to the campus. A couple of cars screeched up, and members of a local gang that called themselves the *Sundrops* piled out of the cars. They were guys from Franklin High School who had peroxided their hair, and one of the things they liked to do was fight.

Roger Jackson and George Elder, senior year

Almost everybody took off running. But running wasn't part of Roger's code. He just told George to stay where he was. Then, when the *Sundrops* were close enough, Roger charged the whole group. He started pummeling the first *Sundrop* he got to, and George's presence was enough to keep anybody else from intervening. After the *Sundrop* told Roger that he'd had enough, the guy's friends were trying to decide whether they should take him to see a doctor.

George was about 6'5" and weighed around 230 pounds, but he wasn't aggressive. He'd never been in a fight. One of the *Sundrops* finally said something insulting that reflected on George's mother, and he hit George in the stomach. Even though George hardly felt it, he didn't want Roger to kid him later on about not hitting the *Sundrop* back. George didn't want to hurt the guy, so he made sure he used his left hand. He thought he could throw a quick jab, and that would be that. But the *Sundrop* moved in at just the wrong time, and George broke the guy's nose. Both of the injured *Sundrops* were taken to a doctor, and Roger and George became instant celebrities. But neither one of them – and especially not Roger – thought it was that big a deal.

There hadn't been a tug-of-war since the debacle at Kinnard's Pond in 1960, and Mr. Redick decided that it was time to have another one. Roger was the president of the student body, and Mr. Redick appointed him to locate a rope. I drove Roger to Nashville, and we went to some business on Broadway that had a rope big enough to withstand the force of almost 300 boys pulling in opposite directions. The rope was delivered to the school later on, and a site – an area beside the bridge on Highway 96 over the West Harpeth River – was selected by members of the faculty as the site of the tug. A news crew from Channel 4 in Nashville came out and filmed the event, and the next morning on *The Today Show*, a nationwide audience saw me and the rest of the Greers get pulled into the river.

The week before we graduated, we had our Baccalaureate service at the Franklin Methodist Church. I don't remember who the speaker was. We sat on the first four or five rows of the church, and the faculty was seated behind the pulpit, where the choir usually sat. They were only about 30 feet away from us. We just had to survive for one more week and we would be safe from demerits, but every one of the teachers was staring at us.

Everything was going okay until Mr. Thompson's wife gave the musical part of the program. She was in her 70s, and her best days as a vocalist were long gone. She started singing some old-time operatic song. It had a lot of high-pitched notes, and I didn't know if I could get through it without cracking up. The teachers knew that everything could go sideways, and they were glowering at us. They might as well have been saying, "If anybody even *looks* wrong, you're in big trouble."

So we were sitting there, and I looked at George Elder, who was sitting in front of me. His neck had turned red, and I knew he was about to lose it. All I could do was cover my mouth and try to keep myself under control. I tried to be inconspicuous, but my body started to shake involuntarily. When I shook, the pew started squeaking, too. And everybody could hear it.

It sounded like Mrs. Thompson was finally wrapping up her performance, but then she started another stanza. It was like, "*Oh My God. No.*" And the longer she sang, the more off-key she got. All the pews were squeaking by then, but nobody said a word. Guys had tears coming down their cheeks, but somehow everybody was able to keep it together. The teachers all knew what we were going through, but they just kept staring at us. It was one of the most excruciating periods of time I ever experienced. One of my aunts was sitting in the balcony, and she laughed so hard that she wet her pants.

A few days later, we had our graduation ceremony in the gym, and then we walked down to the flagpole beside Columbia Avenue and sang the Alma Mater. I hated to leave BGA, but I didn't want anybody to know how emotional I felt. I could've gone to MBA, but I saw MBA as mostly focusing on preparing guys from affluent Nashville families to eventually go into business. BGA was different. At the end of the day, it didn't seem to be about money.

The culture of BGA was shaped by men from rural areas in the South. It seemed like most of them were dedicated to molding students to become the sorts of men they admired. Mr. Thompson had been raised in Pocahontas, Arkansas. Mr. Akin was from a little locale in western Williamson County called Burwood. Mr. Redick was from Camden, in West Tennessee. Mr. Bragg was from McMinnville, in Warren County. And Mr. Smithson and Coach Gentry both grew up in poverty in Williamson County. Along with a few other teachers like Ralph Brown and Jimmy French, they set the tone of what BGA was about. Not that BGA didn't have plenty of flaws. It did. But the way I saw it, the overall intention of the teachers who made up the core of BGA was to instill character traits like honesty, effort, resilience, and authenticity in the students they taught.

I've never stopped thinking about the Battle of Franklin. After my classmates and I gathered around the flagpole on May 29th, 1965, I imagined us as soldiers. We were sixty-eight guys just about to march off and face life.

PAUL CLEMENTS, CLASS OF 1965

1965 Graduation

The information in this narrative came from an interview conducted by Patrick Roberts and Jason Gregg on June 10, 2012, and was supplemented by the editor.

Bill Armistead, Class of 1969

My great-great-grandfather was Joseph Leonard Parkes. He was a banker with the old Harpeth Bank in Franklin. He'd come over on the boat from England at the age of 15. His daughter, who he named Americus Jessie Parkes, married my great-grandfather, George Armistead Sr., who was the editor and publisher of *The Review Appeal*. They were both involved with BGA from close to the time it was founded.

My father, Leonard H. Armistead Jr., was called Bill. His father had gone to BGA, and his great-grandfather and great-great-grandfather were on some of the school's first boards. He started there as a seventh grader in the fall of 1934, and graduated in 1940. He kept all this memorabilia from his high school years – photographs of the football teams he was on, class pictures, and what passed for yearbooks. Back then, BGA really didn't always put out an annual. Sometimes they just took the school newspapers and put them together at the end of the year. That was their yearbook, and it was called the Cannonball.

My father grew up with a guy named Jim Short, but I think Jim was a year older. When they were in the seventh or eighth grade, some older guy bet Jim that he wouldn't eat a dead rat. They put it between two pieces of bread, and he took a bite. I think my father took a bite, too. Those juniors and seniors would coax seventh and eighth graders to do all kinds of stuff. Mr. George Briggs was the headmaster when my father was at BGA. He would play marbles with the students. The agreement was that if anybody could beat Mr. Briggs at marbles, everybody got a day off from school. And the tug-of-war started while my father was a student. I remember seeing a Tug-of-War in the late 1950s. It was held on Main Street. Instead of getting pulled into the Harpeth River, the losing side got soaked with the water from a fire hydrant.

Tug-of-War on Main Street, 1959

Franklin was a small place back when I was growing up. I lived on 3rd Avenue, right down from the square. It was only five or six minutes from BGA. I started going to events at BGA when I was about five years old. If I wanted to walk, I could cut through yards and get there pretty fast. The first events my brother and I went to were football games. The first game I saw was probably in 1955 or 1956.

A lot of BGA supporters would be there, and the visitors would bring along a lot of supporters. My father would stand down by the fence on the BGA side, closest to the main school buildings. We would hang out with him for a while, and then we'd go back behind the stands. We'd play kill the man with the ball and that kind of stuff, and I quickly learned how to keep from getting hurt. Later on I went to basketball games. One time, even though I was only in the sixth grade, I got to ride on the bus with a bunch of students to a basketball game at Columbia High School. When we were driving by CMA, we saw the boys in their uniforms, and we all started screaming, "Bell Hop!"

Back then, Franklin might as well have been 100 miles away from Nashville. Except for a couple of restaurants, Franklin would close down at 5:30. There weren't many doctors, and at that time there were no specialists in Franklin. There were only about six lawyers, and if you had a big legal problem, you had to go to Nashville. Franklin was kind of like Mayberry. There was always someone watching you. Usually, before you got into real trouble, somebody would grab you and tell you to go home. Unless there was a ballgame, the only thing to do in Franklin on a Friday or Saturday night was see a movie on Main Street. Mr. Bowen, who we called Bobo, ran the movie theater. We spent a lot of time there when we were growing up.

My parents divorced when I was about 11, but I had teachers – mainly men – who took me under their wing. When I went to BGA it was just guys. About a third of the students were from Franklin and Williamson County, about a third were boarders, and a third were from Davidson County.

Within a few months after each of us was born, my father had signed up my brother and me to go to BGA. After I graduated from Franklin Junior High in 8th grade, I think 13 of us came to BGA. It was just a great place. There was a lot of camaraderie. Along with the Franklin guys who went with me to BGA, I met people from Nashville and boarding students who would become lifelong friends.

But a lot of my friends didn't want anything to do with BGA. Some guys had gone to Franklin High School, and when I was older, I ended up going to a dance or two over there. When I did, I kept my friends close. There were a lot of guys from the high school who probably wanted to tear into me – just because I went to BGA. They didn't want anybody from BGA coming over there. I'd see a few of my old friends, and I'd say, "Don't y'all get too far away from me. If somebody grabs me, I might need you."

There were some big differences between BGA and Franklin Junior High. Although the classes were about the same size, you weren't getting away with things like not doing your homework. I went from doing homework that took an hour or two, to staying up till midnight or one o'clock every night. It was *quite* a change. Being on time at BGA was very important, in athletics, in academics – in everything. Teachers were always watching you. When I was a freshman, I walked into English class and I got a demerit from Mr. Hainge because I didn't have an ink pen. I got mad, but the next time, I brought a pen. There was always the threat of demerits. If you got too many demerits, you had to serve time in study hall, or work for a certain amount of time.

When I was in the 9th grade, I probably had 90 guys in my class. When I graduated there were 56, and that was after bringing in 15 new students. So after my freshman and sophomore year, several were asked not to come back. Either for academics or bad behavior. It was a wild crowd. Some of the upperclassmen would haze the younger guys. They'd call us street urchins. Every once in a while, in study hall, they'd hang one of us out the window, but nobody bothered us much after we got to be sophomores and juniors.

The study hall was on the second floor of the main building on campus. Everybody had an assigned seat, and you had it for the whole year. At the front of the room was the stage. It was where Mr. Redick stood during assembly, and where we had chapel and speakers and plays and whatever else. The seventh and eighth graders were up at the very front, close to the stage. There was an aisle behind them, and the freshmen sat on the other side of the aisle. The sophomores and juniors sat behind the freshman, and the seniors were in the very back.

The floor sloped up toward the back of the room, and when you were a senior, sitting in the back, you really thought you'd arrived. The library was behind the study hall. Sometimes guys would roll pennies down from the back. If there was a new teacher keeping study hall, or an old teacher who wasn't quite with it, they could get away with it.

I was a freshman in the fall of 1965, and Coach Bill Brown asked Harry Blackburn and I if we wanted to try out for the varsity. I was foolish enough to say yes. We'd been practicing for a week, and the older guys were beating the heck out of me. It was just awful. I kept wondering, *why did I come out here?* The second week, Coach Brown came in and said, "We're going to have a scrimmage tomorrow night, guys. Then he looked at me. "You don't need to come over here. Don't worry about it." Harry was very athletic, and he ended up making the team.

Bill Brown

In 1966, when I was a sophomore, I didn't make the varsity football team. I think there were only had 28 guys on that team. They won the state championship. I was on the B-Team that year, but we practiced with the varsity every Wednesday. They were fast and tough, and it was horrible. We'd all look at each other and go, *gosh almighty, why are we doing this?* Don Denbo would knock me down, and then he'd say, "Are you alright?"

There was a drill where three guys would be standing up, and another guy would run into them one at a time. They would try to butt the guy who was running. One day I had to go against Don Denbo, Steve Robinson, and Johnny Moran. They were all great football players, and they were all *big*. I thought, *Why did I have to get with these three?* Denbo was about five-foot nine, and he was powerful. He just had this *spring*. Steve Robinson was about 6-3 and he weighed over 200. Johnny Moran weighed about 230. I wasn't doing the drill right, and I was hurting. Bobby Gentry pulled me over. He said, "If you don't change, they're going to kill you. You doing it wrong." I finally caught on. I guess the lesson I learned is that you're going to have to do things in life that you don't like, and that they're not really as bad as you think they're going to be.

The rivalry between BGA and Franklin High School was still going on, and every once in a while, guys from Franklin would show up and try to pick a fight with some of the dorm students. But football players like Don Denbo and Harry Ford, who both played at Tennessee later on, also lived in the dorms. One day Mr. Akin said, "I hate to see you boys fighting with them, but if they come up here again and pick on the little boys, that's okay."

I got hurt in my junior year, and I was out for most of the season. Bill Cherry was the new coach, and

Bobby Gentry was the assistant. We were the defending state champions, and we had seven players back who started on the state championship team. We won the first game at Hendersonville, and everybody was excited. But we didn't win another game. At the end of the year, we played Jackson at BGA, and they beat us 40-0.

Mr. Redick was the headmaster when I came to BGA. I knew to watch out for him. He had a canoe paddle with big holes bored in it, and I didn't want to experience that. When Mr. Redick was around, everybody kind of tightened up. One day he got mad about something, and he hit a guy with his fist and knocked him down. Nobody worried about the school getting sued back then. What they worried about was keeping the buildings in one piece. BGA was an old school. The floors in the main building always creaked when you were coming up the stairs to the study hall. I can hear it now.

The first dance I remember was in the gym when I was a freshman. Along with the Exotics, a black band called the Spidells was playing. Everything was going fine, but after about 30 minutes, Mr. Redick went up to the microphone and said, "This dance is over." Everybody kind of looked at each other. He either didn't like the way they were dressed, or the way they were moving, and he just stopped it.

Along with coaching football, Bill Brown was the track coach. Later that year, I was out getting ready for track season. It was February, and it was cold. There were probably eight or nine guys on the varsity.

Bobby Patterson

Those guys were really good. Sam Rutherford was a great distance guy. George Silvey, Harry Ford, Alex Steele, and Jack Milam were sprinters. I looked down near the gym, and I saw Bobby Patterson. He was a senior and he'd won the state championship in the high jump when he was a junior. This is before there were classifications, so there was only one state champion.

Bobby was down there at the high jump pit with a black man. I went to Coach Brown. "Coach, who's the black guy down there with Bobby?" He said, "That's Ralph Boston." Ralph Boston had won the gold medal in the long jump in the 1960 Olympics. He'd gone to Tennessee A&I, and Bobby's father had hired him to coach Bobby. I remember Bobby talking to me one day before a meet. He said, "You nervous?" I told him, "Yeah, I'm always nervous." He said, "Well, don't worry about it. It'll be over fast. It's not like a football game."

Bobby went to Tennessee on a football scholarship. He was big – 6'2" and he weighed over 200. Man, he was something.

The track, which ran around the football field, wasn't 440 yards like most tracks. It was only about 380 yards. Right between the track and the old dormitory, there was a little smoking shack. It was aluminum and it was hot, but if you had permission from your parents, you could go in there and smoke. But I don't know why in the world anybody ever wanted to go in there and smoke.

Mr. J.B. Akin was a big part of BGA. Along with everything else he did, he was the business manager. He was very tight with money. He'd gone to BGA, and he'd been teaching there for years. In the 1940s and 50s he was the only coach the school had. He even lined the football and baseball fields. He was a very nice man. I'd known him from church since I was about 12.

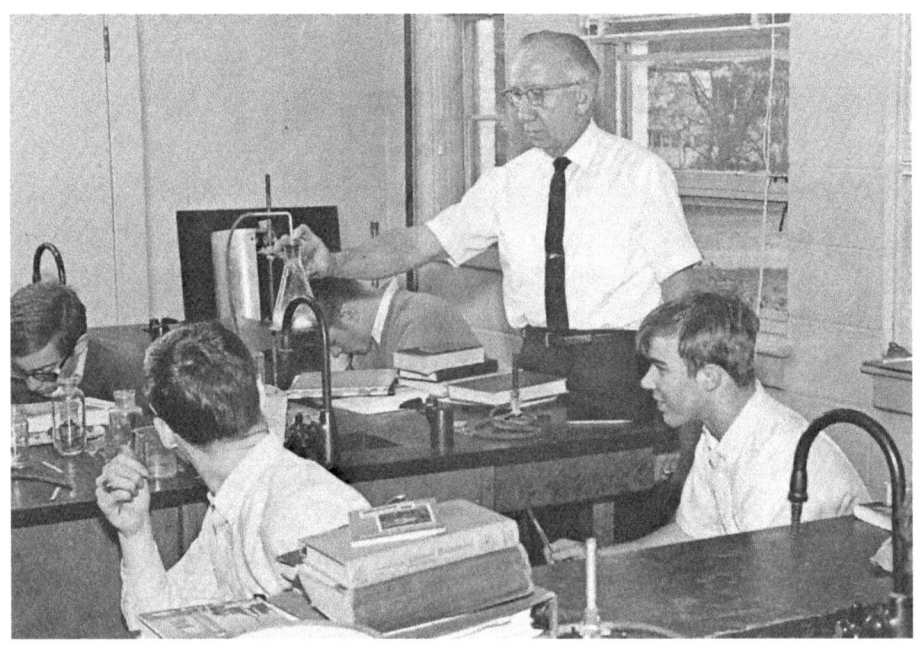

J.B. Akin

Mr. Akin taught chemistry and physics, which I tried to stay away from. I didn't do very well in math and science, so we never crossed paths in the classroom. He knew how to handle everybody. He made the points he wanted to make, but he didn't make people feel bad. The football field at BGA, James B. Akin Field, was named for him. He was a great man.

Bill Bradshaw was another teacher at BGA who stood out. He was the tennis coach, he ran the bookstore, and he drove one of the buses from Nashville. He was also the tennis pro at Hillwood Country Club, and he owned a construction company that specialized in building tennis courts. He taught history and civics. He said exactly what he thought. He thought the communists were trying to take over the United States. If you wove that into a paper you were writing for him, you were going to do fine. But he could be cantankerous. I remember the day he got fired from BGA. He came into class and said, "Well, they finally hung Old Brad." That was near the end of Mr. Redick's reign.

Daly Thompson was an iconic teacher at BGA. He was getting close to 80 years old. He was a BGA graduate and he taught Latin. He had been a wrestler in his day, and he had big hands. If you didn't listen to Mr. Thompson, he'd come over and grab you, and he could throw you across the room. I saw him do it. Mr. Thompson was a no-nonsense kind of guy. He knew what everybody was doing.

Nothing got by him. If he said, "Son, don't make me come to you," you needed to stop whatever it was you'd been doing. He died when I was a junior.

His wife taught tap dancing. She'd bring her class to perform at BGA, and we'd see some of our friends tap-dance. I wanted to get into it because of the girls, and I asked my father if I could take lessons. He said, "You are *not* going to be tap-dancing." *Thank goodness he didn't let me start tap-dancing.* I didn't have any teachers that were women. But I should've taken typing from Mrs. Redick, or speech from Mrs. E.C. Duke. Mrs. Libby Fryar was the librarian for part of the time I was there.

Another unusual teacher was Carl Smithson. He taught math, and math was not one of my subjects. When we were seniors, the bright guys took trigonometry and stuff like that. I was one of the seniors who just took algebra. Mr. Smithson would be teaching at the front of the room, and if he heard something going on, he'd pick up an eraser. He could hit you right between the eyes even if you were sitting in the back row. *Pham!* And if you didn't behave, he'd put you up front. He had a ruler and he'd start hitting you on your hand. *God*, that hurt. I did what I could to avoid that. I made a C in Mr. Smithson's college algebra class. I think I got the C just so he could get rid of me. But when I took algebra in college, I made an A. When I came back and told Mr. Smithson, he looked at me like I was crazy. He just said, "I'm not sure I can believe that."

Mr. Bragg was head of the English department. He had started at BGA in 1950, the year I was born. He taught us Senior English, and we learned how to write themes. We also had to memorize poems from *The Canterbury Tales,* but I can't tell you what they were now. I've put most of that out of my mind. One day something happened, and he said, "Y'all are one of the worst classes we've ever had at BGA." Later on, I found out that he said the same thing about every three years.

Bobby Gentry taught algebra. He'd say, "You're trying to memorize this instead of learning how to do it. Don't memorize it. Let me show you how you do it." He was a great guy. His brother, Jimmy Gentry, taught biology. Most of us hadn't wanted to take biology, but he made it fun. He was also an artist, and he would draw all sorts of things.

The junior-senior prom was supposed to happen in the spring of 1968, when I was a junior. But Martin Luther King was killed in early April, and Franklin was put under martial law. There were a lot of racial problems in Franklin after that. A large part of the black community backed up to BGA, so those seniors just didn't have a prom. But the dances were a lot of fun. There were girls from Harpeth Hall and St. Cecilia and Franklin High School, and some of the guys in the dorm would have dates with girls from places like Columbia or Lewisburg.

Back then, we had high school fraternities. I was a member of Delta Sigma fraternity. I had friends in Nashville who went to MBA, Ryan, Overton, Hillsboro, and Peabody. And I met a lot of Nashville girls because of all the sororities. We'd have dances in the summertime at somebody's house. There might be 350 people there, and we'd hire cops to keep things under control. It was fun, and the fraternity would make some money.

During the summer, I spent a lot of time at Willow Plunge, which was on Lewisburg Pike. It was just past a little hamburger joint called the Gilco. It was owned by the Kinnard family, and my father had worked there back in the 1930s. There were two large spring-fed pools. Part of what I did was work as a lifeguard. The pools weren't chlorinated. They had to be drained every night, and then refilled. But sometimes the pumps that drained them would break down. When that happened, I'd be out there all night. There were big diving boards. There were locker rooms. There was a pavilion, and people would come there to eat lunch. People would drive from miles away to go to Willow Plunge. On the 4th of July there might be 3,000 people out there.

Willow Plunge

And there were dances there at night during the summer. Bands like the Exotics and the Fairlanes. They played a lot of Rolling Stones, Four Tops, and that kind of music. One of the songs you heard a lot was called *Everlasting Love*. It was written by Mac Gayden, who'd gone to BGA in the 1950s. Lots of people from Nashville would come out for those dances. We'd be out there till two in the morning cleaning up. It was close to the Confederate Cemetery, and people would go back and drink beer in the cemetery. They'd trash it, and we'd have to go clean it up. Those were fun times, but Willow Plunge closed after the schools were desegregated in the 1960s. I don't think the Kinnards knew what to do about integration, so they just closed it.

Bunny Akin didn't come to BGA until I was a senior. It was his second time to teach there. I had to take one more science course to graduate, and he taught general science. The first day of class he walked in and saw me. He said, "Come out in the hall for a minute." He looked at me and said, "Now your father and my brother are close friends. But don't think that's going to get you anywhere in this class." I said, "Mr. Akin, I'm just in here to pass this course and graduate."

Before the start of my senior year, J.B. Akin was named the head of the school, but he decided to only serve for one year. He and I got to know each other even better than we had before. I was the president of the student council, and we had to do a lot of things together. One day in July, before my senior year, he called me up. I thought, I can't be in trouble. I haven't done anything. I haven't even *seen* him. He said, "You know, we used to have girl cheerleaders from schools outside of Franklin. What do you think about that?" I said, "Mr. Akin, I think it'd be great." He said, "Well, go get some." I said, "Sir?" He said, "Just go get some." Ruthie Brown was a great friend of mine. She lived down the street in Franklin, and she went to Harpeth Hall. And I was friends with Retha Rudolph. Her brother, Randy, had gone to BGA. And Miriam Woods' brother, Vaughn Woods, had also gone to BGA. so I thought, *Why I don't I just ask them?* I guess Mr. Akin trusted me. As far as I remember, he never asked me who they were.

We had a new coach my senior year. His name was Marvin Franklin. He'd gone to Vanderbilt in the 1930s, and had been a coach up East for many years. Bill Cherry and Carlton Flatt were his assistants. Coach Franklin couldn't remember anybody's name. He saw that it wasn't going to be a very good team, so he resigned before the season even started.

We were supposed to meet at BGA on a Sunday and go to football camp up at Camp Hy-Lake, like BGA teams always had. But Coach Jimmy Gentry showed up and said, "Everybody gather around. I've got some good news and some bad news. The good news is that we're not going to football camp. The bad news is that I'm the new coach." We looked over, and Marvin Franklin was riding away down Everbright Avenue on a bicycle. So Coach Gentry, who was the athletic director, had to come back and coach the team. He didn't want to do it, but he did. Although I respect him for taking over the team, we didn't win a game during my senior year.

There were locker rooms in the basement of the gymnasium. All kinds of things went on down there. They'd hide somebody's clothes, and whoever was missing his clothes would get mad. You'd just come in, hang up your stuff, and go to practice. But Mr. Akin had to deal with a scandal when I was a senior. People were getting their wallets taken. There weren't any locks on the lockers. They were wide open.

Mr. Akin just took the bull by the horns. He said, "We're going to find out who is doing this. It's not going to happen again. We're going to put money in a few wallets, and have somebody watching." Well, they caught the guy. He was one of my classmates. But Mr. Akin didn't kick him out. The guy ended up graduating, and I think Mr. Akin's lenience made a difference in his life.

The competition between the Greers and Platos was a big part of BGA. We had things like track meets and tennis matches. And of course there was the tug-of-war. I was a Greer, and while I was there, we won three of the four tug-of-wars. I remember the year we lost. We started pulling too late. The other side grabbed the rope and started pulling, and it was over in 30 seconds. When they said "get ready," we weren't ready.

BGA Jamborees are another great thing I remember. There would be a track meet and baseball game, and a car would be auctioned off. And there was a fish fry. There would be a crowd of people on the campus that day, and it brought a lot of attention to the school. It was kind of a send-off for us seniors.

I felt a real sense of security at BGA. I really felt comfortable there. It was tough to leave. Everybody else seemed pretty excited, but I had very mixed emotions about graduating. Our graduation was held on the football field at five o'clock. May 30th, 1969. I remember going up in the football stands that afternoon, and just looking around. I was pretty nostalgic about it.

I got a teaching certificate when I was in college. I thought I wanted to come back to BGA and be a coach. I ended up going to law school instead, but I was serious about wanting to come back to BGA.

My family has been connected with BGA for five generations. BGA is a great institution. It's changed over the years, but it still feels like the same place. We've always been just a little different. It has a lot of heritage – families that have been around here for a long time. Battle Ground Academy is one of the best things in my life, and I'm proud of the school. If it hadn't been for BGA, I don't know how my life might've turned out.

The information in this narrative came from an interview that took place on July 20, 2012, and from subsequent conversations.

Bob Smithson, Class of 1970

My father was Carl Smithson. He taught math at BGA from 1952 to 1970. Dad was born in Williamson County in 1921, and he was raised on a dairy farm out near Peytonsville. His father was a very big man. I only have very dim memories of him, but I remember that he couldn't use one of his hands. His children had to do a lot of work on the farm. One of Daddy's jobs was to milk the cows. His father was a disciplinarian. Before he spanked his children, he would bar the door to keep them inside.

There had been a well-known feud in the eastern part of Williamson County between the Bennetts and the Smithsons. People in both families had been killed, and it went on for years. Some members of the Smithson family had been involved in the conflict, but Dad wanted to stay away from all that. That was probably where he got his drive to get an education. Dad had to walk to school. It was a one-room schoolhouse on Henpeck Lane, and it looked like a shack. Because of the Depression, he didn't go straight through high school. After he went to Franklin High School as a freshman, he left home and worked for the Civilian Conservation Corps. He didn't go back to Franklin for his sophomore year until 1941.

Dad got his nickname, *Goat*, when he was playing football at Franklin. The assistant coach was J.B. Akin. Dad butt-tackled, which meant that instead of tackling with his shoulder, he'd butt the runner with his face and his forehead. That was back when helmets didn't have facemasks, and Dad broke his nose in one of the games. There was blood all over the place. The referee called timeout and made him leave the game, but as soon as the bleeding stopped, he went he went back on the field and started butt-tackling again. After that, people called him "Goat."

1941 Franklin team (Smithson #22, front row, 2nd from right)

When he enlisted in the army in November of 1942, he was twenty-one years old, but he'd only had two years of high school. He left around the time his family moved to a small farm out on the Murfreesboro Road. In the summer of 1943, when Dad was stationed at Camp Jackson in South Carolina, his sister accidentally poured some kerosene on a fire, and both she and his mother were killed.

Daddy never would talk about World War Two, but we heard stories about what he did from Hap Rittenhouser, a man we called Uncle Hap. He and my father had served in the same unit – company D in the 398th Infantry Regiment of the 100th Infantry Division in the Seventh Army. Daddy was a sergeant in a mortar platoon, and he operated a 30-caliber machine gun. Along with being a machine-gunner, sometimes he was sent forward to serve as a spotter for mortar teams. He was supposedly the only southern boy – and the only country boy – in his unit.

They were serving in France, and Uncle Hap said they were on the southern side of the Black Forest during the Battle of the Bulge. Their unit was ordered to pull back and solidify their lines, and they were attacked during the night. There was hand-to-hand combat, and although Uncle Hap said they couldn't be sure who was who, he thought daddy might have killed four different people in the fight. And on another occasion, Dad captured seven Germans with a pistol. He won a bronze star for that. He had nightmares about the war for years. When we were living at BGA, he would wake up thinking he was fighting Germans.

Dad's unit had gotten as far as Stuttgart when the war in Europe ended, and the next year he was discharged as a master sergeant. He had served for 39 months. By then he had decided that he wanted to become a teacher, but he hadn't finished Franklin High School. So he went to Mr. Daly Thompson, who had been the principal at Franklin when my father was a student. He was still the principal when Dad came home in 1946. When he asked Mr. Thompson what he should do, Mr. Thompson said, "Let's go talk to Peabody College."

When Peabody wouldn't take him, Mr. Thompson took him to Trevecca Nazarene College, and Dad enrolled there. While he was at Trevecca, he met his first wife, who was also a Trevecca student. They got married in 1948, and my sister was born the next year. But six months later, my father lost his wife. After Dad graduated from Trevecca, Mr. Thompson took him back to Peabody, and helped him get a scholarship for his Master's degree. Dad was a shoe salesman while he was in school, but then the Korean conflict broke out.

Dad was called back into the army, and he was put in charge of a platoon of soldiers with a history of being absent without leave. He was ordered to bring the AWOLs back to camp. He didn't want to bring them in and have them run away again, and he requested that they be kept in the brig until he could round them all up. When he finally got everybody back, he had himself locked himself in a cell with them. There was a knock-down, drag-out fight, and after Dad walked out, there weren't any more problems with AWOLs. He had a way of asserting himself.

In 1951, the year Dad got out of the service, he married my mother. It was too late to get a teaching position, and he went back to selling shoes. Mr. Coverdale and Mr. Redick had come to BGA, and Daly Thompson recommended that Mr. Coverdale hire Dad at BGA. When he started teaching in 1952, we were living in Nashville. Dad would drive the bus that took day students to BGA in the morning, and drive them back to Nashville in the afternoon.

We still hadn't moved onto the campus when a goat was left in Room One. From what I heard, it was an old goat with spiral horns out to the side. It was left in there all night with some hay, and the next morning the room stunk. Dad walked in the room, and I'm not sure, but he might've ended up decking somebody. He supposedly started to walk out, but before he left he said, "I'm going to come back here in five minutes, and this place better be smelling like a rose."

When it came to discipline, Dad followed Proverbs 13:24. "Whoever spares the rod hates his son..." When I was a little kid, I got the switch an awful lot, and I got spankings. And later in life, I'd be talking to Dad, trying to convince him of something. He'd be sitting there, and all of a sudden he'd raise his index finger. Whenever he did that, it meant, "I've heard all I want to hear. Leave me alone while you still can, and go to your room." But Dad also taught me about sports. How to kick a ball, and all sorts of things like that.

In 1959, we moved to 107 Everbright Avenue. The best house on campus was the Briggs' house.

It was on the corner of Everbright and Columbia Pike, and next door, on the west, was Mr. Akin's house. Then there was our house, and the Brown's house was next to us. Beside the Brown's house was the Bragg's house, and the Redick's house was the last one in the row. Our house was directly across the street from the horseshoe-shaped area between the dormitories and the academic building. The horseshoe enclosed a patch of grass, and there were bushes with thorns around the edge of the grass. They had been planted to keep boys from playing in there, but it didn't work. Guys were playing in there all the time.

I was in the second grade when we moved onto the campus, so I became a BGA boy when I was about seven. I remember that when we first moved to BGA, Cannon Mayes was living in the apartment at the back of our house, which later became my room. There was a bathroom, and if the door was shut, we didn't go back there. But after Coach Mayes moved out, that became our bathroom. By the time I was in third grade, I would go to study hall at night with the boarding students. BGA was not just a place for me, it was home.

There was a table for each teacher who lived on campus, and we ate with the boarding students. It was a family. We weren't allowed to sit until the head of the table, my father, allowed us to sit. And from the time I was around eight, I had to clean up the table. Dad was responsible for the four boys at his table, but he considered every student at BGA as his responsibility. He tried to be like a dad to as many boys as he could.

The teachers who lived on campus had rotating responsibilities. On one day Daddy would have to keep study hall. The next day it would be his turn to put the boys in the dorm to bed. There were two different dormitories, and he knew where all the creaky boards were. He'd sneak up and down the halls, and make sure they stayed in bed. If a teacher lived in an apartment in the dorm, he was also responsible for the students who lived there. If you were a munchkin, your room was on the lower level of the old dorm. As you became an upperclassman, you got to move up higher in the building. The upstairs was for juniors and seniors, and that could get pretty rowdy at times.

Being a faculty child meant I had a lot of older brothers, and I'd get picked on. They'd pop me upside the head with their class rings, and I got pretty good at ducking. But I really looked up to the older guys. Bobby Morel was my childhood hero. I remember sitting on the front porch, and listening to my father teach out of Room One. Later on, Dad moved up to Room 13, which was in what we called the new wing. On a lot of nights he would be up in his classroom having help sessions. There might be 15 or 20 kids up there.

When the library and the student area was built, my sister and I used to get in trouble for playing around at the construction site. Daddy was the scorekeeper for basketball games, and we had to sit in a certain place, so he could keep an eye on us. We were expected to be at all the home games. Dad coached B-Team football, and he oversaw the weight room for years. As long as we weren't too much trouble, my sister and I were allowed to go over to the school kitchen. The cooks lived down the street, and sometimes they would walk up the street to BGA. They would sneak us food. They would give us cracklings. Cora Spencer was one of the cooks, and she was wonderful.

On Halloween, the BGA boys would trick or treat at our house. The students couldn't leave the campus, so we always had plenty of candy to hand out. They were like a hoard. When the boarding students went home, I would wander through the halls of the school, looking at the historical exhibits. There were display cases that contained items from the Civil War. There were a lot of Confederate artifacts from the Battle of Franklin. I found minieballs and other stuff in our yard and on the campus. After a while, almost everybody in Franklin knew me. When I was in town, I was always "Carl's boy."

Dad had a gift for teaching mathematics. His approach was to understand when a student would run into difficulty, and he made a rule for each one of those situations. Every student had to write down all the rules in his math textbook. I had a used book, and the rules were already glued inside the cover. But I had to write down the rules again, and then glue them over the old rules.

We'd sit with our hands on our desks, and Dad would walk around the room and ask you to recite a rule. It was serious business. When he said, "Rule time," everybody would think, "Oh no." Because you would get whacked if you didn't get the rule exactly right. You had to give it to him verbatim. Dad had a couple of implements he would use. He called one of them *the wild goose*, and the other one was *the wasp*. The wasp was the slip stick on a slide rule, and he would hit the palm of your hand with it. Sometimes he'd make your hand swell up, but he would ask the guy which hand he wrote with, so the boy could still do his work.

One day I was stuck on a problem, and he hit me in the middle of the chest. He said, "What's the rule?" And he pounded on me until I quoted the rule. As soon as I told him the rule, he stopped. Then he said, "Now, apply it." So we learned to filter through the rules, and identify which one applied. He cut right to the bone. You walked out of class knowing what your mistake was and what rule to apply. There was more involved than just reading a math book. He was teaching his students a mathematical language that he had devised.

Dad did something he called Chalk Talks. A boy would stand at the blackboard and solve a problem.

As soon as Dad saw a mistake being made, he would say, "What's the rule on that?" Sometimes he would get called by a parent who didn't like the way he did things. They saw it as putting too much pressure on their son, but Dad's approach let him correct mistakes immediately.

There was always a game between the boys and Dad, and Dad took it in stride. They would do things like put an alarm clock in his desk and wait for it to go off. And Dad would do crazy things in class. One day he came in acting like he was drunk just for the fun of it. But when he'd say, "Time to go to work," it would get dead quiet, and you would start working.

He'd come home with his papers, and scan through to see who was having a problem. Sometimes he'd write down a little note, and the next day, if you were having problems, you would be at the board working on a problem. He was very hands on.

I remember one night when I was working on my math homework, and it was like two in the morning. He came into the study, and he said, "What are you still up for?" I said, "I'm doing my math homework." He said, "You've been on math since seven o'clock. What was the homework?" I showed him, and I said, "Does that mean I can go to bed?" He said, "You better have every problem." When I walked in class the next day, every kid had every problem. Daddy took up the homework every day, and we never knew whether he was going to look at it or not.

Rockarosa was Dad's farm. It was land out on the Murfreesboro Road that his family had bought back in the early 1940s. He would take boys out there and let them work off demerits. There was a big pile of rocks, and he'd have guys move the rocks from one place to another. Then he'd bring another crew out, and they would move them back where they'd been before. Some of the boys would swear up and down that *Rockarosa* could grow rocks. Dad was the one who named it *Rockarosa*.

Daly Thompson was revered by my father. He was a big man with big, thick hands. When I was an eighth grader, I was in study hall one day, and Mr. Thompson was sitting at the table up on the stage. A couple of eighth graders were sitting off on one side of the study hall, and they were talking up a storm. They didn't know about Mr. Thompson, and they didn't respect him. Mr. Thompson said, "Boys, you need to be quiet over there." They got quiet, but then they started talking again. He said, "Boys, don't make me come to you." It wasn't long before they went back to talking, a few minutes later, Mr. Thompson walked down the steps from the stage and came over next to me.

He looked at me and said, "Mr. Smithson, do you need any help?" I said, "No sir, Mr. Thompson, I'm doing fine." He said, "Alright, son." Then he eased on back to where the boys were talking. Next thing I heard was, *"WHOP."* Mr. Thompson had picked up one of the boys up by the hair, and after he popped him, he dropped him back down in his seat. Then he grabbed the next boy, popped him, and bounced him back in his seat. Then he said, "Boys, I told you not to make me come to you." He never seemed upset. He didn't do it out of meanness. It was just his way of saying, "I mean for you to do what I tell you to do." That was just Mr. Thompson.

Daly Thompson

Whenever there was a school dance, I had to go. I always asked Mr. Bragg's daughter, Becky, or Mr. Naylor's daughter, Sarah. Mr. Naylor was much quieter than the other teachers. He was very intelligent, but he didn't have the big macho personality that most high school boys responded to. Mr. Akin was the school's businessman. He was known for being thrifty. He helped BGA stay solvent. Mr. Redick was very much like a military man, and he had a temper. But in summer school, after lunch, we'd go and sit in Room One, and he would have story time. He told us lots of good stories. He had a generous heart, but sometimes his decision-making process got him into trouble.

When I was going to BGA, there was a controversy about a student named Dan Fleming. He had gotten into some trouble, and his father, Sam Fleming, was a big supporter of BGA. After Mr. Redick let Dan into school, he hadn't done much of anything as a student. Despite that, he was going to receive a degree anyway. The seniors had worked hard to earn their diplomas, and they rebelled over how Dan was being ushered through. Back then, you could stand up and air out grievances, and there was a big meeting of the student body. The faculty didn't say they would do what you wanted them to do, but they would at least take it under advisement.

When BGA made the transition away from being a boarding school, that broke with tradition. And after it happened, the faculty changed. Mr. Bragg was in the middle of all the changes that were taking place. I didn't take the loss of tradition very well. Mr. Bragg became the headmaster when I was a senior, and Dad left BGA when I graduated, which was in 1970. Five years after he left, Dad wanted to go back into teaching. But things had changed. His ways weren't accepted anymore, and that kind of broke a lot of ties for me.

Dad had a reputation for turning out quality students. One day when I was at Vanderbilt, I'd been up late the night before. I was in Calculus class, but I was only half-awake. The teacher noticed that I wasn't playing attention, and he challenged me to solve a problem on the blackboard. All I had to do was look at it to tell him the answer. The teacher said, "Have you had calculus before?" I said, "Yes sir." He said, "Where?" I said, "At BGA." He said, "So you know the Goat?" I said, "Yes sir, the Goat is my father." Then he said something like, "Well, then you can go on back to sleep." All I did from that point on was grade papers for the teacher.

I was going to be a doctor, but I had a gift for mathematics. When I told my father I wanted to be a teacher, he said, "Bob, I'll tell you this. You're never going to make a lot of money that way, but you will never have a more rewarding life than to invest yourself in other people." I'm sorry I couldn't send my kids to BGA. I just couldn't afford it. I would've had to sell Rockarosa. It was our homeplace, and there were just too many memories.

We lived at 107 Everbright Avenue until around 1968, when we moved to a house our dad built. I have very, very vivid memories associated with each and every square inch of the old BGA campus. So much of my life took place there.

The information in this narrative came from an interview that took place in conjunction with his sister, Anne Wallace, on June 7, 2013. Additional information was derived from collateral research.

Anne Smithson Wallace

Carl Smithson was my father. Daddy always wanted to get an education. He started off going to a little one-room school, and later on he fought to go to school. When Dad was growing up, the only way out of farming was education. That was the key to going further in life. But back then, you were expected to work on the farm. That's what you did. Because of the Depression, Daddy left Franklin High School after a year and went to work with the CCC. He would send his money back home, and that helped the family buy the farm on Murfreesboro Road.

After he got back from World War II, he and my mother, his first wife, met at Trevecca College, where they were both students. They married, and I was born in 1949. When I was two months old, my mother got sick. Daddy took her to Vanderbilt, and they said, "Oh, she's just got a virus. Take your daughter home, and come back in the morning." She had acute pancreatitis, and she was dead before they got home. A year or so later, Dad met Bob's mother, his second wife, in Oklahoma City. They married in 1951, and Daddy worked at Carl's Shoes downtown while he finished his education. Once he got the job at BGA, they bought a house on Landon Drive in Nashville.

My brother, Bob, and I grew up on the BGA campus. In 1959, when I was in fifth grade, we moved to a faculty house on Everbright Avenue. I remember how exciting it was to be able to live where dad worked. We had been living in a modern house, and I remember going into the house at BGA. I had a big room with high ceilings. I just thought that was the greatest thing. I remember the boys playing football before and after supper, and before study hall, in the horseshoe across from our house. I wanted to play, too, but girls weren't allowed to play. So I ended up climbing every tree on that campus.

Each faculty member had a table, and we ate with the boys every meal. I learned very early not to be late to a meal, because if you were a girl, all of the boys had to stand up when you came to the table. I felt very safe back then. I knew all the boarding students, and everybody who lived on our street.

I remember when Dave and Marky Wood got married. The first place he taught was BGA, and we helped them move into a little two-room apartment in the old dormitory. She was so beautiful. And Ralph and Helen Brown lived in the apartment in the new dormitory. Coach Brown whistled all the time. Teachers lived in the apartments first, and some would eventually graduate to a house. It was a matter of seniority. One night, Helen was watching a football game. She felt terrible, but she sat through the whole game. It ended up that she had a ruptured appendix, and they had to take her to the hospital.

When I was a little older, I used to babysit their sons, Mike and Wink. Helen Brown became the dietician at BGA, and one of my fondest memories was going over to the school kitchen. That's where the black cooks showed me how to make biscuits, and there would be chitlins cooking on the back of the stove.

When I was 12, I was having a lot of stomach aches. It had been going on for two or three weeks, and I kept telling Dad that my stomach was really hurting. One morning I got up and went over to have breakfast at 7:30. When I got to the table, I said, "Dad, I just can't eat. I feel terrible." So he went out to wait for Dr. Guffee, who always brought his boys to school. A little later, Dr. Guffee came in to examine me. He put me up on our table, and he said I had appendicitis. He drove me to the hospital, and operated on me that morning.

I remember going to church. The boarders went to the Methodist church every Sunday. They walked to church in groups. They would sit in the balcony, and they knew better than to get loud up there. Dad sang in the choir for years. He had a beautiful voice. We sat in the pew facing the choir. He could see everything we were doing, and we didn't want him to look at us the wrong way.

We got spankings, and Dad used the belt. When he pulled off his belt, watch out. But he played with us, too. He loved playing monopoly with us. We might play it the whole weekend. He also played with us outside. He'd do things like build snowmen with us. And my parents would take us to Willow Plunge in the summer. A lot of BGA people had summer jobs there, and we would stay all day.

Part of what he gave us was a love of travel. He loved to take us places. We traveled every summer for two weeks. I have been to every state in the Union, except Hawaii and Alaska. We would go to all the museums and historic places. And when we were older, when he had his construction company, he would take us abroad with him. He gave us a sense that Franklin was a wonderful place, but there was also a world out there that we needed to know about.

Daddy loved music, and he was determined that I would learn to play the piano. I started taking piano when my parents bought me a piano for my sixth birthday. I took lessons until I was a senior in high school. He made me practice an hour a day, every day, and he would sit and listen. One of his favorite songs was *Blueberry Hill*, and he loved hearing Kate Smith sing *God Bless America*.

Girls could only attend summer school at BGA, and my dad made me take two courses that were taught by Daly Thompson. He loved Mr. Thompson, and I took an eight-week vocabulary course, and my first year of Latin, from him.

And I learned math from my father. He said, "Ann, you have a lot of ability in mathematics. You've just got to use it." He didn't like the way I was being taught by my teachers, and when I came home I'd have daddy's math class. I was taught one way at school, but when I went home, he taught me "the right way." I'd go back to school the next day, and when I put the problems on the board the way Daddy showed me, I'd get into trouble. I quickly learned to do them dad's way for dad, and the other way when I was in school.

But it was because of dad's rules that I really learned math. When I was taking Algebra One, plenty of nights were full of tears. I might as well have been one of his students. I had to learn all of his rules, and I had to be able to say them fast. He didn't let me just sit there and think about it. Students he had taught found higher math to be much easier than it was for most students. He gave them the foundation, and once the foundation was there, they could apply it to whatever level of mathematics they were learning. No matter how high the math goes, the rules don't change.

Every fall, when the new students came to BGA, there would be a big dance. They didn't know anybody in the community, and local girls would be invited to come and meet the boys. That was always a big thing for me. Mom and dad would dress up and go to the dances, too. I remember my first kiss. It was on our front porch, and the boys who had end rooms in the dormitory were up there watching. So when I got my first kiss, the boys started whistling and catcalling, and heckling.

I loved watching graduations on the front lawn. The boys who were graduating would gather at the pole down by Columbia Pike, and sing the alma mater. They would all be standing in a circle around the flag pole with their parents and faculty, and with the big boxwoods behind them. I thought it was beautiful.

I always knew I was going to be a teacher, but I was determined that I was never going to teach math. Ever. When I got my degree, it was in Elementary Education. But once I started teaching, I realized that my gift was math. So I started teaching math, and my brother would say, "Here I am with the math degree, and you're the one teaching math." We were brought up to revere education, and that's why Bob and I became teachers. We both grew up believing that teaching was one of the highest callings you could have.

Along with his understanding of mathematics, one of Daddy's gifts was his presence. People, and especially students, understood that he meant business. He even had a certain walk. I would be down at the gym when I was little, and even though I couldn't see him, I could hear daddy coming. He had a very pronounced gait.

After BGA moved, I went back to the old campus on Columbia Avenue. We grew up there. It had been our extended home, and it was being destroyed. When I saw what was being torn down, I cried and cried and cried. I had so many memories there.

From time to time I'll meet one of Dad's former students. He'll say, "I have your dad to thank. He was so hard, but he helped me get where I am today." That's a pretty good legacy. They have told me they would have failed math, or dropped out, or been kicked out of BGA, if Daddy hadn't said, "Come to my house tonight. We're going to work on this together." He was very demanding, but a lot of his students loved him dearly.

One of the things Dad was able to do was see your potential beyond what you could see yourself. He wasn't going to let you get by with being less than he thought you could be. He was determined that you were going to rise to your potential. That's what a good teacher does. Make you rise above what you think you can do.

The information in this narrative came from an interview that was done on June 7, 2013 with Anne's brother, Bob,

John Bragg

My great-grandfather, Charles Washington Mooneyham, was from Spencer, a little village northeast of McMinnville. He joined the Confederate Army, and he may well have come across the land that would eventually become the old BGA campus. During the Battle of Franklin, his cavalry regiment was in reserve out along Carter's Creek Pike. After the battle, he was in one of the units that advanced through the area where BGA would be built.

He lived to be 90. I was only four years old when he died, but I remember him from our family reunions when he lived in Rock Island. Grandpa Mooneyham had a long white beard, and he would wear his Confederate uniform. He would sit in a rocking chair out in the yard, and all of the young folks would gather around. He told stories about fighting Yankees. He would always end up getting out of his chair and throwing his arms up. One day, I saw that he was missing his right index finger. It had been shot off, maybe at Chickamauga. I was so young, it scared me to death.

My mother, who taught school before she married, died in 1932. I was seven years old. About six months later, my sister came down with polio. My father remarried a year or so after that. I went through elementary school and the first two years of high school in McMinnville. My father was also a former school teacher, but at that time, he was in the nursery business. He wasn't able to give me much personal attention, and I was never close to my stepmother.

I was a free spirit. My grades were good, but I didn't study much. I would sneak out at night to play. It was decided that I needed to be shipped off to school, and I spent my last two years of high school at Sewanee Military Academy. One morning at breakfast, my father said, "John Alden" – he called me by my double name – "I have some news for you. You're going off to school. I'll give you three choices – Sewanee Military Academy, Columbia Military Academy, or Battle Ground Academy." Our first visit was to Sewanee, and I just told him that Sewanee was fine. Since he ran a nursery, he worked out a deal to pay part of my tuition with landscaping.

SMA was a great experience for me. It turned my life around. Back in those days, hazing was common, particularly in military schools. Even though it was frowned upon officially, hazing went on. My free spirit sort of waned, and it didn't take me long to conform. I was on the honor roll most of the time that I was there. I was tall enough, but when I was at Sewanee I only weighed 125 or 130 pounds. I was not big enough to play varsity football, so I played on the B-team. I also played B-team basketball, but I was on the varsity tennis team and I ran cross country.

Although we competed against BGA, I didn't make any trips to Franklin. But I remember seeing the old BGA school bus when they came to Sewanee. BGA gave SMA fits in football and basketball. I remember seeing George I. Briggs, the BGA headmaster. He was a very distinguished looking white haired gentleman. He looked old, but he wasn't even 60 at the time.

I graduated from Sewanee Military Academy in 1943. Two weeks later, I was inducted into the army. Basic training lasted 13 weeks, but they held me over to help teach the next group. So my 13 weeks turned into 26 weeks. The original group I trained with went to Europe. They were in the Normandy Invasion, but I missed that, They sent me to the Pacific instead.

I went to Caledonia, which is about 750 miles off the western coast of Australia. I was assigned to the 147th regimental combat team. Although I was in the Army, my unit was attached to the 5th Marine division. After the Marines invaded an island, our job was to go in and mop up. After Allied forces took the Admiralty Islands, the invasion of Iwo Jima took place.

I'll never forget my 20th birthday, March 20th, 1945. That's when I stepped ashore on Iwo Jima. The Marines were coming off as we were going in. We saw a lot. We had to go in and get the Japanese out of the caves. A third of the total Japanese force were still alive. They were underground. The whole island was just a honeycomb of caves.

My first night on Iwo Jima, we had to dig in. We started digging foxholes. Iwo Jima is an inactive volcano, but you didn't have to dig very deep until you got to hot sand. We couldn't stay in the foxholes, and we started digging slit trenches. Our raincoats were rubberized on the inside, and we put them down on the sand. Then rubber would get hot, and we'd have to come out the trench. After my first night, when daylight finally came, there was a Japanese grenade in my trench. While I was dozing off, a Japanese soldier had probably come looking for water, or food, or arms. Or whatever.

Going into the caves to get the Japanese out was something that… I still don't like to go underground. And I do not like to be in close spaces. It was a hopeless and helpless feeling. We just didn't know what was around that next turn. The Japanese were dedicated soldiers. The byword of the Japanese soldier on Iwo Jima was to take ten enemy with you. Get ten before you are killed, or before you commit Hari-kari. I saw a lot of Hari-kari, mainly with grenades. But I kept thinking that I'd make it back home.

I spent six months on Iwo Jima. The island was supposedly secure when we left, but there were still some Japanese hiding underground. I think the last Japanese soldier on Iwo Jima surrendered in 1947. After Iwo Jima, we went to Tinian to help finish up the airbase there. It was the airbase from which the Enola Gay would be launched. From Tinian, we went to Okinawa, where we went through two major typhoons. Typhoons were as bad as the Japanese.

Japan surrendered on September 2, 1945, but I was still in Okinawa, waiting for the magic ship to come. At the end of October, a Dutch freighter that had been converted into a troop ship finally came. We were motored out to the ship in LCMs and LCTs, and we had to climb the nets to get on the ship. The waves were high, and the boats were bouncing against the ship. It was dangerous. Two men were killed trying to board ships. After two days of trying to board ships, the captain finally said he'd give us one more try, and then he had to move. We made it on the third try.

On the way back to America, we got the first fresh eggs we'd had in two years, and mutton from Australia. On the voyage back, I was browsing through the little library they had on the ship. Then I came across a book called *30 Days to a More Powerful Vocabulary*. I thought it was a great tool to expand the mind. And they piped in music. I particularly remember the song, "Don't Fence Me In," by Doris Day. They played it all the way to the states.

We were supposed to go to San Francisco, but there was a longshoreman's strike and the port was closed down. We were diverted up to to the mouth of the Columbia River, and we disembarked in Portland, Oregon, and were taken to Vancouver Barracks on the Canadian border. So many troops were coming home that they were unable to process us. Then we were shipped by train all the way down to Fort Bliss, Texas. Everybody wanted to get home for Christmas, and we were all looking at the calendar the whole time.

After I was processed at Fort Bliss, I got on the train to Tennessee. I arrived in Nashville on December the 24th, and then I had to drag my barracks bag all the way from Union Station to the Greyhound Station. I got my ticket to McMinnville, but all the buses were filled. Then I saw a lady sitting in the window. She was motioning for me to come to the door of the bus. It was Elizabeth Clarke, who was my second grade teacher. She insisted that I take her seat. She said, "I'll get a later bus, even if it's tomorrow." I got to McMinnville at seven o'clock on Christmas Eve, and called home. When my sister answered, she dropped the phone. It was a very emotional time.

My father insisted that I go to University of Tennessee to study horticulture, and then go to work with him in the nursery business. But that's not what I wanted to do. Although I wanted to take pre-law and go to law school, I gave in to his wishes and drove to Knoxville to enroll. Then I saw that I would only be taking agriculture courses. No English or History classes. And I was assigned to live in a Quonset hut. That was the last straw, and I went back to McMinnville.

The next week I started college at Sewanee. Nine-tenths of my friends in college were also veterans. It was just, "Where were you? I was in such and such place." And that was it. We'd talk about Sewanee. About fraternity life. We just didn't say much about what had happened during the war. I think there's a relief valve somewhere in the human psyche. It was certainly true in my case. I just tried to forget those things. I had a life to live.

After I graduated from University of the South in 1949, I went to the University of Virginia and did graduate work in History and English. Instead of going back to work with my father in the nursey, I thought I might want to teach. I was very engrossed in my academic work both at Sewanee and Virginia, and the personal touch of the professors had a lot to do with creating my interest in teaching.

Sewanee Military Academy didn't have an opening, and I went over to Castle Heights to see if they needed a teacher. While I was there I ran into Jonas Coverdale. I had known him at Camp Hy-Lake. I had never been a camper at Hy-Lake, but it was near Rock Island and I'd spent a lot of time at the camp. So when I told him I was looking for a job, he said, "I've just been hired at Battle Ground Academy. I'm looking for an English teacher. Before you make a decision, I'd like to talk with you." So we set up a time and I went to Franklin.

When I got to Franklin, I drove down Main Street. I saw Gray's Drugstore on the right, and I stopped to ask where the campus was located. The druggist was Mr. Frank Gray. He was an old, white haired man, and he was behind the counter in the back of the drugstore, filling prescriptions. He came up and introduced himself, and after I told him why I was there, he started talking to me about BGA. He was on the board of trustees, and we ended up talking for about an hour.

The original campus had been on the east side of Columbia Avenue, almost across from the Carter House. But the original building had burned in 1902, and the school was established on the west side of the road, a couple of hundred yards further away from Franklin. The first time I set foot on the campus, the school was very much the way it had been since 1903. The buildings were run down, and they smelled old inside. At the time, BGA had 105 students and six faculty members.

When I sat down with with Jonas Coverdale, he didn't know much more about the place than I did. He was new to the school, but after about an hour, I decided that BGA was as good a place as any. I thought I was getting a very handsome deal. My first salary was $90 a month, and that included room and board. Jonas Coverdale was head of the junior school at Castle Heights when the BGA board hired him to come to Franklin. He was the man the school needed at the time. He was not a great academician, but because he had Camp Hy-Lake, he knew boys and what it took to make them happy. He also knew how to hire a good faculty.

Original School Building, 1889

Three men were already teaching at BGA when I started. J.B. Akin had graduated from BGA in 1926, and he had come back to teach and coach in 1942. He was the head coach in football, basketball, and baseball. And Ralph Naylor, whose father had been the president of Emery and Henry College in Virginia, had married the daughter of BGA's former headmaster, George Briggs. The other returning teacher was Patrick Wade.

J.B. Akin's wife, Katherine, was the school's Secretary and Treasurer, and there was an old African-American maintenance man. He must've been in his 80s, so there wasn't much maintenance he could do. Each teacher was supposed to clean up his own room at BGA. J.B. Akin didn't usually have an assistant coach, and he would recruit students to help him clean up the gymnasium. In those days there was no money. That's sort of the way the school was run. It was very personal.

I just wish his students could have known Ralph Naylor as he really was. He could do a little bit of everything – even fly a plane. Where the old Williamson County Hospital was, out on Carter's Creek Pike, there was an airstrip. Ralph would go on Sunday afternoons and rent a little plane, and he'd fly around Franklin.

Ralph was very smart – very brilliant – but he was absent-minded. You'd say one thing to him, and it would remind him of something else. Ralph had an upstairs class adjacent to the old study hall, where he taught his English classes. He had a habit of coming into the classroom right after lunch, raising the window, and spitting. Well, one day a student came up with a prank. He raised the window before class. So Ralph came in and closed the window, and then he spit on it.

Another one of his talents was photography. He developed his own film, and he used one of the rooms in the school building as a dark room. One day a student opened the door, and Ralph was standing there in the dark. When he asked Ralph what he was doing, Ralph said, "Well, everybody has to be somewhere." Ralph was also a musician. He could listen to a recording – like a Tommy Dorsey album – and point out nuances that most people wouldn't hear.

First Year as Teacher (1952)

When I came to BGA, I was assigned to live in the dormitory. I had 50 boys to look after. I married the next year, and Coverdale gave me one small additional room. We didn't have much living space, and Jane and I lived in the dormitory for about two years. Paul Redick lived on Everbright Avenue in a house the school owned that was called *Westover*. But then Paul's father-in-law, Mr. Hayes from Huntsville, Alabama, built a home for Paul and Betsy on the BGA campus.

So Jonas Coverdale said, "John, I'm sending you down to live in *Westover*." I thought, Hallelujah. I was feeling great, and I started to walk out the door. Then he said, "But wait a minute. I'm also sending ten boys with you." I can picture that as if it happened yesterday. Jonas Coverdale had a way of doing that. When it came time for a raise, it was never as much as you wanted, but when he finished talking to you, you felt sorry for him, and you wanted to give part of it back.

But there is something I will never forget about Jonas Coverdale. One time we had to take my wife, Jane, to Vanderbilt Hospital for emergency surgery. Coverdale called me into the office, and handed me his personal check. It simply had his signature on it. Nothing else was filled out. He and his wife, Gertrude, were going to New York. He said, "You may need this while I'm gone." And I did need it. He was tight in the way he ran the school financially. He had to be. But when it came to the human element, he was very generous.

It's hard to explain what the athletic program was like in the 1950s and the early 60s, and even before that. The school was small and the faculty was small, and there was very little money available. J.B. Akin was a one man athletic program. He had no assistants. He was the football coach. He was the basketball coach. He was the baseball coach. He was the track coach. But he turned out great athletic teams. During the mid 1940s, right before I came to BGA, the T-formation was a new football formation. J.B. was astute, and he studied up on the T-formation. He was the first coach in the Middle Tennessee area to use it, and it caught our opponents off guard. They had no defense against it. In 1944 BGA went undefeated due to that.

In addition to his coaching, J.B. taught Chemistry and Physics and Biology. If he had students who were deficient, they had to go to afternoon study hall. If his star player was academically deficient, that star player would be in afternoon study hall, not out on the football field. That's the way the school was run, and that's the way the athletic programs were run. J.B. and I were very close friends. He was a great fellow.

Paul Redick was basically a good man. He had been teaching with Jonas Coverdale in the Junior School at Castle Heights, and he also taught classes in the Senior School. History was his main field. Paul had been an athlete in college. He'd gone to UT Martin, in West Tennessee. He was from a little West Tennessee town called Camden. Paul wanted to coach, but he wasn't a coach, he was a teacher.

When Jonas Coverdale was offered the job at BGA, he had a law degree from Vanderbilt, but he'd never gotten a Bachelor of Arts or a Bachelor of Science degree. He did not have the academic credentials required by the Southern Association of Colleges and Schools, so he was not eligible to be head of the school.

So Jonas Coverdale brought Paul Redick with him, and Paul was given the title of headmaster. Coverdale took the title of president. So during Paul's first years, he was listed as the headmaster of the school, but he was just a history teacher. He was Jonas Coverdale's assistant. I think Paul realized that academically, he didn't measure up to the standards of BGA. In addition to his degree from UT Martin, Paul got a graduate degree in Physical Education from Peabody College. Although he knew his history course well, he was not academically oriented.

Carl Smithson came to BGA in 1952, and he was one of a kind. Carl was much like Paul Redick. He did not really have an academic background, but he had a degree in mathematics from Peabody College. Carl wanted to teach more than anything in the world. In years past, Math had been one of the strongest programs in the school, going all the way back to Dr. Bill McGavock, who graduated from BGA and had later become Chairman of the Math Department at Davidson College. And Glenn Eddington was one of the greatest math teachers of all time. So these were the teachers that Carl Smithson followed.

What Carl did not know, he made up with in effort. He studied the subject hard, and he usually had a good student in his class that he could learn from. I remember when Carl first started teaching. He had a student named Tom Clarkson. Tom was brilliant. When Carl really got stymied on a math question, he'd say, "Tom, go up to the board." Tom would do the problem, and it was sort of a joke. But it didn't take Carl long, and he caught up. Carl's approach was to keep ramming it in to the brains of his students until they got it. He made them repeat it until they were sick of it.

And intimidation was a part of it. Throwing erasers at them. Pulling their hair, and so forth. Today you'd be sued for that, but the students he turned out in math didn't have a problem with math in college. We had three Burton brothers at BGA. Larry Burton, Jim Burton, and Mike Burton. Larry had a law degree and had just started practicing law when Carl had Mike, the youngest brother, in class. Mike was making faces in class one day. He was sitting on the front row, and Carl finally turned around and slapped Mike out of his seat. Mike wasn't hurt, but Larry had learned that that was against the law.

The next thing I knew, Larry was in my living room with his mother. Larry was saying, "I'm going to sue Carl Smithson first, and then I'm going to sue Battle Ground Academy." When he got through, I started talking to Larry about his experiences with Carl in math. Then I said, "How did you do in math at Sewanee?" He recognized that he'd learned a lot from Carl Smithson. And we talked about Carl and his B-team football teams, and that the kids he coached loved Carl. Larry and his mother finally decided that there were better ways to resolve the situation than suing the school or suing Carl. We decided that if Carl apologized to Mike and to the student body, that would take care of things. It was hard for Carl to do, but he did it.

Daly Thompson was one of a kind. He came to BGA from Pocahontas, Arkansas. He was already a year or two older than most of the students in his class. He graduated from BGA in 1910. He was a good football player and a good student. After he finished at BGA, he went to Vanderbilt and graduated from there in 1914. Then he came back and taught at BGA until he went off to World War I. After the war he went back to teach in Arkansas. But while he was at BGA, he and Captain Tom Henderson had become good friends. When the principalship became available at Franklin High School, Captain Tom and a few citizens in Franklin got Daly to come back and interview for the job, and he was hired.

When I first came to BGA, Daly was still principal at Franklin High School. We were having conflicts with Franklin High over recruiting certain of their football players. Jimmy and Bobby Gentry were coaching at Franklin High School, and there were some hard feelings for a while. But when it came time for Daly to retire from Franklin High School, he wasn't ready to stop teaching. So he was hired to come to BGA and teach Bible and Latin. He was a Latin scholar, and he had learned his Latin at BGA under Daddy Peoples.

The boys loved Daly Thompson, but he took no foolishness. That led to an incident I'll never forget. Bill Pope was taking Latin. Bill was very much of a cut-up, and on that particular day, he was sitting on the front row in Daly's class. Bill was doing something like making faces. Daly had corrected him two or three times, but Bill kept it up. Mr. Thompson had his Latin book in his hand, and he handed it to Bill. When Bill reached out and took the book, Daly slapped him right out of his chair.

The moment he did that, he knew he had made a terrible mistake. Daly just left the room, and I happened to be coming down the hall. He said, "John, I have… I've made a big mistake. I should've known better. As principal of Franklin High School, I wouldn't have allowed this." After he told me what he'd done, I said, "Well, Mr. Thompson, I'm sure Bill deserved it." But Daly was very upset about it. The next day the Cannonball, the school annual, was being dedicated. And it was being dedicated to Daly Thompson. I get emotional when I tell this story. When the dedication was read from the annual, the first person to stand and yell and cheer was Bill Pope.

As much as I hated to do it, I had to use the paddle on occasion. But I always called in another faculty member as a witness. And before I did anything, I would telephone the parent and explain the situation. I'd say, "We've tried everything else, and nothing has worked. I'm willing to try this, but if you don't want me to try it, I'll just send Junior home." They always said, "Go ahead. Do your job."

Every Monday night there was a faculty meeting in the old library. The meetings would start at seven o'clock and last until about ten. The faculty would sit around two or three tables that had been pushed together. There was a list of the entire student body. There were only about 125 students at the time, and every boy in school would be discussed. Their academic work, their behavior, or if they were having problems of any kind. If they were having problems in their home life, that was discussed on a very confidential basis. But we pretty well knew every boy in school, and knew as much about them, academically, as there was to know. This was done in some fashion up until the time I retired, but as the school got larger, not every student was discussed at length anymore. It couldn't be done.

In a sense, the faculty was one big family. But we were human. As in all families, there were disputes and there were arguments. But by and large, we stuck up for one another. If somebody needed help, he would get that help.

In the early years of my tenure, Saturday School was a part of BGA. The students who were required to attend Saturday School had academic deficiencies, or demerits to serve off. The academic part of Saturday School was in the morning, and lasted until about noon. Demerits would be served off in the afternoon. At first, demerits were mainly served off by working on the campus. Cleaning up the school building, and things of that nature.

Then it got to be where a teacher would say, "Well, my lawn needs cutting, or I have some work that needs to be done at my house." Carl Smithson had a small farm out off Murfreesboro Road. It had pasture land, and a lot of rock. He called it *Rockarosa*. Some students would look forward to going out to Carl's place and working on his farm. I lived on campus, and I had kids helping around the yard.

I liked the writing aspect of teaching. I tried to expand the minds of my students by having them read the classics. That made my teaching of literature much more meaningful. When I started teaching English, I went to Jonas Coverdale and gave him a list of books that I wanted to order. He said, "That's no problem." But he didn't expect what I said next. "I need thirty copies of each book."

Les Miserables, Pride and Prejudice, and on down the line – I had all those books put in the library. And I hadn't forgotten about *30 Days to a More Powerful Vocabulary*, the little book I'd read on the way home from the war in the Pacific. By the time I started teaching at Battle Ground Academy, it had come out in paperback. I ordered those books for my entire senior class. For twenty years it was a corollary to my Senior English course.

I always went through the vocabulary portion first. That expanded their minds more, and because of their expanded vocabularies, they could understand more of what they were reading. Then they could express what they had learned through their writing. I learned a lot about students through their writing.

One of the things I enjoyed was when the class wasn't prepared to take a test, or discuss a certain assignment. I would say, "Close your books." I would go to the board, and write a phrase on the board. I would say, "I want a 45-minute theme, a 250 word theme, on this subject. On whatever it means to you." I would pick themes out of the air just to see what they would come up with. I enjoyed that very much. Then there were term papers. I was big on research. I used Campbell's book on footnoting. I was teaching college level work to high school seniors. It took with some of them, but there were some it didn't take with.

One particular student would come to me, and grit his teeth. He would say, "I'm not going to read that book." I'd tell him, "That's fine, but you won't get a credit in English 4." There were times when students got somebody else to write reports for them. So I'd select a scene that only someone who had read that book would know. Then I would have them write everything they knew about that particular scene. That sort of separated the sheep from the goats. CliffsNotes just didn't cover that. I was always battling CliffsNotes. But my approach took with a great many students. I've had students come up to me and say how much they enjoy reading today, and they thank me.

I'm not saying I was a good English teacher, but I tried. I never talked about what happened in places like Iwo Jima and Okinawa. People have wondered why I didn't tell my students about those experiences. Well, I was never asked.

I was big on memory work. I had my students memorize the first eighteen lines of the prologue of Chancer's Canterbury Tales in Old English. The credit for that belongs to Bruce Jackson, who was a math teacher at BGA during my first year. One night, in my room in the dormitory, Bruce and I were talking about our classes. I was having trouble with certain students in poetry readings. And Bruce said, "You're teaching Chaucer. Have you ever thought about having them memorize part of the prologue in Old English." I may have said something like, "I'm not that cruel." But the more I thought about it, the more I liked the idea. I met all kinds of opposition, but they had to stand in front of the class and recite the passage from the Canterbury Tales

There were a few liberals on the BGA faculty, but most of the teachers were conservative. We had a young teacher, Billy Bradshaw, and Billy Bradshaw was an arch-conservative. He and I would have arguments about my outside reading. He thought I was too liberal in the books that I had my students read. We had discussions about it, and sometimes they were heated. He thought *Brave New World* was a liberal book, and Billy would criticize me in his classes for having students read books like that. That finally got to our librarian, and she said thank goodness we had somebody who was trying to expand minds through literature.

I will never forget the day of Kennedy's assassination. I was in a 4th period English class on the main floor, part of where the old library had been. I heard some commotion in the hall, and about that time, the bell rang to end the period. When I stepped out of my classroom, someone said that President Kennedy had just been shot. Then of course everything was in an uproar. It was a Friday, and we let boarding students go home.

Bill Bradshaw

Jonas Coverdale retired in 1959, and Paul Redick was the headmaster through most of the 1960s. There was a lot of conflict on the faculty. There was unrest. Paul was a good man, but he felt like the only way he could run the school was to divide and conquer. He kept the faculty in an uproar. He would line up his supporters against those who didn't support him. There was eventually a conflict between J.B. Akin and Paul Redick. They were both good men, but very different men. They were both my friends, but I was closer to J.B. Akin than I was to Paul Redick.

J.B. came to me one Friday afternoon in 1968. He told me, "John, I've come to the end of my rope, I don't think I can work any longer with Paul. I am going to submit my resignation. I'm going down to see Stewart Campbell at the bank." Stewart was on the BGA board. Stewart and J.B. had been in school together as students, and had stayed close. So J.B. went to see Stewart Campbell, and he outlined his reasons for retiring. That he could not get along with Paul anymore, and that he didn't agree with the way the school was being run. So he handed his resignation to Stewart.

Stewart took it, but he said, "J.B., I've always believed in doing things after really thinking them through. I'm going to take this resignation and put it in my desk drawer. I'm going to think about it a while, and I want you to think about it a while." J.B. came back to the campus, and being the man that he was, he went to see Paul Redick. He told Paul exactly what he had done and why. Paul was hot-headed, and he just vented his emotions. He said something like, "Well, we'll see about that. I'll just go down and turn in my resignation. And we'll see which one the board wants to accept."

J.B. Akin

So Paul went down to the bank and handed Stewart Campbell his resignation. Stewart told him the same thing he'd told J.B. – that he'd think about it. Both resignations were given to the board of trustees, and the board decided to accept Paul Redick's resignation. They gave J.B. Akin the title of President and Headmaster. But J.B. did not have the proper academic credentials to be a headmaster. He had to go back to school. He went to Middle Tennessee State to take the educational courses he needed to meet the requirements of the Southern Association of Colleges and Schools to be the head of a school.

J.B. was not in good health at the time. He made the trip back and forth to Murfreesboro every day all summer long, while he tried to do his job at BGA. After the end of the school year, J.B. had a nervous breakdown. He went to his internist in Nashville, who was a former student of his. He was told that he needed to rest, and he was hospitalized.

Joe Pinkerton was Chairman of the Board, and he asked me if I would step in for J.B. until he felt like coming back. Then the board decided that they needed to go ahead and start their search for a headmaster. One of the trustees met with the BGA faculty, and he told us that the board was going to hire a new headmaster. I decided that I would put my hat in the ring. One of my supporters was Kirby Primm.

The selection committee could not come to an agreement about whom they were going to hire. When the board convened, Kirby Primm met them as they were entering the room. He was standing at the door. As Stewart Campbell passed through, Kirby said, "Stewart, we're going to select a headmaster tonight." Stewart was on the selection committee, and he said, "We are?" Kirby said, "Yes. And that headmaster is going to be John Bragg." So the meeting started, and after the selection committee reported that they had not come to an agreement, Joe Pinkerton opened the floor for discussion. The first question was from Kirby Prim. He asked Jonas Coverdale what kind of teacher I was. Coverdale gave his report, and one by one, the trustees stood and made comments.

Some of the old trustees had come out of the woodwork to be at the meeting. Wirt Harlin Sr. had not attended a board meeting in twenty years. Hubert Wyatt had not been to a meeting in fifteen years, and Glen Overby also came. They all supported me. The vote was held, and the count was eighteen to three in my favor. That was how I became headmaster.

Around the time I became headmaster, I was living in the house that George Briggs built at the corner of Columbia Pike and Everbright Avenue. One morning I was having coffee in the breakfast room, and I saw some young men with metal detectors. They'd dig a hole and pick up whatever it was they'd found. I spent a lot of time running off people like that. Civil War artifacts needed to stay on the BGA campus.

I briefly taught Senior English during the first semester I was headmaster. But I would be interrupted with school business that had to be taken care of right at that time, and that was unfair to the students. I really couldn't do both, so I stopped teaching. In my 40 years at BGA, the happiest times that I had were my first 19 years – when I was a teacher. But my 21 years as headmaster were great years. I thoroughly enjoyed what I was doing, but I had more fun and enjoyment when I was a teacher.

Well, I knew what I had gotten into. The biggest part of being headmaster was financial. The school had no money. There had never been an organized effort to raise money. The first thing I did was institute a fundraising campaign. Kirby Primm got Dr. Andy Holt, the President of University of Tennessee, to come down and make a talk to the BGA community. As a result of that campaign, we got enough money to build our first new building, which we named People's Hall. That campaign brought parents and trustees and students together, and unified the school.

Mrs. Matilou Duke

I was also able to help upgrade our speech program. I had decided that every student in school should be able to stand before the student body, and express himself – without being scared to death. So in consultation with Matilou Duke, we developed a program. Every freshman would take a speech course for one semester. Part of the curriculum was that every student would stand before the student body and make a speech. No exceptions. Every freshman dreaded that day, but every freshman did it. I'm proud of that.

That was one of the first things I discussed with the board after I became headmaster. One of the young trustees frowned on that particular thing. Sam Fleming was at that particular meeting, and when he spoke everyone listened. He said, "In my years at BGA, the course that meant the most to me was speech. And he said, "When I went to Vanderbilt, speech stayed with me more than any other course I had." When we dedicated the main academic building, we dedicated it to Sam Fleming. When I told Sam I wanted him to speak at this dedication, he said, "Let me think about it, but I'd prefer not to do it." But when he called me the next day, he said, "I'll do it. I'll make the talk." And he gave a great talk to the student body. His wife told me he had worked harder on that than anything she'd ever seen him work on.

One of the most traumatic things I had to do took place right after I became headmaster. We were faced with a dormitory problem. BGA was both a boarding school and a day school. There were excellent students wanting to come to BGA, but because we had to fill the dormitory with boarding students, we had to turn away a lot of day students. Financially, we had to have a full dormitory, or we couldn't operate. We needed that extra income. So we had to take students who were not as well-qualified as some of the day students we had to turn away. Then several other private schools were started. With the advent of schools like Brentwood Academy in 1969 and Franklin Road Academy in 1971, there was more and more competition. So BGA was at a crossroads.

Sam Fleming

I realized that something had to be done. My recommendation to the board – something that I hated to do – was to close the boarding operation. The idea of closing the dormitory was met with vehement opposition – even by some members of the board. Former students like Allen Steele, who was a good person and a good friend, couldn't see the school operating without being a boarding school. But when I showed the financial side to the board, it was pretty well decided.

I had Sam Fleming's support, and although the vote was close, my recommendation carried and we closed the dormitory. As painful as it was, it had to be done. But we had to allow our boarding students to remain until they graduated, and we put them in private homes on the campus.

During the 1960s, BGA had begun playing against integrated high schools. We had some individuals on the faculty that were very, very, conservative, and our headmaster, Paul Redick, was one of them. He didn't want BGA to even play against a school that was integrated. But that had to change.

According to Southern Association of Standards, Rules, and Regulations, the Board of Trustees can't run the school. They hire the administrator, and if they don't like the way the administrator is doing things, they can fire him and hire someone else. Even though the board did not make decisions regarding who to admit, I wanted their consent. So after I came up with a proposal that BGA should begin to admit black students, J.B. Akin and I presented it to the board. Although there was some disagreement, a majority of the board was in favor of the proposal.

Our first African-American student applied for admission to BGA in 1971. His name was Mike Holland. He was a great young man, and he had a supportive family. His mother and father were tremendous people. Michael was a basketball player, and our freshman team was playing against Franklin at Franklin High School. I was walking across the basketball court to get to the BGA stands, and one of the BGA fathers cupped his hands and yelled out, "Hey, John, when are you going to take another (n-word)." Mike Holland's parents were in the stands, and you could hear a pin drop. I just shook my head. I kept walking and got in the stands, and watched the second half. And the son of the man who yelled eventually became a very close friend of Mike Holland.

Mike Holland

As time went on, I learned about the Bookers, an outstanding African-American family that lived in Franklin. Monroe Booker, who was a World War Two veteran, and his wife, Mary, were co-owners of a service station on Carter's Creek Pike. They had twelve children. When we played Franklin High School in basketball, a lot of the time they would beat us like a drum. And the biggest competition would come from a Booker. Around 1980, I learned that their youngest son was about to be a freshman, and I went to see his parents. I said, "I'm tired of your children beating up on us in basketball. I'm here to talk about your son, Barry. We'd very much like him to come to BGA." All of their older children had gone to college, and one of their sons had gone to Harvard.

Mr. Booker said, "Well, I'm interested in hearing what you have to say." The next thing I said was how much help I could give him financially. It wasn't long before he came to the conclusion that Barry should come to BGA. Barry was a superior student and outstanding athlete during his time at BGA, and later at Vanderbilt.

Barry Booker

In addition to bringing an end to boarding and integrating the school, the other major change that occurred while I was headmaster was the admission of girls to BGA. When the school was founded in 1889, it was an all-boys school. But females were soon admitted, and they would be part of the student body for most of the next forty years. The last girls to attend BGA graduated in 1929. There were no female students at BGA from the 1930s through the end of the 1970s, but in order for BGA to survive – and to be the school we wanted it to be – we needed to bring girls back to BGA. Enrollment was down, and so was the quality of the students we were getting. In private schools, there was a trend was toward coeducation.

In order to give them ammunition, I suggested to the board that we needed to know how the BGA community felt about the school becoming coeducational. The survey revealed that there was overwhelming support for bringing girls back. The next thing was acclimating the boys to the changes that were coming. At first, the boys were against it. But the girls came back in 1979. During the first noon meal held in the new dining hall, the boys all sat at one end of the room, and the girls were at the other end. The second day, it had sort of integrated a little bit. By the third day, they were thoroughly mixed up, and by the fourth day, we were trying to keep them apart.

The saddest parts of my time at BGA were when there was a student death. In 1974 a freshman named Steve Rudolph had some kind of embolism on the football practice field. It was a condition that ran in the family, and he just collapsed on the field. They came running to my office. I went with him in the ambulance to the emergency room at the Williamson County Hospital. I was in the room when he died. The family still hadn't gotten there, and I had to meet them when they came. I think that was the most traumatic thing I faced.

Another tragic incident happened at the tug-of-war in 1985. The rope broke that year, and we had to discontinue the tug, and do it a different time. But John Mark Knabe, who was a sophomore, got in the car with another one of our other students. They went further out on Highway 96 to turn around, and there was a car wreck. He was killed instantly. And again, I was there before the parents got there. The Knabes were marvelous people.

The Board of Trustees wanted me to stay on, but when I became sixty-five—after forty years—I thought that I had paid my dues. I had just built a home on the Tennessee River, and I wanted some time to enjoy it.

When the decision was being made about whether BGA would move to a new campus, I pretty well stayed out of that. I was very much involved in the old campus, sentimentally and emotionally. It had been my home for almost forty years.

When I came to BGA in 1950, the dining hall was in the basement of the old dormitory. All the meals were served family style, and the students would eat at a family table. There was the Coverdale table, the Redick table, the Naylor table, the Brown table, and the Bragg table. Four or five students would eat at my table. My daughter, Becky, came along in 1955, and as soon as she was old enough to eat in the dining hall, she suddenly had a lot of big brothers. That's the way it was. BGA was a family.

But I knew that the school was geographically hemmed in. Just before I became headmaster, the board was interviewing other candidates for the job. All four of the individuals they interviewed for the job recommended that the campus be moved. That was way back in 1969. That may be one reason why the board hired me, because they weren't ready to shell out all that money. The Board of Trustees was not ready to pull up stakes and move. We couldn't expand anymore. My recommendation to the board was that Ron Griffith would be the right man to lead that effort. It had to be done.

One of my former students, Rusty Wilkerson, stood up at a reunion of the class of 1955. He said, "Mr. Bragg, I still want to know why you had us memorize Chaucer's *Canterbury Tales*. What good did that do us?" I said, "How many times in your life have you mentioned to students who went to other schools that you memorized part of *Canterbury Tales*? And how many times have you found that they had to do the same thing?" Rusty said, "Not once." I said, "That's right. And that makes you unique. Just look around you at all of these distinguished people. And Rusty, you're one of them."

Every year I hear from students – going all the way back to my earliest years. It's usually around Christmas. Letters from former students mean a lot to me. I had impressed some of them without realizing it at the time. I thought some of the students I heard from had hated my guts. And a few recipients of my paddling have come to me over the years. Whoever it is will usually back up, but there will be a smile on his face. There isn't any animosity, and I'm so glad.

Sometimes, in my dreams, I'm still at school and there's some unresolved problem that's bugging me. Then I wake up and I realize that I'm no longer headmaster. And I'm relieved. But so many of my dreams are about the old school. About the old campus. About my early days. When I go by the old campus, so many memories come back. I'm surprised at how fast my forty years at BGA went by.

The information contained in this narrative came from an interview that took place on April 27, 2012, and from articles written by John Bragg. He died in Franklin in 2018 at the age of 93. He was survived by his daughter, two grandchildren, and a great-grandchild.

Index

A

Abercrombie, Eugene, 47
Abernathy, Bill, 232
Academy Street, Franklin, 239
Adair, Beegie, 220
Adair, Billy, 210–11, 213, 215, 217, 220
Adams Street, Franklin, 160
Akin, Bobby, 54, 63
Akin, Damon, 218
Akin, James Boyd (J.B.), 19, 73, 97, 115, 124, 138, 140–42, 148, 157–58, 162, 192, 257, 260, 278
Akin, Janice, 20, 158
Akin, Jimmy, 33
Akin, Katherine (Mrs. J.B. Akin), 19-20, 158, 278
Akin, Millard Fillmore, 19
Akin, Vance, 155
Akin, William Burnett ("Bunny"), 106, 112, 132, 259
Alden, John, 275
Allen, Danny, 225
Allman, Duane, 218
Allman Joys (Allman Brothers), 218
Anderson, Bill, 155
Anderson, Gary, 78, 80, 132, 186, 195, 202
Andrews, Capers, 30
Argonne National Lab, 99
Armistead, Bill, 2, 252, 317
Armistead, George Sr., 252
Armistead, Leonard H. Jr., 252
Armistead III, 317
Arno, Williamson County, 11

Arrington, Williamson County, 15
Ashland City, Tennessee, 19, 157–58
Ashland City High School, 68
Ashworth, Elbert, 120, 145
Ashworth, Richard, 145, 151, 155
Atkins, Chet, 230
Atomic Energy Commission, 99

B

Baccalaureate service, 249
Baker, Bill, 2, 25, 27–29, 31–34
Baker, Ruth Huddleston, 34
Barber, Michie, 130
Barnes, Steve, 247
Barney, Jim, 91
Bassham, Jim, 232
Bate, Senator William B., 1
Battle Avenue, Franklin, 68, 78, 103
Battle Ground Academy, 1–3, 6, 9, 11–12, 15, 18, 22, 35, 39, 42, 45, 47–48, 50, 52, 58–59, 69
    84–86, 115, 123, 131, 134–35, 137, 157, 159, 166, 208, 237, 246, 261, 275, 277, 280, 282
Battle Ground Academy relocated, 2
Battle of Franklin, 1, 5, 12, 17, 19, 52, 239, 243, 250, 266, 274
Baugus, Caroline, 207
Baxter Seminary, 62
Baylor School, 6, 70, 72, 90, 95, 125
Beaman, Barbara, 195, 201
Bean, Boston, 32
Beasley, Bubby, 216
Beasley, Earl, 110
Beasley, John, 133
Beasley, Padge, 193
Beasley, W.J., 208
Beasley Town, Franklin, 208
Behar, Moises, 161
Belle Meade, 198
Benedict, Buddy, 76, 176, 180, 197–99
Bennett, Coach John, 132–33, 239–40
Bennett, Jerry, 95

Bennett Family, 95, 240, 262
Benton County, Tennessee, 102
Berry, Chuck, 180, 195
Bethesda, Tennessee, 110, 129–30
Beziat, Rick, 230
BGA gym, 98, 139
BGA Museum, 33, 135
BGA Orchestra, 31
Bible class, 10, 58, 119, 124, 146
Big Sandy, Tennessee, 154
Birmingham, 18, 67–68, 72
Blackburn, Harry, 255
Blackwell, Frank, 215
Blankenship, Don 110
Blankenship, Ouida, 9
Blubber Derby, 226, 248
Blue Creek Road, 88
Boaz, Lula Mai, 13
Bo Diddley, 155
Bond, Tom, 13
Bonehead, 222
Booker, Barry, 289
Booker, Monroe, 288
Boston, Ralph, 256
Bowen, Mr. ("Bobo"), 254
Bowman, Jodie, 211
Bradley, Owen, 131
Bradshaw, Bill, 214–15, 224, 232, 242, 244–46, 257, 284
Brady, Dorothy, 22–23
Bragg, John, 24, 108, 117–18, 120, 124–29, 131–32, 142, 147–48, 154–55, 179, 181–82, 192–93, 201, 248, 268–69, 290–91
Bransford, Joanna, 30, 33
Breezy Hill, Williamson County, 142
Brentwood Academy, 181, 287
Briggs, George Isaac, 5–7, 18–19, 26–29, 31–33, 39–40, 42–43, 45–46, 48, 50, 53–54, 59–62, 84–85, 124, 127, 137, 143, 145, 159, 209, 253, 275
Briggs, Jane, 6, 44–46, 127, 129, 142, 279
Briggs, Matilda Harrison, 5
Briggs, Sarah Ewing (Mrs. Ralph Naylor), 28, 74, 142

Briggs, Susie, 145
Briggs gymnasium, 143
Briggs house, 47, 50, 117, 145, 264
Brindley, Susan, 201–2
Brothers, Russell, 64
Brown, Allen, 198
Brown, Bert, 210, 213, 215, 217, 240
Brown, Cannon, 47
Brown, Caroline, 85
Brown, Coach Bill, 223, 244–45, 255–56
Brown, Coach Ralph, 70–71, 83, 130, 132, 138, 154, 176–78, 184–85, 187, 197, 199–200, 202–5, 239, 243–44, 255–56
Brown, Helen (Mrs. Ralph Brown), 72, 83, 193, 271
Brown, John, 154, 178
Brown, Kinnard, 64
Brown, Larry, 78, 81, 183, 194–95
Brown, Lula, 207
Brown, Major Campbell, 207
Brown, Mike, 83, 271
Brown, Ruthie, 260
Brown, Tommy, 140, 183, 188
Brown, William Henry ("Uncle Henry"), 28, 61, 84–86, 117, 208
Brown, Wink, 83, 271
Bryant, Alton ("Altie"), 29
Buford, Gaston, 14, 17–18, 35, 37, 69, 88, 98
Buford, Jim, 18
Burton, Jim, 161–62, 188, 199, 280
Burton, Larry, 78, 195, 202, 280–81
Burton, Mike, 280-81
Burwood, Williamson County, 19–20, 68, 157, 250
Burwood Elementary, 68
Burwood Methodist Church, 20
Butter Bowl, 76, 162, 177, 185, 241

C
Caffey, William, 17
Calvin, Buddy, 247
Camden, Tennessee, 102–4, 250, 280

Cameron, Bob, 139, 142

Campbell, W.C., 224

Campbell, Jim, 137

Campbell, Lillian, 170–71

Campbell, Patrick, 137

Campbell, Stewart, 73, 137, 143, 181, 284–85

Campbell, Winder, 137, 141

Campbell School, 137

Camp Hy-Lake, 75–78, 100–101, 103, 124, 126, 131–32, 152, 176, 183–86, 198, 238–39, 277

Canterbury Tales, 108, 179, 214, 248, 258, 283, 290

Capps, Walter Reed, 87

Carlisle, Dorinda, 158

Carnegie Tech, 99

Carnton, Williamson County, 86

Carter, Jerry, 218

Carter House, Franklin, 277

Carter's Creek Pike, 20, 245, 274, 278, 288

Carthage, Tennessee, 79, 108, 203, 241

Casey, DeBow, 149, 155, 162, 238

Casey, Dudley, 110

Casey, Nelda, 164

Castle Heights Military Academy, 62, 75, 90, 100, 103, 108, 118, 124, 176, 183, 198, 277, 280

Centerville, Tennessee, 127, 147

Centre College, 81–82

Charades (band), 217

Chattanooga, 6, 63, 69, 110, 167

Cherry, Bill, 139–42, 197, 199, 255, 260

Cherry, Winky, 247

Chubby Checker, 219

Citadel, 149, 167, 171–72, 175

Clapton, Eric, 219

Clarke, Elizabeth, 276

Clarkson, Tom, 143, 280

Clarksville, Tennessee, 6, 192, 199

Clements, Kate, 292

Clements, Paul, 238

CliffsNotes, 283

Clinic Bowl, 76, 80–81, 141, 187, 195, 199, 204, 243

Coasters (music group), 155, 219

Cobb, Tony, 218

Cody, Josh, 36, 73, 133

Cohn High School, 154

Coleman, Angela Martinez, 196

Coleman, John, 189, 195–96

Colton, Jesse, 49

Colton, John, 190

Columbia, Tennessee, 19, 52, 79, 109, 124, 141, 187, 189, 203, 208, 236, 258

Columbia Avenue, 5, 62, 117, 130, 133, 142, 145, 250, 273, 277

Columbia High School, 109, 139, 253

Columbia Military Academy, 72, 77, 90, 275

Columbia Pike, 28, 89, 129, 148, 170, 210, 265, 273, 285

Comer, John, 80

Compton, Robert, 14

Compton, Sam, 14, 16

Cook, Jeff, 217

Corley, Bob, 168

Corner Drugstore, Franklin, 32, 44, 160, 195

Cotton, Park, 30

Cotton, Walter, 12, 14-15

Courtney, Richard, 14, 18

Courtney, Robin, 61

Coverdale, Gertrude, 124

Coverdale, Jonas, 72–73, 75, 100–101, 103–4, 107–10, 118, 124–27, 131–32, 138, 147–48, 154–55, 176–77, 183–84, 208–9, 264, 277, 279–80, 284–85

Crenshaw, Bob, 91

Cripple Derby, 248

Crockett, Coleman, 120, 126–27

Crouch, Willie B., 147

Crowell, Glenn, 57, 211, 213–15, 217–19

Crowell, Mickey, 161–62, 199

Cuban Missile Crisis, 224, 245

Cuban students, 35, 54, 58, 103, 110, 126, 137, 147, 149, 155

Culbreath, Bill, 30–31

Cumberland College, 75, 103

Cummins Street, Franklin, 114

Custer, Bridget, 218

Cutrer, Richard, 204

D
Dachau, 248
Dan German Hospital, 191
Daniel, Jack, 30
Daniel, Rod, 180
Darlington School, Georgia, 6
Davidson College, 58, 131, 280
Dawes, Jimmy, 96
Daytona Beach, 218
De La Beckwith, Byron, 245
Denbo, Don, 65, 255
Dickens, Mae, 31
Dickerson, Willie Spencer, 208–9, 317
Dickinson, Don, 227
Dodd, Coach Bobby, 204
Domino, Fats, 155–56
Dotson, Bill, 140
Drifters (singing group), 155, 219
Duke, Mrs. E.C. (Matilou), 258, 286
Duncan School, Nashville, 62, 101, 118, 120, 126, 138
Dunkerley, Bob, 202

E
Earl's Fruit Stand, Franklin, 142
Eddington, Glenn, 29, 37, 57–58, 61, 65–66, 68–69, 87–88, 92–94, 97, 99–100, 108, 116–18
Edgar, Richard, 52
Eggleston, Mary Ed, 121
Elder, George, 16, 221, 248–50, 317
English, Claiborne, 35
Ensworth School, 111
Everbright Avenue, Franklin, 29, 54, 68, 96, 128, 260, 264–65, 269, 271, 279, 285
Everhart, Mike, 247
Everhart, Tommy, 75-76
Everlasting Love (song), 259
Evers, Medgar, 245
Exotics (band), 217–19, 256, 259

F

Fairlanes (band), 216, 259

Fair Street, Franklin, 107, 110

Farnsworth, Russell, 180

Father Ryan High School, 43, 81

Finger, Bill, 232

Fiveash, Tom, 76, 177, 186, 197, 199

Five Points, Franklin, 27, 32, 44, 150

Flat Creek, locale, 85

Flatt, Coach Carlton, 260

Fleming, Dan, 213, 268

Fleming, Sam, 14, 73, 75, 143, 213, 268, 286–87

Florida State, 149, 165

Fly, Percy, 165

Ford, Alvin, 81, 187, 202

Ford, Coach Turney, 43, 62, 108, 157

Ford, Harry, 65, 255–56

Forrest, Nathan Bedford, 124

Fort Granger, 56

Fort Knox, 172

Fowler, Calvin, 110

Fowler, Charlie, 77, 80–82, 110, 185, 202

Fowlkes, Betty, 218

Francis, Jack, 195

Franklin, Coach Marvin, 260

Franklin, Tennessee, 6, 9, 12–18, 21–23, 26–31, 42, 46, 48, 50, 52–54, 56–59, 62–65, 68, 77, 84–87, 90, 93–94, 103, 106–7, 110, 112, 116–17, 121–22, 124–26, 128–29, 133, 136–39, 141, 147–48, 150, 154, 156, 159, 165, 168, 170, 177, 181, 189–90, 208, 210–11, 216, 218, 225, 238, 240–42, 248, 252–55, 258–60, 263–64, 266, 272, 275, 277–78, 281, 288, 291

Franklin County, Tennessee, 76, 79–80, 204

Franklin Elementary School, 63, 137

Franklin High School, 68, 74, 107, 114–15, 129, 145, 157, 209–10, 254–55, 258, 263–64, 281, 288

Franklin Junior High School, 160, 189–90, 192, 210, 254

Franklin Road, 92, 94, 142, 150, 165, 170, 178, 184, 240

Franklin Road Academy, 287

Franklin Rodeo, 23

Franklin Theater, 63, 130, 141, 160, 195

Franklin Library, 28

French, Coach Jimmy, 132, 176, 178–79, 230, 239, 243–44, 246, 250
Fryar, Libby, 258
Frist, Dr. Thomas, 23

G
Galdo, Otto, 147
Gale, Stanley, 120, 138, 140–41
Gallatin, Tennessee, 31
Gardner, Gretchen, 141
Gayden, Hamilton, 124
Gayden, Mac, 147, 180, 259
Gentry, Bobby, 59, 61, 66, 158, 255–56, 258, 281
Gentry, Cindy, 317
Gentry, Jimmy, 107, 215, 224, 227, 248, 250, 258, 260
Gentry, David, 44
Gentry, Peggy Sweeney, 66
Georgia Tech, 154, 204–5
German, Dan, 22, 191
German, Mildred, 98
German-Rice Hospital, 22
Geshke, Terry, 197, 199
Gilco (Drive-in), 64, 148, 164–65, 195, 202, 216, 258
Giles, Frank, 71, 89, 94
Gillespie, Dickie, 194
Girls Room (accomodation), 12, 15
Gracey, Pete, 36
Graham, Robert, 136
Granbury Street, Franklin, 208–9
Gray, Billy Fey, 120
Gray, Frank, 13, 15, 277
Gray, Mary Lee, 57
Gray's Drugstore, Franklin, 277
Grayson, Zeke, 43
Green, Coach Jack, 205
Green, John, 53–54, 56
Green, Walter, 317
Greer-Plato basketball tournament, 96, 130, 150
Greer-Plato track, 89

Greers, 26, 63–65, 88, 93, 95–96, 111, 130, 142, 150, 165, 170, 178, 227, 234, 242, 248–49, 260
Gregg, Jason, 2, 251
Greyhound bus, 81, 110, 276
Greystone (BGA residence), 35, 68, 87, 89–90
Griffith, Ron, 290
Grimes, Charles William ("Tiger"), 116–18, 120, 128
Grimes, Ronny, 211
Griswold, Nelson, 15, 96
Grizzard, Winston ("Weenie"), 243
Guffee, Albert, 21–22
Guffee, Betty Jane, 23
Guffee, Dr. Harry, 21–24, 52, 76–77, 80, 168, 190, 196, 205, 227, 255, 272
Guffee, Harry Jr., 23
Guffee, Jane McGee, 21
Guffee, Paul (Class of 1929), 22-24
Guffee, Paul (Class of 1961), 22-24, 78, 81, 132, 186, 188–90, 194–96, 198-202, 204-06, 279-80, 284-85
Guffee family, 168
Guiton, Tom, 149, 153–54, 170

H
Hainge, Allen, 254
Halloween, 33, 52, 141, 155, 160, 265
Haney, David, 53
Hard Bargain (Franklin neighborhood), 85
Hardcastle, Loy, 217
Harding Road, 29, 129
Hardy, Sam, 153
Harlin Bob, 93, 96, 98
Harlin, Wirt Sr., 285
Harlinsdale farm, 98, 107
Harpeth Bank, 252
Harpeth Hall School, Nashville, 134, 258, 260
Harris, Bob, 158
Harrison House, Williamson County, 5
Hartsville, Tennessee, 141, 190
Harvey, Will (grandfather of Glenn Eddington), 57
Hasty, Don, 193–94

Hatcher, Abe, 147, 169
Hatcher, Kathryn, 11–15
Hatcher, Milton, 11
Hatcher, O.C., 223
Hawkins, Box, 140, 161
Hayes, Jimmy, 104
Haynes, Emma Wooten ("Mama Haynes"), 51–52, 68, 124, 132, 153
Haynes, R.E., 51
Hays, Elizabeth, 103
Helm, Tommy, 120–21
Henderson, Captain Tom, 159, 241, 281
Henderson, Mazie, 14
Henderson, Thomas Perkins Jr., 159
Henderson, Tom ("Captain Tom"), 159, 241, 281
Henderson, Tom (Thomas Perkins Henderson III), 238, 241–42, 245, 247
Henderson, Tom Jr., 159
Henderson Family, 14, 241
Henderson Invitational League, 245
Henderson Invitational Tournament, 245
Hendersonville, Tennessee, 77, 152–53, 256
Henpeck Lane, Williamson County, 262
Herbert, Bill, 140
Herd, Hal, 186, 190
Hettie Ray's (Nashville nightclub), 29
Higgs, Barbara, 121
Highway Pup (Nashville beer joint), 129
Hillsboro High School, 142, 148, 176, 181, 258
Hillsboro Road, 22, 29, 46, 247
Hillsboro Road bus, 240
Hillwood High School, 232
Hinkle, Carl, 36
Hoffa, Jimmy, 14
Holland, Mike, 288
Holt, Andy, 286
Holt, Spencer, 63, 77, 80, 204, 248
Hoskins, John, 33, 38
Houghland, Calvin, 232
Howlett, Maxie, 12–13
Hudgins, Howard, 216

Hudgins, Mike, 142, 148-49, 155, 159–60, 163, 165, 175, 199
Hudgins, Tom, 190
Hull, Secretary Cordell, 222
Hume-Fogg High School, 100
Huntsville, Alabama, 103, 229–30, 279
Hutcheson, Bob (Class of 1950), 93
Hutchinson, Robert, 42

I
Ingram, Doc, 31
Interurban bus, 31, 50, 94
Iquitos, Peru, 174
Ironing Board Sam, 232
Irwin, Harris (Franklin policeman), 160
Isaac Litton High School, 80–81, 187, 195, 204
Isaacs, Billy, 96
Iwo Jima, 45, 169, 248, 275–76, 283

J
Jackson, Bruce, 126, 283
Jackson, Jack, 217
Jackson, John, 224, 247
Jackson, Roger, 239–40, 246, 248–49
Jenkins, Virgil, 32
Jenkins, William, 110, 117
Jennings, Bob, 12
Jenson, Paul, 217
Jewel, Asa, 190
Jewell, Johnny, 81, 202
Jim Crow South, 86
John Birch Society, 245
Johnson, Dob, 140
Johnson, Gerald ("Momma"), 71, 90–91, 158
Johnston, Howard, 181
Jonas Coverdale, 115
Jones, Ira, 62
Jordan, Albert, 73
Jordan, Billy, 93

Jordan, Coach Nance, 33, 35
Jordan. Uncle Bob, 106
J.R. Watkins Company, 13

K
Kefauver, David, 227, 230
Kennedy, Kathleen, 11
Kennedy, President John F., 215, 224, 232, 284
Kennedy, R.V., 129
King, Martin Luther, 258
Kinnard, Claiborne, 64
Kinnard, Judy, 188
Kinnard family, 191, 258
Kinnard's Pond, 242, 249
Kirkpatrick, Bill, 42
Kirkpatrick Kirk, 194
Kirkpatrick, Lucilius, 42
Kirshner, Alan, 104, 120, 138
Knabe, John Mark, 290
Knight, Bob ("Bub Nut"), 212–13
Knox, Britt, 148–49, 153, 155, 161, 167, 171, 175
Knox, Faye (Mrs. Britt Knox), 175
Knox, Phoebe, 167–68
Knoxville, 276
Korea, 110

L
Lackey, Dianne, 180
Lambuth College, 223
Lance, Tommy, 97
Lavin, Mike, 110
Lawrenceburg, Tennessee, 70, 141, 230
Laws, Hiram A., 135
Lea, Bob, 15
Lea, Milton, 15, 85
Lebanon, Tennessee, 62, 100, 103
Levering, Marilyn (Mrs. Stephen Plonka), 235

Lewis, Jerry Lee, 219
Lewisburg, Tennessee, 193, 221–22, 228, 231, 258
Lewisburg Avenue (Lewisburg Pike), 10-11, 13, 21, 45, 86, 114, 129, 137, 148, 241-42, 258
Liberty Road, Williamson County, 57
Ligon, Ronald, 140
Lillie, Theodore, 13
Linville, Jimmy, 139
Little Richard, 195
Little Texas, Williamson County, 22
Little Willie John, 155
Lockridge, Billy (member of the Spidells), 218
Lucas, Petey, 87

M
Mackey, Lee, 40
Magyar, Jose, 110
Main Street, Franklin, 106–7, 110, 148, 253–54
Mallernee, John, 244
Manchester, Tennessee, 76
Marshall, Courtney, 14
Marshall, Gilbert, 96
Marshall County, Tennessee, 85
Maury County, Tennessee, 86, 207–8
Mayes, Coach Cannon, 133, 138, 155–56, 166, 176, 186, 190–91, 194, 242, 265
McCall, Jane, 44–45
McCall, Tom, 44, 97–98, 110
McCall Electric, 44, 46, 96, 98
McCallie School, 6, 62, 67, 70, 72, 90, 95
McCord, Darris, 109, 158
McCord, Ernest, 132, 239
McDaniel, Gordon, 59, 62
McEwen, Mrs. Lee, 11, 13
McGavock, Bill, 280
McGavock farm, 86
McGugin, Coach Dan, 23
McGugin, George, 199
McKeand, Susan, 132
McKee, Erwin, 120

McKeel, Dick, 88, 158

McMillan, Robert, 230

McMinnville, Tennessee, 103, 122, 148, 154, 250, 274–77

Mechanized Death (film), 248

Memphis, 6, 11, 16, 45–46, 48, 223

Memphis University School, 65, 187

Methodist Church, Franklin, 10, 124, 129, 133, 272

Mid-South Athletic Association, 69, 90, 113, 125

Midway (BGA residence), 68–69, 89

Milam, Jack, 65, 256

Miller, Albert, 207

Miller, Green, 207

Miller, Lula Brown, 207–8

Mills, L.I., 190

Millsap, Ronny, 219

Minton, Pete, 179

Montague, Van Bettis, 41–42, 46, 62

Montgomery, Phelps, 96, 117

Montgomery Bell Academy, 63, 65, 75, 78, 101, 126, 129, 176, 183, 197, 199, 236, 238, 250

Mooneyham, Charles Washington, 274

Mooney School, 6, 78

Moran, Johnny, 255

Morel, Bobby, 76, 78, 80–81, 185, 187, 202, 243, 265

Morrison, Whitehall, 78, 81, 187, 195, 202

Moss, William, 13

Motlow, Jack Daniel, 30

Mount Carmel, Williamson County, 85

Mount Pleasant, Tennessee, 77, 204

Munson, Larry, 81

Murfreesboro, Tennessee, 285

Mustelier, Henry, 110

N

Napier, Bob, 169–70

Natchez Street, Franklin, 86

Naval Academy, 225, 233

Naylor, Ralph, 89, 95, 119, 127–28, 142, 147–48, 164, 180, 184–85, 201, 212–13, 223, 231, 268, 278

Naylor, Mrs. Ralph (Sarah Ewing Briggs), 28, 74, 142, 268

Night Train (1960s TV show), 232
Ninth Avenue, Franklin, 209
Nolan, Mike, 18
Nolensville, Williamson County, 124, 160
North Brothers Drug Store, Franklin, 57
North Carolina State, 81, 188
North, Frank, 27

O

Oak Ridge, Tennessee, 75
Odom, Jimmy, 95
Old Hillsboro Road, Williamson County, 110, 247
Oliver, Cecil, 44
O'Neill, Sutton, 224
Overby, Glen, 285
Owen, Coach Tommy, 65, 197
Oxley, Coach John, 210, 223–24, 246

P

Palacio, Jose, 54
Parish, Jim, 247
Parkes, Americus Jessie, 252
Parkes, Joseph Leonard, 252
Parmer, 78, 197–98
Paschall, George, 14
Patterson, Bobby, 256
Patterson, Don, 214, 233–34
Patterson, Jack, 204
Patterson, Jimmy, 104
Payne, George, 178
Paz, Pedro, 78, 139–41, 155, 161–65, 170, 175
Peabody College, 10, 50, 67–68, 74, 79, 103, 111, 127, 180, 205, 264, 271, 278–80
Peabody Demonstration School, 101
Pearl Harbor, 44, 222
Pearson, Mike, 211–12
Peebles, Regen, 187, 203
Peoples, R.G., 6, 12, 19, 85–86, 281

Peoples brothers, 9
People's Hall, 286
Peoples School, 15
Perkins, Carl, 148, 219
Perkins, Sam, 85
Pettus, E.L., 57
Pewitt, Gale, 92, 99
Phelps, Kenneth, 117, 221, 227–28, 231, 236
Phillips, Bert, 81, 186, 195, 202, 210
Pile Drive, 245
Pinkerton, Joe, 285
Plasman, Dick, 62
Platos, 63–65, 88, 93, 96, 130, 142–43, 150, 165, 170, 178, 242
Plonka, Stephen, 224, 229–30
Pocahontas, Arkansas, 9, 133, 250, 281
Poindexter, Professor J.E., 35
Pointer, Bud, 89
Pollard, Jerry, 142
Pope, Bill, 281
Porter, Dale, 136
Porter, Jerry, 233
Portland, Tennessee, 62, 276
Post Hotel, 32, 124
Postlethwaite, Willis, 32
Poston, Barry, 180
Poteete Family, 114
Presbyterian Church, Franklin, 18, 58, 129
Presley, Elvis, 148, 170
Presley, Sallie, 86
Primm, Kirby, 285–86
Pryor, Lillie, 125
Pulaski, Tennessee, 76, 185, 189, 241
Pursell, Joe, 32

Q
Quebeck, Tennessee, 100

R

Ramsey, Buck, 175
Rasmussen, Nicky, 194–95
Rasmussen, Walter, 140
Ratteree, Coach Pride, 171
Rau, Howard, 70
Red Grill (Franklin Restaurant), 129, 141
Redick, Bill, 81–82, 132, 198–200, 202, 206
Redick, Paul, 75, 80, 102–5, 118, 126–27, 132–33, 138–40, 147–48, 162, 168–69, 176–78, 184, 198–201, 213, 218, 227, 233, 243, 249–50, 256–58, 279–80, 284–85
Redick house, 190, 199, 265
Reynolds, Jack, 63
Rhea, Rascoe, 230
Rice, Tandy, 22
Ripley, Tennessee, 41–43, 46
Rittenhouser, Hap, 263
Riverside Military Academy, 159
Roberts, Dan, 98
Roberts, Patrick, 2, 251, 317
Roberts, Sarah, 12
Roberts, Soapy, 179
Roberts, Susie Lee, 6, 142
Roberts, Walter, 12, 55, 145
Robertson, Dan, 96
Robertson, Stephen ("Bear"), 232, 246
Robertson Academy, Nashville, 184
Roberts Watch, 55, 228
Robinson, Steve, 65, 255
Robinson, Tom ("Butch"), 70, 91, 96–97
Robinson, W.T., 35
Rockarosa farm, 267, 269, 282
Rock Island, Tennessee, 274, 277
Romney, Hervin, 153, 170
Rose's Grocery, Franklin, 18
Ross, Bill, 62
Rudolph, Retha, 260
Rudolph, Steve, 290
Rue, Harrison, 32
Rue, Waitt, 32

Rutherford, Sam, 256

S

Saturday School, 60, 178, 282
Schmitt, Jack, 91
Sewanee, 50, 142, 275, 277, 281
Sewanee Military Academy, 90, 120, 158, 192, 275, 277
Seward, Douglas, 95
Sewell, Bob, 116
Sewell, Jimmy, 211
Sewell Electric, 116
Shackleford, Burton, 77
Shackleford, Duke, 76–78, 81–82, 186–87, 192, 200, 202, 243
Shanlever, Charles, 124, 162
Shapard, Joe, 233
Sharpton, Valeria, 115
Shelbyville, Tennessee, 193
Shinkle, Mike, 194
Short, Jim (Class of 1940), 253
Short, Jimmy (Class of 1965), 211
Short, Robert Mord, 48, 50
Silhouettes, 216–17
Silvertones (band), 180
Silvey, George, 65, 256
Sinclair, Richard ("Mouse"), 197
Sloan, John, 183
Smear (game), 241–42, 245
Smith, Flem, 161, 168
Smith, Gary, 40
Smith, Jerry, 217
Smith, Jim, 230, 247
Smith, Stefan, 211
Smithson, Bob, 262
Smithson, Carl, 74, 114–15, 126, 142, 147–49, 155, 163–64, 169, 184, 200–201, 211–12, 219, 231–32, 244–45, 258, 262–63, 280–82
Smithson, Etta Poteete, 114
Smithson, H.C. (father of Carl Smithson), 114
Smithson, Howard (Class of 1957), 169

Southern Association of Colleges, 280, 285

Southwestern University, 6

Spangler, Ralph, 158

Sparta, Tennessee, 77, 103

Spencer, Cora, 128, 265, 317

Spencer, Cora Miller, 128, 132, 207–9, 225

Spencer, Tennessee, 274

Spencer, Walter, 208–9

Spidells (music group), 218–19, 256

Spring Hill, Tennessee, 207–9

St. Andrews School, 96, 149

Steele, Alex, 256

Steele, Allen, 287

Stewart, Boardman, 211, 214, 222–23, 231, 244, 284–85

Stone, Stein, 36

Strahl Street, Franklin, 145

Stumb, Larry, 152, 156, 170

Stutts, Odis, 101

Sullivan, James, 42

Sundrops (local gang), 248–49

Superconducting Super Collider, 99

Sweet Thunder (band), 219

Sweetwater, Tennessee, 104

T

Tague, Nell, 6

Tanksley, Allen, 211, 214, 216–17

Taylor, Teresa, 218

Telstars (band), 216

Tennessee A&I, 209, 256

Tennessee River, 102, 290

Tennessee Tech, 121, 171

Terry, Johnson, 153, 155

Thompson, Daly, 8–10, 65, 73–74, 77, 133, 135–36, 168–69, 178–80, 193, 201, 212, 222, 231, 239, 244, 250, 257, 264, 267–68, 281

Thompson, Bob, 221, 231

Thompson, Kenneth, 31

Thompson, Mrs. Daly ("Ouida'), 10, 133

Thompson, Sarah Evelyn, 10
Thompson, Scipio, 136
Thompson's Station, Williamson County, 85–86
Tippins, Jimmy, 130
Tobacco Bowl, 141
Tolbert, James, 30
Tomlinson, Billy, 80–81, 204
Tommy, 70, 76, 120, 183–84, 188
Tompkins, John, 238
Tompkins, Sid, 81, 187, 202
Torrence, Joe, 80–81, 202
Trabue, Charles, 76, 78–81, 132, 186–87, 197–98, 202, 204, 243
Trevecca College, 115, 270
Triune, Williamson County, 57
Tug-of-War, 63, 130, 142–43, 150, 165, 170, 178, 186, 226–27, 249, 253, 260
Tullahoma, Tennessee, 76, 204
Tulloss, Mary Sam, 13

U

University of Tennessee, 19, 45, 68, 103, 157, 276, 286
UT at Martin, 280

V

Valients (band), 216
Vanderbilt University, 9, 14–15, 22–24, 62, 73–74, 77–78, 81–82, 98, 133–34, 138–39, 143, 178–81, 187–88, 194–96, 200–202, 205–6, 234–35, 237, 269–70, 280–81
Viet Nam, 172, 174, 235
Voorhees, Mary DeGraffenreid, 28–29, 33

W

Wade, Patrick, 68, 88, 97, 278
Wagner, Diane, 218
Wagon Wheel (Nashville club), 29
Walker, Coach Peahead, 72
Wallace, Anne Smithson, 269–70
Wallace, Guy, 27

Waller, Ben, 110
Wall Scholarship, 107
Wantland, Hal, 203
Wanzer, Philip, 40
Ward Belmont School, 45
Warfield, Charlie, 181
Warren County, Tennessee, 250
Washington & Lee, 244
Watkins, Arthur, 6
Waynesboro, Tennessee, 123, 126, 134
Webb, Sawney, 12
Webber, Johnny, 184
Webb School, 12
Welch, Nancy, 218
Wells, Tommy, 154
West End High School, Nashville, 121
West Main Street, Franklin, 27, 137
Westover (BGA residence), 35, 43, 68, 101, 129, 153, 279
Whitaker, Martha Hatcher, 11, 16, 317
Whitaker, Nelson, 15
Wilkerson, Rusty, 290
Wilkinson, Bub, 76
Williams, Dorothy, 115
Williams, Martha, 27
Williamson County, Tennessee, 11, 19, 22, 74, 85, 93, 115, 250, 254, 262
Williamson County Hospital, 278, 290
Willow Plunge, 64, 191, 200, 216, 218–20, 242, 258–59, 272
Wilson, Florence, 51
Winchester, Tennessee, 80
Winningham, Geoff, 244
Winstead, Amy, 85
Winstead, Samuel, 85
Winstead Hill, Williamson County, 5
Wood, David, 123, 125, 129–30, 176, 239, 241, 243
Wood, Margie (Mrs. David Wood), 132, 271
Woodbury, Tennessee, 175
Woodlawn High School, 68
Woodmont Boulevard, Nashville, 218
Woodmont School, Nashville, 238

Woodring, Tuck, 184, 186, 202
Woods, Vaughn, 260
Wooten, James Council, 52
World War I, 239, 281
World War II, 33, 50, 63, 74, 108, 270
Wyatt, Hubert, 285

Y
Yates, W.C., 20

Z
Zion Cemetery, Maury County, 209

Acknowledgements

A number of individuals made important contributions to this book. Both Patrick Roberts, who left BGA to become the headmaster of Palmer Trinity School in Miami, and Jason Gregg, a graduate and a senior member of the BGA staff, understood that recording the recollections of graduates could help Battle Ground Academy preserve its history. Jason contacted graduates and recorded videos of the subsequent interviews. And along with asking questions from time to time, he warehoused the interviews for an entire decade. When the project was reactivated, he scanned numerous images from old yearbooks and school newspapers. Bill Armistead (Leonard H. Armistead III) is a member of the fourth generation of his family to have served as a board member of BGA. He is Life Trustee of the school, a perennial benefactor, and in addition to providing financial support for the transcriptions, was a continuing source of encouragement for this project. My daughter, Kate Clements, was diligent and patient throughout the long and frequently arduous process of transcribing the interviews, and along with laying out each page, she designed the book's compelling cover. My wife, Ruth, was kind enough to proofread most of the narratives, and she identified numerous errors that I never noticed. Marcia Fraser, who recently retired as head of Special Collections at the Williamson County Library, contributed her considerable expertise and guidance regarding the process of putting the book into an electronic format in order that it could be printed. Further help was given by the library staff, and especially Paige Hurley and Lane Collins, who patiently helped me navigate seemingly endless technological issues. In writing *Battle Ground Academy: A Monument to Education*, Cindy Gentry created an important source of information for this book. By compiling the articles of Miss Jane Owen into the multi-volume set, *Who's Who in Williamson County*, my friend, Rick Warwick, County Historian, made that treasure trove of information easily accessible. Rick also shared helpful historical information and several photographs, as did our friend, Walter Green, a 1967 graduate of BGA. I appreciate the help of Rose Cox and Willie Dickerson in providing a photograph and information about their mother, Cora Spencer. And my 1965 classmate, Dr. George Elder, made a significant contribution by providing the interview he conducted in 2004 with Mrs. Martha Hatcher Whitaker, who graduated from BGA in 1925, and died the following year at the age of 98. Finally, I am grateful for all those who took the time to share their recollections of what BGA was like "back in the day".

www.ingramcontent.com/pod-product-compliance
Lightning Source LLC
Chambersburg PA
CBHW051325110526
44582CB00004B/103